DAN CARTER

DAN CARTER

THE AUTOBIOGRAPHY OF AN ALL BLACKS LEGEND

with Duncan Greive

headline

For Honor, Marco and Fox

First published in Great Britain in 2015
by HEADLINE PUBLISHING GROUP

6

Cataloguing in Publication Data is available from the British Library

Hardback ISBN 978 1 47222 894 9
Trade Paperback ISBN 978 1 47222 895 6

Typeset in Minion Pro

Printed and bound by CPI Group (UK) Ltd, Croydon CR0 4YY

Headline's policy is to use papers that are natural, renewable and recyclable products and
made from wood grown in sustainable forests. The logging and manufacturing processes
are expected to conform to the environmental regulations of the country of origin.

HEADLINE PUBLISHING GROUP
An Hachette UK Company
Carmelite House
50 Victoria Embankment
London
EC4Y 0DZ

www.headline.co.uk
www.hachette.co.uk

Contents

Publisher's Note

In New Zealand the 'number 10' position in a rugby team is known as the first five-eighth or first-five, and 'inside centres' are known as the second five-eighth or second-five.

Writer's Note

My introduction to Dan Carter was under somewhat bizarre circumstances. 'To celebrate the launch of their new smart fabric,' the press release read, 'Jockey Performance are making Dan available for a limited series of one-on-one interviews . . .'

I'd read this kind of interview before. You go along, chat with Dan Carter about rugby, then, in small italicised print at the bottom, you mention that the interview was 'furnished by Jockey' or similar. That didn't seem very much fun to me. But I liked the idea of doing a serious in-depth interview with Dan Carter and his life in underwear. So did Simon Wilson, my editor at *Metro.* We accepted Jockey's kind invitation.

I was summoned to the Langham Hotel, in central Auckland, and eventually ushered up to a two-room suite which Jockey had put on for the event. There were half a dozen or so young women there, led by a beaming Sara Tetro, still glowing with the fame of her hosting stint on *New Zealand's Next Top Model.* Off in the corner sat DC, looking worn out, but amiable.

My time came. I sat down with Dan, and spent 15 minutes asking him about his life in undies. 'What were the first undies you ever wore, do you remember?' 'How about during your teenage years?' 'You must have a huge collection — how many pairs do you reckon you've got?' 'Are there any undies you just wouldn't wear?' Etc.

He was a really, really good dude about what was a ridiculous and somewhat intrusive line of questioning. I walked away pleasantly surprised, and wrote up a very silly feature of which

I remain quite fond. There was no part of me that imagined I'd ever be allowed in a room with him again, what with my having revealed myself as being such an alarming clown.

It was quite the surprise when, around a year later, I received a phone call from Warren Adler. I didn't know him prior, but he had worked with Ruby Mitchell, a good friend. We discussed what a fine human she was for a couple of minutes, before he got to the crux of the matter: he worked for Upstart Press, a new publishing house founded by ex-Hachette staff. Would I be interested in writing a book about a prominent New Zealand sportsperson?

I replied that it depended on who that person might be. In my head, there were maybe two or three people who would occupy the middle ground between 'important enough to have a book written about them' and 'someone I'd like to write about'. Dan Carter was one of them.

This was driven less by what I knew of the man than what I didn't. He was arguably the biggest star in New Zealand sports, and certainly its most visible. There he was, floating on a wall doing a bad impression of a heat pump. Smiling up at me from my mum's fish oil capsules. Taking a hearty swig of Powerade after a near-miss on a mountain bike. He was everywhere! But what did I know about him?

I knew he was probably the most consistently prodigious backline player of my lifetime. That he was the highest points scorer in international rugby by a huge margin. That he was also the highest points scorer in Super Rugby, an arena in which he had won three titles. That he had twice won the prestigious International Rugby Player of the Year award and had been nominated on two other occasions. That he was considered both stunningly attractive and incredibly modest. And that his second test performance against the Lions in 2005 was quite possibly the greatest game a rugby player has ever assembled.

But I also knew that his body had betrayed him cruelly, when he needed it most. And that when that happened, he seemed to shrug it off. To recap the three things I knew: 1. He was everywhere. 2. He was a rare sporting genius. 3. He appeared to have no emotions.

It seemed inhuman. Yet, the man I'd met a year earlier had been funny, self-effacing, tolerant. He had none of the born-to-rule jock energy of some other rugby players I'd met. So I knew there was a contradiction between his public image and the reality of his person. That's inevitably true of all prominent people to an extent. But I had a suspicion it was particularly true of Dan Carter.

Adler asked that I send through a few features, so that he and Kevin Chapman, the head of Upstart Press, could assess my suitability for the job. I did, and a couple of weeks later I heard back. They liked my work, and could reveal that it was indeed Dan Carter they were scouting for.

I was flattered, excited — and worried. I'd never written a book before, and had hoped that if I ever did I would be able to do it in many years' time, once I had some clue how it was done. But an opportunity like this would likely never come along again, I reasoned. So why not take the meeting at least?

I walked up the road from my home in Kingsland to a café near the top of Mt Eden Road. Typically, I underestimated how long the walk would take, and arrived sweaty and a little dishevelled on an unseasonably hot day in October. I walked out the back, and found Dean Hegan, Dan's agent, and Dan himself. The three of us talked for 40 minutes, generalities mostly, before Dean excused himself and left Dan to it.

We spoke for a further hour, discussing what he and I might want from a book. I was struck by how much he seemed to care what I'd be getting from it. Whether it was the right time for me. If I was happy for my first book to be the autobiography of a rugby player. It seemed to come from a place of empathy and care, which I appreciated, but also a baseline shrewdness: is this person the right one to entrust with my story?

We exchanged contact details, and he drove me home afterwards, which, again, seemed nice. Over the coming weeks Upstart and Dan's agents at Essentially continued to negotiate — no contract was yet in place — while Dan and I continued to talk via email and Skype, operating under the assumption that the deal would get done, and that I would write his book.

Throughout that time I thought often of the possibilities of the story. As a journalist I had almost never written about rugby, despite loving sports, and the game. I found its presentation in New Zealand very dull, the All Blacks aside. I reflexively dislike the central control model of the NZRU, preferring the wild west private ownership model you find basically everywhere else in the professional sporting universe. I thought that fundamental distortion spread down into boards, which allowed ordinary coaches and administrators to remain in situ for far too long, and the players, who seemed aloof and distant. There seemed to be a wall up, and I couldn't be bothered trying to scale it. So I wrote about basketball and MMA and cycling and golf. Anything but rugby.

Writing Dan's book represented a tantalising opportunity to be smuggled into the heart of the operation. Rugby was a huge part of New Zealand life, and one that had undergone a radical transformation post-1995 — one which Dan happened to be there to witness first hand. He was one of the two or three most pivotal figures within the All Blacks during a period of great change for that awe-inspiring team — one which I, for all my misgivings about rugby's structure, loved unequivocally.

Beyond the attraction of the broader backdrop was the personal story of the man. As we went back and forth, I became more and more certain that he would speak very openly about the realities and frustrations of life as a professional athlete at his level. That behind the perma-smiling face lay a real human, with doubts and dreams and failings, and that we would be able to tell that story.

As I write this, having just submitted the manuscript, I think we have. There were moments along the way when I became convinced that wouldn't happen. I was busy starting and running a website, 'The Spinoff', throughout the year. Plus I'd never written anything longer than 8000 words, and had no idea how it was done.

There were debates about whether to publish for Father's Day 2015. This would be deeply problematic, as Dan would still be under contract and obligation to the NZRU at that point, and thus necessarily more reticent. More to the point, his story would be unfinished — he still harboured dreams of playing one last World Cup, though his body was failing him at the time.

I also thought that, whatever his intentions, it was inevitable the book would be watered down to something insipid. I knew a number of other people would read it pre-production. I thought their input would spook Dan from his planned candour.

In the end, none of that seemed to have any profound effect on what we created. I say 'we' because even though I typed the book, Dan has been deeply involved in every facet of its creation. After I'd signed on I heard horror stories of players and coaches who grudgingly gave the barest minimum time to this kind of project. Who wouldn't even read the proofs, and then find themselves in shocked denial of something written in their autobiography.

Dan wasn't like that at all. He is the busiest person I've ever met, yet gave countless hours to me and to this book. There were long stretches in Taupo and Christchurch, the latter taking in a trip to Southbridge, where I met his mother and father. I know the route to his house in Auckland well at this point, and there are dozens of emails, text conversations and Skype records to attest to his dedication to this project. That mightn't seem like much to ask of someone for their autobiography — but from what I've been told, it's exceedingly rare for an athlete to be as engaged as this in their book.

That doesn't mean I didn't find it challenging to write. After initial discussions about the third person, it was decided that the market wanted it from Dan's perspective. That meant not only that most of the tools I normally rely on as a feature writer were out of reach, but that I would have to figure out how to reveal the scale of his achievements despite his extreme reluctance to ever acknowledge the greatness which is manifest within him. The idea of ever failing to appear humble seems to fill Dan with a mortal dread, even when he's talking casually about accomplishments which would be utterly alien to the vast majority of us.

I would have to do all that within his voice and vernacular. I'm still not sure whether I accomplished it. But I know that Dan gave his all to this project, and that it contains truths about himself, his teams and his era to which the vast majority of his fans won't have been privy. I hope this book goes some way to opening up the secret world of the All Blacks and Dan Carter, and in so doing helps demonstrate the effort and the strain which has shaped his life.

Duncan Greive, September 2015

Prologue

First

All I had wanted was to put my hand on the trophy. To have played a role in winning it. To feel a part of the Rugby World Cup experience, while being something close to fully fit.

For so much of the past year that felt impossible. Not worth thinking about. I was so far behind Crudes and Beaudy. Playing out of position for the Crusaders, my leg giving me lingering trouble.

Now, I'm sitting here, a few hours after the fulltime whistle. A Cup Winner's medal around my neck. Man-of-the-Match in the World Cup final, my last game for the All Blacks. A scenario I'd never even have dared imagine.

One thing we talk about over and over with this current All Blacks side is about never focusing on the outcome. We view the outcome as a function of following our processes. That might sound a little dry to some, but looking back at every major loss we've had over the years, they mostly started with us thinking too far ahead of the game. That's a big part of the emotion I'm feeling right now: the absence of a battle I've been waging all week. In fact, to a certain extent, it's one I've been waging since 2011: never think of the stakes; never think of the outcome.

For four years this moment has been a long way off, and often deeply improbable. I'd sit down with Gilbert Enoka, our mental skills coach, and he'd help me get away from my thoughts, designing a programme to cover a few weeks, or a day. Even hours at times.

This week was a different kind of psychological challenge. What was looming wasn't a rehab, or a selection, or a test. It was what I'd wanted my entire life. I've dreamed of this moment ever since I saw David Kirk's All Blacks light up the country in 1987.

Think too hard about the magnitude of that desire — and how it would be boiled down into 80 minutes — and you'll be overwhelmed. So for the past week I've been constantly avoiding thinking about the Saturday at Twickenham. Instead, it was always about whatever was directly in front of me.

This morning I woke up and logged out of my social media accounts. I wanted to shut out all the expectations. Of fans, friends and family. Even the fact my All Blacks career was ending. To think only about the game, and how we, as a team, would like to play it.

The opening whistle was a relief, when it finally blew. Before then it was about controlling and directing my thoughts; now they would respond instinctively to what came at me on the field.

Some games take a while to reveal their character. You don't immediately know what you're in for. Not this one. You knew that it was a final, and everyone on the field had ratcheted up their physical commitment to its maximum potential. That was obvious from the start. I didn't have to make many tackles early, but was in awe of what my teammates were doing to the Wallabies.

The collisions were ferocious. Jerome made a big tackle. Then Conrad. Then Brodie. All of them were just so dominant. It set the tone for the whole match, a degree of effort unlike anything I've ever experienced before. It was everything I wanted the game to be.

Early on I got hit late. Nothing too serious, but enough to wind me, and make me determined to make them pay from the kick. Not long after, I copped a high shot. This time within range of the posts. Each time I got up determined to nail the corresponding penalty.

I want to make every kick — but I knew with each of those that the best way to remove the target from my back was to get up and make sure I made them pay.

The game began to open up. Nehe scored in the corner, finishing off some brilliant work, the perfect way to head into the half. During the break we were deeply focused on starting well. Thanks to Ma'a's amazing run, we did. That try put us up 21–3. Exactly where we wanted to be. But it also meant we began to take our foot off the throttle. You could sense the team relaxing a little, yet we felt powerless to stop it. A little was all Australia needed. After Ben got carded the Aussies surged back. They were immense through that period, and tactically brilliant. The two tries came so quickly, and that lead we'd ground out vanished in minutes.

We regrouped as 15 men after Ben returned, needing to reassert our authority over the game. It wouldn't be easy. I was absolutely buggered at that point. I like to think I'm one of the fittest guys on the team, but my legs were just so heavy. We couldn't let them know that, or allow fatigue to dictate our decision-making.

From the restart, logic might have suggested we kick the ball long and play for territory. That's what we'd done with Ben off. But it hadn't worked, and we decided to attack with the kick and go short.

I didn't get it quite right, but somehow the very act of making an aggressive rather than defensive decision helped us snap back into the right mindset. We tried to set up for a dropped goal, but couldn't get the position right. Still, I felt confident.

Then, two minutes later, Aaron hit me with a pass unexpectedly. Not having thought about what I'd do with the ball freed me up to play more instinctively. I made a snap decision to go for the dropped goal. I wanted that seven-point margin back. It sailed over.

A few minutes later we were awarded a penalty just their side of halfway. Richie and I debated whether to go for the corner. I decided to have a shot. It was at the very limit of my range; but I felt that, with the adrenalin of the day, I should have just enough to get it across. Again, it worked.

That gave us 10 points, and breathing space. Not enough to relax — we'd learned how dangerous that was already — but to play with an edge, a confidence. Then, as the minutes wore down, Beauden scored a try to take it beyond doubt. I lined up the final conversion, knowing that the game was beyond their reach. I was struggling to contain my emotion when Liam Messam came out with a tee. He asked: 'Are you going to kick it with your right?'

He was reminding me of a conversation I'd had with Aaron Smith an eternity ago, way back at the start of the Cup. I'm a leftie, but for years I've practised kicking with my right foot. Not for any serious reason; I guess it just goes back to the kind of backyard ball tricks you do as a kid. I had said to Aaron that I'd love to kick one right-footed before I retired. Even saying it aloud felt like a premonition.

And here I was: my final kick in test rugby, the game beyond doubt. I never wanted to do anything to disrespect that incredible Wallabies side. But the idea felt irresistible: like a line running straight back through this World Cup, through the personal pain of 2011, and the team's pain of 2007. Through the Bledisloes, and the Lions series. Through my whole career.

Back to where it all began for me. On a muddy section, alongside my parents' house in Southbridge, where rugby was just the most fun a kid could have.

At the end of my international career, a line back to the very start.

I had no choice. I lined it up. Walked in, planted and swung through with my right.

And, just like that, it was over.

1
Playing Until the Night Stopped Us

In the midst of the yawning expanse of the Canterbury Plains lies a small town named Southbridge. It lies 50 kilometres south of Christchurch, beyond the base of Lake Ellesmere, near the top of the Canterbury Bight. The Carters and Brears — my mother's side — have been born, grown up and died around here for generations.

Southbridge is in the heart of the region, a rural town that exists to service the surrounding farming community. There's one pub, one café, one petrol station. There used to be two dairies, but now they've both closed down. It's a couple of dozen streets and 700 people. I can't imagine a better place to have spent my childhood.

I was born on 5 March 1982, in Leeston Maternity Hospital, just down the road — the same place my Mum and Dad came into the world. Leeston's just another small town, but to me it was always a big deal — with more people, more shops, and a high school I would eventually attend. As close as the towns are, and as much time as I've spent there, Leeston is still the opposition to me. As soon as I was old enough to understand such things, it was drilled into me that Leeston was a team we just had to beat during rugby season.

As a kid, Southbridge was a giant playground. I had a tight-knit group of friends, and each year our world would get a little bigger. First the street, then the block, then the rugby club — in time we had the run of the whole town. We'd sleep out in ditches or in my neighbour's treehouse — where we'd conduct little séances — mostly scampering back home once the excitement wore off and fear set in. We biked and walked every inch of it, outdoors in blazing heat or bitter cold. It was complete freedom, the quintessential small-town upbringing.

Both my parents come from big families — my dad Neville's one of six, and my mum Beverley one of five — and there were cousins on every street, most closely bunched in age. This would sometimes get a bit awkward when I got older, as we were related at some distance to half the town. Kiss-and-catch is a bit freakier when you aren't certain of your family ties. But as a youngster it was great, as I had an in-built set of friends. My sister Sarah and I existed both as a duo and also as part of the huge gaggle of kids which turned up at every family occasion. We were a big, unruly mob, and we would convene at various points throughout the region for birthdays and holidays.

When I was young we spent a lot of time on my grandparents' farm, out nearer the coast, where the Rakaia River meets the Pacific. They had a sheep farm, which was a huge part of my childhood — another area I could roam and explore. I remember the sadness which came when they sold it in the late '80s — it became too hard to run and they retired to Hornby. Luckily I still had my dad's family just down the road.

My 'hood was Broad Street, a wide, quiet stretch of tarmac

running toward the south-eastern edge of town. My grandparents lived a hundred metres away, and we'd spend countless hours around there, doing typical country stuff like inflating a tractor inner tube and playing with it for hours. My cousin Jackie and I would walk past our grandparents' place each day on our way to school, often stopping in on the way home. When I grew older I was allowed to ride as far as their place, and leave my bike there before continuing on foot. Eventually I was considered old enough to bike the whole way.

Dad grew up in my grandparents' house, at the town end. When he and Mum got married they bought a section on the next block and, a couple of years before I was born, Dad built the house I would grow up in. It had a small renovation a few years back, but is otherwise unchanged since he put it up in the late '70s. So Dad has always lived on Broad Street. I imagine he always will.

Despite it being a farming community, we're not a farming family. Dad became a builder at 18, and has been one ever since. Half the houses in town he's either built or worked on. When I stopped by in January he was rebuilding the local fire station. On most days you'll find him somewhere around town, making something or fixing it up. Mum's a teacher at Springston Primary. She's taught throughout the surrounding towns, and most people in the region under 40 or so will have had a lesson from her at one time or another.

For most of my childhood Mum was a reliever at the district's various primary schools. This was problematic for me growing up, as she'd occasionally be called on to relieve my classes. I wasn't a naughty kid — at least, I rarely got caught — but no one likes having their mum teach them. I was never quite sure whether to misbehave — because she is your mum and you want to push the boundaries a little — or whether to be an absolute angel and save the grief.

I loved school, but much more for the social side than the academic. Most of what knowledge of the world I possess — business, maths or science — has come through the experiences I've had as a rugby player, driven by curiosity or necessity. While I was at school I cruised through class, counting down the minutes until the bell rang. I would live for lunchtime and after school. I just wanted to be playing with my mates more than anything, rather than being locked up inside. Three o'clock meant running ourselves ragged from that moment until the last rays of light disappeared.

While we did some biking and hide and seek-type stuff, even from a young age it was sport which gripped our little gang — me, the Connells, the Taylors, the Whitfords. We would play cricket all summer and rugby all winter. The only time off I had came when I was four and badly broke my arm. I was around at a mate's house and we were all bouncing on the trampoline. I got pushed while in the air, landing awkwardly on my arm, off to the side of the tramp. The bone popped out through my skin near the elbow — a gnarly compound fracture. I was in hospital for a while, and told I had only a 50 per cent chance of regaining use of my arm. Luckily it came right. It was a rough year — I also fell off the fort at playschool and got stitches through one of my eyebrows. I still have the scar, which people assume is an old head knock from rugby.

Sport is central to small-town New Zealand social life. It really is what binds small towns together: the clubrooms as adults, the fields as kids. Maybe it was different in the big cities, but there wasn't a lot else to do. With just so much space and parks around every corner, we all had land to play on. Even at my primary school there's so much grass — you could fit four rugby fields in the grass area of Southbridge Primary, a lot for a hundred-odd kids.

I suppose I was naturally sporty, but I put a huge amount of my success down to the way Dad encouraged me. My mum always talks about it — right from when I was a wee boy, Dad was wanting me playing with a rugby ball. He was a very hands-on father; there was always a ball around and he was always willing to play with me. Not because he wanted me to be an All Black — because he was a sportsman himself. He loved rugby and was happy to have a wee boy to teach the game. As soon as I could walk he wanted me kicking the ball — that was his next mission. 'Cool, he's walking, big tick — let's get him kicking.' Apparently I used to try to tackle Mum around the legs from a very early age as well. It's just in my blood, I guess.

Rugby was the centre of social life, too. If you weren't playing sport you weren't really part of the community. Our family has always been deeply involved in local sports — one sevens side was entirely made up of Carters: Dad, his four brothers and a few cousins. Dad's a Southbridge rugby legend — a life member, on the committee at 17 and part of the club forever. He played for Ellesmere, our district side, and Canterbury Country for many years, and has done time coaching every Southbridge side, from under-7s, to women's, to seniors. He played over 300 games of senior club rugby, into his late forties, and still plays golden oldies today, at 60. It's just what he does. There aren't many people in the region's rugby scene who haven't come across him on or around the grounds. That includes All Blacks coaches Wayne Smith and Robbie Deans. In fact, Deans kept him out of the Canterbury

Country side for a decade because they played the same position. Back then if you were on the bench it was unlikely you would make the field. You were only getting on for an injury.

So many of my early childhood memories are of being down at the rugby club with Dad. I started playing when I was six — Southbridge midgets in the morning. Playing with my mates, having the time of my life. Dad was a purist, so the night before I had to get the nugget out and clean my boots and have my kit all laid out for the next day. I got so excited on Fridays. We had a takeaway ritual — fish-and-chip Fridays — but game day was all I thought about. I wanted to go to sleep just so when I woke up it would be here.

It was by no means solely about playing the game, either; it was about the whole experience. Once I finished with the midgets I'd race upstairs for the after-match. Then we'd go and help set up the goal pads and the flags for the senior game. I was in awe of the senior rugby players; they were hometown heroes to us kids.

While the senior game played we split time between watching, enthralled, and having our own little games on the sideline. Our attention spans weren't that great. As soon as that senior game finished we'd hit the field and be out there playing until nightfall.

Eventually Dad would come down and tell me to get the pads. This was a big deal: if I collected the flags and the goal pads, I could go upstairs and claim a free Moro bar or Coke — a big prize. There was a big social scene around the clubrooms and I adored every minute of Saturdays as a youngster. Rugby dominated life, and even Sundays would often be claimed by the code. Dad is a lifelong volunteer firefighter, so he used to play a lot of rugby for the Fire Brigade team or Combined Services at various tournaments, turning out against the Police or the Army. It was another day of rugby, so I was happy.

Dad's a pretty easy-going guy, but he works bloody hard. He works long hours without complaining. He's a club stalwart, volunteering without a second thought for any work that needs doing, and that extends to the town as a whole — he'll do favours for anyone. But despite all the various people and organisations that needed him, he was always my number-one supporter. He would drop me at training, coach me, even play alongside me in certain teams. He was always there on the sideline, watching and supporting. His rugby ideology ran straight down into me — all my discipline around fitness, getting in shape prior to the season, running cross-country — that came out of his teaching and ethos.

Even to this day I haven't played a game for the Crusaders or the All Blacks without hearing from him ahead of kick-off. It was always a phone call, until the last couple of years, when he discovered text messaging. Nearly three decades into my playing career he's still intimately aware of my games, and has been a huge inspiration of mine throughout my childhood, my career and my life.

I can sense just how proud he is, coming from such a strong rugby family, that I've made the All Blacks and had the career I've had. I know I'm living his dreams as well — that he would have done anything to have played for the All Blacks. The team meant so much to him, and while he never made it himself, being able to watch his son play for the team brings him huge satisfaction.

The 1987 World Cup was when I first became aware of the All Blacks. They were hazy, so distant. The rugby players I saw in the flesh every Saturday were those I looked up to. But on the rare occasions I saw the All Blacks play I knew there was something special about them. One of my earliest rugby memories was John Kirwan scoring his length-of-the-field try against Italy. And David Kirk wiping out the corner flag on his way to winning the Cup. I'd replay the videos over and over, watching specific moves then sprinting outside to try and replicate them. Maybe it's because those highlights have been played so many times since, but in my mind they remain clear, and even today I can still recall the energy and excitement of the tournament.

Southbridge had our own All Black in '87 — Albert Anderson. Alby was a giant of the club, back when All Blacks were playing club rugby and NPC. I used to see him around the clubrooms a lot when I was really young, which was awe-inspiring to all of us kids. So I'm the second All Black from Southbridge.

Back in '87 was when I began to obsess over certain players. I would be out after games imagining I was Kirwan scoring tries, or Grant Fox kicking goals. It meant I kicked pretty well, even as a seven and eight year old I'd knock them over from 35 or 40 metres on the angle. Dad reckons that was when people started to lean over and tell him I'd be an All Black, but I was blissfully unaware of any expectations. As a halfback I would pretend to be Graeme Bachop, because of his pass — the best ever, I reckon. Then later, as I started to play a bit of first- and second-five, Andrew Mehrtens. I idolised Mehrts, had his poster on my wall, and generally thought he was about the best player on the planet. Little did I know that in a few years we'd be lacing up our boots alongside one another.

The road to that moment truly began in '88, the year following the World Cup, when I officially started playing. Even though I was running around, mostly playing touch rugby and league — each easier to play with small numbers — it was rugby proper that was the ultimate in our town and in my family.

Despite that, and despite our proximity to Christchurch, we didn't often make the trip in to Lancaster Park. My first game would have been when I was five or six — Fiji versus Canterbury. I went with Dad and a friend and it was pretty special attending such a big game. Taking in the sound and passion of the fans, the scale of the stadium, the quality of the Canterbury team. A year or two passed before I turned out for my first rep game there, for Canterbury Country. I would have been all of eight or nine years old. We played across the field. I remember being in the changing room and the unimaginable thrill of getting my Canterbury Country jersey.

The day is still so clear in my mind, but the result has faded. We probably got a hiding. Canterbury Country always did it tough against the City boys; they were so much bigger than us. We would always lose by 30 or 40 points, but it never mattered to me back then.

I loved the games, but I didn't love every part of them. I used to cry all the time, probably two or three times a game, because I was so small and my opponents so huge by comparison. But I would always just go on tackling. I was told that old cliché: the bigger they are, they harder they fall. It's been used to get little guys to do mad things forever, and it worked on me. Tackling those monsters hurt like hell, and I hated it. There would be times that I would just completely muck it up and get flattened, but that's how you learn at that age. I still maintain that my technique came out of that period, a tiny kid always trying to tackle giants.

I've never been one to make big hits in a game, but I know I'm having a good defensive game when I'm tackling really low. That started back then. I'm not particularly big even now, but didn't grow to my current height until I was about 19 or 20. That's why I played halfback growing up, as I was always the smallest on the field. I played there right through from midgets up until fifth form, when I finally had a crack at first-five.

For all the rugby I played competitively as a kid, though, it was dwarfed by the hours I spent playing with my mates. That's what I put my skill-set down to — those countless hours after school. When I was very young we'd head to the rugby club to play. A group of six to eight of us played league, bullrush, touch or rugby — whatever we had the numbers for. We'd do it down the park, but Mum wanted us close to home. There was a section alongside ours where my parents grew gherkins, bottling them to sell for a little extra cash. Then one summer my dad planted grass, so from then on we effectively had a rugby field alongside our house. That was our afternoon ritual for nearly a decade. I wonder how my life might have turned out if they'd never made that sacrifice. I likely wouldn't have played nearly so much, and might never have acquired the skills I did without that endless repetition.

My mum must have had cause to regret their decision when she did the laundry, as it was filthy work. We used to put the sprinkler in the corners of the goal-line so we could slide and score big tries, playing for two or three hours straight, until it got dark and Mum told us to come inside. We'd be covered in mud, soaked in sweat, utterly spent. But even then I'd be trying to practise my goal-kicking. It was truly the dominant part of my childhood, for years and years. I never got into video games, never really watched much television. An oval ball, a few mates and a patch of grass and I was set for hours.

Those games we played for pure pleasure were probably the reason I became an All Black. We were essentially running drills without knowing it: that's where I learned to tackle, where I learned to pass, where I learned to kick. A couple of my younger friends became part-time tackle bags. Shane Taylor and Derek Whitford were commandeered to hit up the ball, over and over, just so I could take them down.

I'd also work on my place-kicking, using the house as stand-in for goalposts. This meant the ball would come rolling back down the roof and over the guttering. Dad would've had to replace it any number of times, but he never complained. I just figured he was a builder, so it was easy for him.

That might have been part of what motivated him to create what remains to this day the best present I've ever received. On the morning of my eighth birthday I hopped out of bed and walked down the corridor to our kitchen. Dad gestured over his shoulder towards the field, telling me to look outside. Standing there, gleaming in the morning sun, were a pair of professionally made rugby posts. They were a replica of the goals down at the club — expertly painted in blue and white, the Southbridge colours. The posts remain standing today, and have become a bit of a local landmark — Mum and Dad will look up from breakfast and see tourists taking photos of them from time to time.

That redoubled my obsession with place-kicking. From then on every spare minute was spent kicking goals from all angles. I would practise in front, then move next to the house, where I had to kick over two fences to get over the cross bar. There was another angle, kicking over some trees and the driveway. Back then there were no kicking tees; you made bird's nests of grass or piled-up mud.

Those days are so vivid to me, even now, and remain the foundation of my game. I wasn't aspiring to be an All Black back then; it was pure youthful enjoyment and fun. That's where I built up the base of skills that has helped me through 13 years of professional rugby.

New Zealand rugby is mostly pretty good at identifying talent, and giving it a chance to shine. High school, district, region, island and national sides: there are plenty of opportunities for talented players to turn it on and push up the ladder. Look into the background of most All Blacks and you'll find selection for key age-group teams peppered throughout their playing CVs. We seem to know who is coming and how they'll develop, and be able to ferret out quality players no matter how deeply they're buried.

That's why, regardless of what I've gone on to achieve in my life, I didn't grow up with serious ambitions within the game. People might think that's false modesty, but my early record would bear it out. I did well enough through age-group sides, but never seriously threatened to break into any of the truly important teams through primary and early high school. I wasn't particularly bothered by that. It was just a fact of life, and I never really thought much of it at the time. Which isn't to say I wasn't confident that I was one of the better players in Ellesmere — more that our country region wasn't anything like the rugby hotbed that Christchurch was, so you weren't really sure where you stood.

By high school I had developed the rudiments of my style. I was still playing halfback, especially early on, and doing a lot of the kicking. My attacking game had developed to the point where if I didn't score a try in a match I'd be disappointed. The rep teams I made were the same ones my dad had played for — Ellesmere and Canterbury Country. I never made Canterbury teams.

The most anticipated games each year were always within the district. There's no team you want to beat up on more than your neighbours up the road. As I've said, I grew up knowing we had a great rivalry with Leeston. It was good-natured, but taken pretty seriously — we were never allowed to wear red and white, because those were their colours.

It doesn't go too far; we're all friends with one another, really. But within the club rugby environment it was extremely serious. The Southbridge–Leeston rivalry stretches back decades. As a kid you grow up and you hear the adults saying 'You can't lose to Leeston' — it's drilled into you over and over. So at an age-grade level, the games you'd get the most nervous about were the Southbridge–Leeston derbies.

Other in-district games were played against Lincoln, Darfield and Waihora. Springston was always a hard game — it's near the Burnham army base, and the sons of those military men were big and tough. You knew you were up against it travelling there. Each age group ran for two years, and I played from the beginning of primary right through to the end of high school. You had a year when you were tiny, and out of your mind with fear, and another when you were the big kid and looking to beat up on the new kids. That dynamic ran right through school.

I drifted through high school making various rep teams, loving rugby but never dreaming that it might be a career. It wasn't until I was in about sixth form, when I was at Ellesmere College in Leeston, that I was selected for a Hanan Shield districts team. Me and a mate of mine, Philip Dawson, made a regional tournament in Christchurch. All of a sudden I was lining up against players from New Zealand Secondary Schools, young stars who'd been known as special players their whole lives. It was my first time playing against a whole side filled with quality, but also surrounded by legitimate talent from numbers 1 through 15. To my surprise, rather than being overwhelmed by the step up, I relished it. It was the first flash that rugby held more for me than the solid but unspectacular career I'd had to that point. I was determined to see how far I could go.

2

Teenage Kicks

My attempts at teenage rebellion were classic country stuff, and almost comically small-time. I used to steal Mum and Dad's milk money. Just a bit each day, until I had enough to buy a pie and Coke on the way to school. As a group, we'd sometimes roam the streets, looking to entertain ourselves. One of our favourite games was throwing stones onto people's roofs, until the owner would come out — at which point we'd all sprint away. That's what passed for troublemaking in Southbridge in the '80s.

Probably the most memorable piece of rebellion came during a lip-synching competition at Ellesmere College. I decided to do something completely out of character, egged on by a good friend, Phil Cave. We liked a bit of mischief, he and I. For some bizarre reason we decided I should dress up in a little miniskirt, and run through 'Pretty Woman'. He was on stage, and I would walk past, looking flirtatiously at him. Then, near the end, he tripped me over and came in behind me and started mock thrusting. To this day I have no idea why we did it. The whole school erupted, and we won the award for 'best audience reaction'. But we got sent to the principal and were given a pretty severe telling-off. Which I can understand — it wasn't a great look, in front of the whole school.

Later my friends and I started sneaking alcohol from our folks. We were around drinking from a young age, and you start to get into the culture of it in your early teens, especially when you start making the First XV and other rep teams. The first time I had a couple of beers I would probably have been 15. I loved the confidence it gave me, cutting through my natural shyness and allowing me to be much more open and engaging.

Pretty soon my mates and I would start figuring out ways to get a little drunk in small groups. It started with 'pitching a tent'. We'd throw it up in someone's yard, and their parents would think it was all innocent. Or maybe they knew what was going on and just turned a blind eye. Regardless, the main reason you'd pitch a tent was to have a few drinks with your mates. One of us would make a bottle of rocket fuel, by mixing a little of all the spirits in their parents' liquor cabinet. It was absolutely disgusting, but it did the job.

As we got older things became a bit more organised. There'd be parties at the school hall, or at people's houses when their folks were away. Much as we enjoyed it, drinking wasn't a big part of life — just something we'd do when we could, driven by boredom and opportunity.

With the exception of my 'Pretty Woman' performance, I was terrified of getting picked out. I always kept my head down, tried to stay out of sight and mind. Even in subjects I enjoyed, when I was certain of the answer I'd never raise my hand. That continues to this day, even in team video sessions or other group scenarios. I'm happier kicking a goal to win a match in front of 80,000 than answering a question in front of a couple of dozen. It doesn't make much sense, but it's always been that way. The field is my safe place, a haven where I'm at ease and confident.

Obviously this has changed to an extent. It's impossible to be an All Black and fail to develop some interpersonal skills. I'm now able to yarn with sponsors, media or members of the public in a way which would have frozen me in place in my teens. It's one of the many strange side effects of being a professional sportsperson — it functions as an epic, high-level self-improvement course.

Life changed markedly with the end of primary school. At Southbridge Primary you knew everyone in school; there was only one class per year, so you were guaranteed to be with your mates. Ellesmere College was away up the road in Leeston and form one to seven. My friends came up with me, but we were split into three different classes. For the first time I was in a different class from most of the friends I'd had my whole life, and I didn't like it at all.

The first three years were tough. I was terrified of the older boys, who looked like grown men and came from further out around the district. I longed for the days when the whole school was made of friends and relatives. That changed markedly in fourth form, when I entered both the First XI and First XV.

At Ellesmere I realised I was a better than average sportsperson. Through high school I played as much cricket as rugby, and was pretty handy at both. I wasn't the only one — a guy named Brendon McCullum was pretty useful at both codes too, as I'd discover soon enough. Even though we're friends now, he still makes sure to remind me of that fact when we catch up.

I played Canterbury Country cricket as well as rugby, and felt very strongly about the game. I loved that it was both an individual and a team sport, and the intricacies and duration of the battle between batsman and bowler. I also loved the social element of it, the camaraderie and conversation which comes from the length of time a game takes to play out. I made Canterbury Country senior level and Southbridge Seniors before I was forced to give up the game after sustaining a stress fracture in my back at 17.

Before I quit I did well enough to get a six-wicket bag for the Southbridge senior side, which meant I had to shout the rest of the team a crate. This was a little awkward, as I wasn't yet old enough to buy alcohol — I was 17, and the drinking age still 20 — so Dad had to step up.

I had a pretty active social life by then, and occasionally my life got out of balance. There was one incident in particular that still gives me chills to this day. I went out on a Friday night to a house party, only making it home in time for a couple of hours' sleep. I woke up and played cricket all day, then went straight back and stayed up most of the night again. I was sober driver for my mates, but it was another very late one, which meant I had to drive to the West Coast to play rep cricket on the back of four or five hours' sleep for the whole weekend. I was meeting everyone in Sheffield, which is just past Darfield — about 50 kilometres or so north of Southbridge. I was driving down familiar roads, barely keeping my eyes open. I kept nodding off, and should've pulled over. But I knew I was almost in Sheffield, so continued to push on.

The next thing I knew I woke up and I was on the other side of the road, on the grass verge. I freaked out and slammed on the brakes. The car fish-tailed over the road to the other side, and ended up about a metre from a fence post. Adrenalin coursed through me as I thought about what might have happened had I woken up a split second later, or there had been oncoming traffic. I looked down at the skid marks and felt a huge wave of relief and fear. I drove on to Sheffield, shaking and soaked in sweat, and told my friend he had to drive. Regardless, I couldn't sleep after that, because I was still freaking out.

Ironically I got a few wickets and a half century, one of my better days' cricket. But the whole day I felt sick from the adrenalin and shock, and never drove in that condition again.

My last few years of Ellesmere College saw me start to push the boundaries a little. The First XV environment can sometimes mean trouble — the youngest players in the team learn the habits of the eldest pretty quickly. Just as in any team, the senior guys set the tone, and the new entrants wouldn't dream of trying to change anything.

In fifth form we started to occasionally bunk the last couple of classes to head into Christchurch. At least, we thought it was Christchurch. We were only really going as far as Hornby, with its mall and its McDonald's. We thought we were pretty bad ass, but really we were just some nervous country boys dipping our toes in the city.

That would change the following year, thanks to my selection in the South Island Schoolboys side. To me it was a bombshell, albeit a very welcome one. There was a huge jump between the district and sub-regional sides I'd played in through my youth and the South Island team. I was excited about representing the country boys of Southbridge in a team dominated by guys from Christchurch and Dunedin, but I certainly didn't see it as a marker of things to come. So it was a surprise towards the end of the year when a couple of city schools approached me about transferring to play rugby.

I was offered the chance to play for St Andrew's and Christ's College, two well-regarded and well-funded private schools, but I never seriously considered either. The school I chose was Christchurch Boys'. For some reason, despite my only having spent my final year there, I'm more associated with CBHS than Ellesmere. I've always found that pretty funny, particularly given how my year went. I'm still proud to have attended, but in terms of my formative years as a rugby player, they all happened out in the country.

Christchurch Boys' is a public school in Riccarton with as proud a rugby history as any school in the country. That was part of the motivation, for sure, but if I'm honest it was as much driven by the fact Ben Jones was also coming in for the year. Even though he's from Ashburton, he was already a good mate, and remains among my closest friends to this day. We were both swayed, too, by the presence of Doug Tausili, another guy I knew from age-group rugby, who attended the school. We have remained close ever since, and each was among my groomsmen. The idea of us three combining to play for one of the best rugby schools around was immensely appealing. Without their company I doubt I would've had the courage to take up the offer. Then who knows how my life might've turned out?

Christchurch Boys' was a culture shock. It's between Riccarton and Fendalton, with big, beautiful houses, wide streets and kids who'd grown up in that world. It was a long way from Southbridge, and I'd traverse the distance in my mum's Nissan Pulsar diesel. It was an hour each way, which seems a hike now I look back, but at the time I never thought twice about it. At that age you've got nothing but time anyway. The Pulsar topped out at 127 km/h, flat-footed. I remember this because the only time I got pulled over for speeding was on the way into school one morning, in the midst of one of the numerous dead flat, dead straight roads between home and school.

Even though Christchurch Boys' is this establishment school, I still felt at home, because there were so many boarders from the country. There were farm boys from Dunsandel who might have done a couple of years at Ellesmere — it was a good mix of people, which meant no one felt too isolated. I was also helped acclimatise through the two nights a week I spent with my maternal Auntie Teena, after rugby trainings.

In time, I ended up spending many evenings with Doug's family. They're a big Samoan unit, and embraced me like one of their own. I was still a skinny kid at that stage, and they told me taro was a 'natural steroid' — the reason island boys were so strong. I would eat piles of the stuff, though I don't know how much good it did me.

From my first day at Christchurch Boys' I threw myself into sports, to the point where the principal called Dad and asked, 'Are you sure he wants to come to school here?' Apparently I'd only attended five of the first 15 days of term one. It wasn't that I was wagging — I'd just signed up to every code going, and had been at various tournaments. So while it wasn't my best year academically, I enjoyed the range of sports immensely. Particularly the rugby. At least, I did until the Christ's College game came around.

Christchurch Boys', like many serious sporting schools, never lets you forget its proud history. There's one particular corridor, to the left as you walk in the main entrance, which is crammed with memorabilia from its various sporting triumphs. I remember walking down there on the way to meet the principal as I was being recruited, and feeling this weight come on me. There are All Blacks jerseys from the likes of Andrew Mehrtens and Daryl Gibson, ancient game balls, shields and dozens of polished silver trophies. Compared to Ellesmere, which has a few scattered cups in the PE staff room, it was a different world.

This all meant you were deeply conscious of how important each game was — that your actions would be recorded and reflected upon, that you were building on a proud history. Either adding to it or detracting from it. Before now, most of my teams were underdogs. Southbridge was a small town, Country a second-tier union. We won more than we lost, but we were never the dominant team, the presumptive champion. And as passionate as our fans were, there were somewhere between a few dozen and a couple of hundred.

I was completely unprepared, then, for the intensity of the atmosphere which sprang up around the Christ's College game. They were our arch-rivals, the private school which thought they were better than everyone — at least in our minds — and the relationship between the two schools was characterised by an intense antagonism which engulfed the entire school the week of the game, and completely dominated game day. The year prior we had come second in the country and, with a number of key players returning, expectations were high that we'd have a handy win over Christ's.

Unless you've experienced the great rivalries of New Zealand high-school rugby you can't truly appreciate how keenly all this is felt. The games have been played for over a century and are often shown on national television. We taught the whole school our haka, out on the tennis courts, earlier in the week. There was just nothing else on anyone's mind, and I loved the intensity of it all.

The day dawned crisp and clear, perfect conditions for rugby. There was a school-wide assembly, during which our caps were given out in an elaborate ceremony. The team was given a half day off school to prepare, which was a huge privilege and drove home how important this game was. Around lunchtime we made our way to Christ's — who were hosting that year — piling into minivans and making the journey in near-total silence.

When we arrived, the atmosphere was unbelievable. Old boys from both schools filled the sidelines, drunk, loud and chanting. Police and security were everywhere, which was understandable given how feral and tribal the crowd was. There were sixth and seventh formers on megaphones, yelling abuse at one another. There is a tradition of chanting the opposing schoolboys' nickname, something obscene. It's ridiculous and gross — but part and parcel of that white-hot atmosphere.

Before the game started both schools performed mass haka, facing one another, which made me realise how many people the team had on its back for this one. The chants were echoing round the ground, just like they do every year. When we started playing, the abuse from the spectators was constant, and only increased as the game went on — still one of the most intense environments I've ever played in. It made us players incredibly tight. Every time I made a mistake or missed a kick the crowd would go crazy, and it started to affect us all. Doug Tausili was a Christchurch Boys' legend. He'd been in the First XV for three years and he tried to take over the game on his own, taking every free kick or penalty and putting up huge up-and-unders to try to help us regain possession. I understood the desire, but it really wasn't working.

We were a long way out of sync. I remember Ben Jones, who was lightning around the field, slicing through looking for a short ball when I'd elected to pass it long. The ball hit him in the head. Meanwhile Christ's were just playing out of their minds — I don't think their kicker, Greg Norris, missed all day.

It was so frustrating, watching us fall apart and feeling powerless to reverse it. We had an incredible team, including my future All Blacks teammate Adam Thomson. Christ's were handy, too, with another soon-to-be All Black in James Ryan at lock. He was huge for them, doing most of their kicking for field position as well. At halftime, our coach, a gruff, deep-voiced man named Phil Robson, tried desperately to snap us out of this panic. As a professional, you have techniques you use to get out of the 'red head' — All Blacks mental skills coach Gilbert Enoka is a genius on that front — plus the experience of having done it before. But as schoolboys you freeze and never thaw out. We simply got rolled, losing comfortably in the end. Just to show how much of a shock it was, Christchurch Boys' has yet to lose to Christ's since.

The dressing-room was a morgue. Everyone was in tears — we were stunned by the gap between our plan going in and what had transpired on the field. People were more upset, and crying for longer than I've ever seen since, including World Cups. No losses hurt so badly as the ones in schoolboy rugby, probably because at the time that's almost all you have in your life.

Once we picked ourselves up we went to town, partying all the harder because of what we'd been through. We went out with the Christ's College boys, which sounds crazy, given how much we hated them just a few hours before. But once the final whistle was blown all that stuff slides away, and we ended up having a great night. It started at a teammate's house, whose parents were relaxed about us drinking, before we tried our luck in town. It all helped erase the pain of the loss.

Despite the defeat to Christ's, we still played well enough to win the Christchurch competition. For a school with a tradition like ours, though, that wasn't a huge deal — it was expected, to an extent. The bigger prizes were the national competitions. If we wanted to begin to make good our loss to Christ's, that was where it would have to happen. Our key inter-schools matches were against Christ's, Timaru Boys', Otago Boys' and Wellington College. We won the other three games, which gave us back some confidence, then returned to Timaru, to play the round of 32 for the New Zealand Top Four Championship.

We'd beaten them handily earlier in the season, and despite having lost Adam Thomson and Ben Jones to the New Zealand Schoolboys team, we were very confident we could repeat the victory. Man for man we were as talented as any school team in the country, loaded with future provincial and Super Rugby players. When we played well we were a machine. And the loss to Christ's made us burn with desire to prove our worth.

What we hadn't reckoned on was the pitch. When we got down there, Timaru had transferred us to their number two ground, which seemed strange, given the importance of the game. When we arrived we saw why. It remains the muddiest field I've ever seen in my life. Within seconds of kick-off both teams were head to toe in thick brown mud, and completely indistinguishable from one another. Kicking for goal was impossible, even from directly in front. Timaru exploited the confusion expertly, to their credit. They would whip around to the other side of the ruck and pick up the ball, and the poor ref would have no clue which team had picked it up, and so never called the penalty.

We lost the game, and were furious afterwards. With the Christ's game we were beaten by a better team on the day, no question. Against Timaru it felt more like sabotage at the time. Now though, I think we just let it get to us. If we'd just got on with the game, rather than getting distracted by anger at the conditions, we'd have had a much better chance at winning.

With the loss went our chance to impress selectors looking at the team for higher honours. There was a nervous wait to see whether selectors would retain faith in us, or pick guys who'd advanced deeper into the tournament. Thankfully the selectors kept faith with me, and I was again picked for the South Island schoolboys — though kept out of the starting side by the selection of McCullum, who frustratingly still hadn't left rugby alone to concentrate on cricket.

It meant that our year had ended in bitter disappointment — still one of the worst years for Christchurch Boys' in recent memory. We all sat in the sheds and bawled our eyes out. It was one of the lowest feelings I had ever experienced around rugby.

We watched the rest of the results come in, resentment growing all the time. Otago Boys' and Wellington College, each of whom we'd beaten by 30 points, made the Top Four. With rugby done, the rest of the year seemed a bit pointless. My academics, never particularly strong, had withered away by that point. I sat four bursary subjects, passing two, and did 'sports science', a sixth-form certificate course for rugby and rowing boys, which I ended up topping.

I really didn't work anywhere near hard enough, and by the end wasn't even turning up to some classes. It's a big regret of mine that I failed to complete a couple of bursary subjects. I did some good around the school, coaching junior rugby and certainly didn't get into trouble. But when you spend class time at a mate's place or playing table tennis in the common room, you're not giving it your all, and not taking advantage of the opportunity school represents.

Having let my school work go, and having had rugby fall apart, I went into the last weeks of school pretty despondent. You were supposed to start planning what you would do after school. There were plenty of boys heading to uni — everyone seemed to have a plan — but what was I going to do with my life? It never crossed my mind to contemplate being a full-time rugby player. I understood that was an option on some level, but it was still so new. Rugby had only been professional for five years, and I hadn't really considered it as a viable career at any point. I didn't understand the marketplace for talent, didn't realise that Super Rugby players and All Blacks were playing rugby as jobs. I was so naive, and filled with doubt about my ability. I simply had no idea what I was going to do.

FINAL YEAR DIARY: London, 4 November 2014

Recorded via Skype just after the All Blacks touched down in London, following their 72–6 victory over the USA Eagles at Soldier Field in Chicago.

This is my last northern hemisphere tour. But it was also my first visit to the US with an All Blacks side, running out into a sold-out NFL stadium in Chicago. For the most part we play in familiar countries, against familiar opponents and at familiar stadiums. Not last week — none of us has played the Eagles, or in the US, and no All Blacks team has ever played in Chicago. The week has been extraordinary. We went to a Blackhawks hockey game, and felt the passion of the Chicago fans. They screamed the national anthem, with a level of intensity you'd never see in New Zealand. All for a regular season NHL game.

The same thing happened on Saturday. We took the field and were instantly in awe. A packed stadium, with over 60,000 people watching, in a country which barely knows rugby exists. There were maybe 5000 or 10,000 Kiwis, but the majority were Americans, there out of curiosity as much as anything else. They sang their anthem with the same kind of ragged emotion we saw at the Blackhawks, which helped lock us into the game's importance. It was doubly affecting for me, as I'd been included in the playing side, something which looked unlikely earlier in the week.

Mentally it has been so liberating, the transition from hearing critics doubt whether I should even be making the tour to getting 30 high-quality minutes. I haven't been so excited to play in years — as reserves we warmed up after halftime, but I just didn't stop. Too much energy. That might have been why they put me on around the 50-minute mark. And also why I made a couple of mistakes early on. You can be over-hyped.

The nerves came, too. I haven't been able to train with the team all year. Even though I've been in camp a bit, you need to run the moves at full pace with the team. It was all pretty new to me, so it was more about just fitting in and not mucking it up, rather than driving the show too much. So I was lacking preparation, and I'm going to be lacking preparation for the rest of the year. But just to have some minutes feels amazing, after such a messed up couple of years.

Before each tour we create objectives for it. As usual, one of the focuses was to dominate every opponent. The current All Blacks team strives to be the most dominant side in the history of world rugby. That's what we've worked towards for the last couple of years. For the team, having evolving goals helps keep you fresh and engaged. Another focus for us was to treat this tour as a test run for the Rugby World Cup in 2015. We play very little knockout rugby, so it's good to simulate it where you can. That's one of the most challenging things about the World Cup — you get through your round robin play and then you're into the quarter-finals. If you don't win that then you go home.

Usually the game before the knockout stage is a slightly easier one, so this tour represented an ideal opportunity to replicate the feel of a World Cup. The USA game is like the last round robin game; it's a weaker opponent, ahead of the London game against England, which we're treating as effectively a quarter-final match — a do or die.

Following that we get another opportunity to do the exact same thing: repeat the round robin-to-quarter-final feel against Scotland. It's also played in Edinburgh, close to Newcastle, where we've got a game during next year's World Cup. It helps to familiarise yourself with regions ahead of time. The following week we have to travel to Cardiff, something we'll likely do next year for the quarter-final. Going into the games with that mentality helps us stay locked in for the tour in a way we might struggle to otherwise, after such a long season.

We're staying on Kensington High Street, at the same hotel we always do. Often we make camp on the outskirts of cities, and the focus on rugby can get a bit much. Here we can train, talk and focus — but also escape into London and get away from the game for a few hours when we need to. The routine of touring can make locations blur into one another. Today's a Tuesday, and will run a good 12 hours. All the tens will meet with Fozzie [Ian Foster], the backs coach at 8.30 am, to run through strategy ahead of a presentation this afternoon. From there I head straight off to a full body gym session. Following that I've got some time with our physio, just to rehab some minor injuries. Next I see a massage therapist to work on my leg injury.

I'll break for a quick lunch, then do a half hour of pre-workout, called 'trigger point', getting strapped at the same time. We have a quick team meeting, where Aaron Cruden, Beauden Barrett and I will deliver our strategy for the week

— the game plan, the key areas of focus. After that it's on to the bus for a ride to training. We'll arrive at 2.30, train for two hours, then hit the pool for recovery. After that we've got an activity, a team-bonding exercise known as clubrooms. We all wear our club jerseys, tell stories, have a bite, a drink and a laugh. I'm clubrooms president, so will help organise that. We'll wrap that in the early evening, then I've got a series of stretches to run through before bed. Every minute's spoken for.

3

A Short Walk on the Wild Side

My year at Christchurch Boys' was tough. It was some of the first really high-level rugby I'd played, and between the pressure and losses in some key games, I started to lose touch with the simple, expressive pleasure I took in the sport. In its place came some self-doubt, and a sense that I'd let down those who'd believed in me and given me opportunities. I wanted to get away from that feeling, and spent most of the year doing just that. I was working, playing colts rugby and having a good time. I had no designs on selection to higher grade sides — I was back to playing rugby for the same reasons I had as a kid: for the sheer love of the game.

I spent much of 2001 indulging in the aimless freedoms that suddenly appear in your life when school ends. My Southbridge friends had a flat, a real dive, and I'd stay there two or three nights a week through that first year out of Christchurch Boys'.

It was a party flat. We'd drink some beers at home, then head into town, often with just enough money to buy a shaker or two between a group of us. Other times we'd just hang around the flat and get hammered. I slept on a scungy mattress in the hallway, among empty bottles and pizza boxes, normally peeling myself up off the floor to return to Southbridge the following morning.

We acted the way kids do when they're away from adult supervision. When you finished your beer you'd just smash it on the wall, the ground or in the fireplace. We were mindlessly destructive — we just didn't know any better, or didn't care. One time we were waiting for a cab which never came, so took out our frustrations by completely demolishing the front fence.

The neighbours probably don't remember us very fondly. Neither would the landlord. It was the kind of flat where people had locks on their rooms, which tells you a lot. We had one mate, Richard McMillan, who went away diving, so he locked his room, and begged us to leave it alone while he was at sea. Of course, the minute he left we smashed his door down and put muddy footprints all over his wall.

I think the worst we ever got was a cold winter's night when a bunch of country people had come into the city for a night out. We lit a huge bonfire in the backyard. You're not meant to do that in the middle of town, it turns out, and inevitably someone rang the fire brigade. They arrived and began hosing down our creation. We just stood around, blasting the Prodigy's 'Firestarter' at full volume, thinking we were the funniest guys in the world. Looking back, I'm embarrassed, because of Dad's role as a volunteer firefighter. I know how bad it is to be called out on a Saturday night to deal with some drunken idiots. But at the time we didn't know any better. It was a pretty grimy lifestyle, but exactly what I needed at that point in my life.

That was my first year flatting without having any major commitments and, though I didn't know it yet, also my last. I didn't have to pay rent — didn't have to pay for anything beyond beers, gas and food. During the day I worked a succession of labouring jobs. I dug potatoes and yams, and helped out my dad a bit. That didn't last long. He's a real craftsman, but I just couldn't ever be as precise as the job demanded, which frustrated both of us. I left and went to work for another builder. That, if anything, went even worse. I turned up wearing running shoes instead of proper work boots. Within a few hours I'd stood on a nail and had to go get my foot fixed up. I was off-site for weeks. They must have thought I was such a clown.

I drifted around a lot. There was a spell at Boss Sauce, making mint and Worcestershire sauce in vast quantities, before a longer stint at CRT, the rural supply store. I was mixing seed and grains for farmers, which I probably enjoyed more than any other job through that period. Mainly because hefting 25 kilo sacks around a warehouse was pretty good training for rugby. But none of the jobs really grabbed me, none felt like anything more than a means to an end. It was just hard manual labour.

Later that year I got my own place with some friends I'd met through High School Old Boys, my rugby club. They were going to uni, and found a house near the University of Canterbury. It was a pretty ordinary brick-and-tile bungalow, with a small backyard and a detached garage. The bedrooms had already been claimed when I showed up, but I wanted to move out of home pretty badly, so moved into the garage. It was bitterly cold and entirely lacking in creature comforts — the lawn outside was often my loo. But it beat the hallway of my mates' flat, and was my first real home away from home, so naturally I loved it.

Even though I wasn't at uni, the rest of the flat was, and it felt like the whole area was just filled with students. Midweek parties were a big part of the social scene, which suited me perfectly as a rugby player, fitting in well with the rhythms of training and playing. I'd party with my rugby mates on Saturday night, and my student mates during the week. During the day we'd often gather for massive games of touch on the University fields. They'd last hours, and frequently end with a keg split among 20 thirsty young guys. Later we'd head to a house party, or sometimes down to the student bar, The Foundry, on pushbikes. If it was a Thursday you'd always find us at a bar named Nancy's. Those were some of the happiest and most carefree days of my life.

You might think that my rugby would suffer from the strain of such a heavy social schedule, but I think it actually helped. It sounds a little crazy, but years later when I'd talk with Gilbert Enoka, the All Blacks' outstanding mental skills coach, I'd remember that era when he talked about how important it was to be able to relax and let go of stress when seeking high performance. The previous year I'd been a knot of worry ahead of some Christchurch Boys' games, and as our season began to fall apart, the expectations became all I thought about. This year I was playing with the kind of freedom I had known as a kid.

Coming out of school, I'd been asked to play senior rugby for High School Old Boys. But even that seemed like too much pressure, so I decided to turn out for the club's Colts side instead. This time there was no expectation on me, and not a lot on the team — it was the senior side which absorbed all that. Away from the spotlight, I quickly found the groove I'd been missing since my last days with Southbridge age-group teams. I was scoring tries and kicking goals from first-five, and our team ended up with a pretty good record. I played well enough to be selected for Canterbury Under 19s that year.

It was a great feeling, but I still felt like I was a long way outside the system — the really good young players were in various New Zealand squads, or members of the NPC or Canterbury Colts team. Despite it being a step up, the Under 19s weren't a high-priority team for the region, and training wasn't all that different to club rugby. So while I enjoyed my season immensely, I didn't feel like it meant much in terms of my future aspirations within rugby. They were still largely parked.

That started to change towards the end of the year, when I received an unexpected phone call. It was from Rob Penney, an ex-Canterbury player who has gone on to an outstanding coaching career with Canterbury, Munster and now the Shining Arcs up in Japan. Back then he was running the Canterbury Academy, the feeder into the region's NPC team. He asked me to come and train with them over summer.

I was blown away. I'd never really thought about playing rugby as a career, particularly after a fairly ordinary year with Boys' High, and missing the New Zealand age-group teams. I was living in my garage and playing rugby for fun, and never imagined for a minute that anyone important was watching me.

The Academy was a very serious, sharply run organisation. They trained in early mornings and evenings, around work and study commitments, but in the same facilities used by Canterbury and the Crusaders during the day. I leapt at the opportunity, and found the regimen suited me perfectly. I've always loved training, but at club colts level back then it was pretty basic — predominantly drills, with not much in the way of strength or conditioning work. Canterbury Academy was another level entirely.

That's when I realised what hard work was, what it felt like, and how I'd respond to it. It was the first time I had really trained hard through a summer and gone through a serious pre-season. I thrashed myself like never before, and felt the physical rewards. We were doing hill repeats and I found I was always near the front. I was also doing serious weight training for the first time in my life. I started summer around 78 kg, and within a year was closer to 90 kg — not far off my playing weight today. It was a transformational few months.

I got addicted to the discipline of it, and began training my butt off. It was because I had a focus — I wasn't throwing the ball around with my mates any longer, I was working towards something bigger. I felt so fortunate to be given this chance, and a lot of that came from having had that year outside of this world. Normally kids would get recruited right out of high school and go through a three-year Academy cycle. Maybe if that had happened I'd have been more complacent about the opportunity. But that year of working bad jobs and playing lower grade rugby meant that I was very aware of what the alternative was.

Towards the end of summer I got asked to trial for the Crusaders Development side. This was the best possible outcome, and a huge step up from Old Boys colts. I was humbled to even be asked, but surprised myself by making the squad. This was my first taste of semi-professional rugby, at least in terms of the environment, but in truth I felt like I was just there to make up the numbers. There were a couple of other first-fives, Charlie Hore and Cam McIntyre, who were well above me in the rankings. They had played to a pretty high level, including NPC for Canterbury.

I was sure that my main job was to watch and learn. But Charlie and Cam both got injured early in the season, so I ended up starting. The team was a serious proposition. We were playing warm-up matches to all the Super Rugby games, on all the legendary New Zealand stadiums, most of which I'd only ever seen on TV. Eden Park, Jade Stadium, Carisbrook. Some of the most famous rugby grounds in the world.

My summer with the Academy meant I went into the 2002 season transformed, a different athlete to the one who had turned out the previous year. My newfound size meant I could be that much more physical and effective in the tackle, and shrug off the attention of defenders more often. I was surprised to find that the transition wasn't too challenging. If anything I found it easier as a playmaker, because rather than being among a handful of quality players spread throughout the team, almost everyone was of a good standard and did their jobs.

This was the first sign of what would become a self-reinforcing feedback loop in my career. Every time I stepped up a grade, I felt instantly at home. The game almost grew easier, in a perverse way, due to the sheer skill of the whole team. It meant I had more space and time to make decisions, and more confidence that my teammates would be able to execute whatever I could throw at them. We were a strong team, with a number of future Crusaders involved. By the end of the season I felt pretty comfortable in the team, and we played well enough to win the competition.

All the same it was still a shock when I heard I had earned a trial for the New Zealand Colts side to play the Under 21 World Cup that winter. Maybe I was naive about the attention which was being paid to my performances at that stage, but I just thought I wasn't on the national selectors' radar. This isn't false modesty — just a reflection of where I felt I was in the pecking order at the time. You have to remember that I had never made a New Zealand Schoolboys or Under 19s side. I hadn't even been given a trial for a national side to that point, and my one season of major high-school rugby had been a disappointment. Guys like Cam McIntyre and Luke McAlister were already nationally known, and had made a bunch of age-group sides. There was simply no good reason for me to consider myself their peer.

The invitation, then, came as a surprise, but also made me more determined than ever before to make the most of it. To my mind there was every chance that this would be my only shot at this level, so I went in extremely focused on making it count. After the way things ended at schoolboy level, this felt like a shot at rugby redemption, a door I had assumed was locked fast looking ever so slightly ajar.

The trial took place at the Institute of Rugby in Palmerston North. I'd heard a lot about this Institute of Rugby — it was regarded as a breeding ground for top players, where the best raw talent went to be finessed into professional form. It was home to All Blacks camps between tests, and built specifically for the sport at the highest level. To go there for a trial was an incredible feeling. You lived and breathed rugby all day for as long as you were there. It was exhausting, but exhilarating, too.

I bunked in with other guys in a series of bedrooms, and all the facilities you needed were right on your doorstep. There were rugby fields and an athletics track, where we went through a battery of tests, from sprints to three-kilometre runs. That's where my summer with the Academy really paid off — I leaned hard on my fitness base, and was normally in or around the top group through those cardio-based tests.

We played a couple of games, obviously, but what I remember most vividly is the selection at the end. There were nearly 50 of us at the trial, but only 30 or so made the squad to travel. We gathered in a function room, and sat in a big group, all wound tight with nerves. As each name was read out you'd have to leave the room and go into the indoor training area. Hearing my name called was the most extraordinary feeling. Having been on the outer of the elite New Zealand sides throughout high school, it was an overwhelmingly validating feeling to have made this squad.

Sean Fitzpatrick was the manager. He'd been the All Blacks captain throughout my teens, and was the iconic player of his generation, a physical embodiment of all the All Blacks stood for. Just being in the room with him made my head spin. He came out and told us we were this year's New Zealand Colts team. I didn't really hear much else — the emotion was too much to absorb. As soon as we were released, I called Dad and explained what had just happened. We were both reeling.

Things seemed to happen very quickly after that. I returned to my garage to pack, before flying up to Auckland for camp ahead of the tour. At the start of the year I had barely left the South Island. My only trip overseas had been a cricket tour to Australia. I'd never even been to Auckland. Now, I had two weeks there before we travelled on to South Africa.

We stayed at the Novotel in Ellerslie, and trained every day. I revelled in the intensely structured NZRU environment. Even though we weren't getting paid, I felt like a professional rugby player because I was living and breathing rugby. That is what I loved most about the experience: the biggest passion in my life was rugby and to be able to do that all day was amazing. It was all laid out for us — we were given all this great free gear, and training at the best gyms, or on rugby fields in mint condition. That bog in Timaru felt a long way off. Our days and minds were swept clear to allow us to focus on the game alone. And all the while we knew that there was a World Cup waiting just around the corner.

I remember being very aware of the contrasts. A year earlier I'd been playing club rugby for the Colts, just throwing the ball around with my mates to have a bit of fun. No cares — but no ambitions either. Suddenly I was staying in flash hotels, training and playing with the best young players from around the country. I thought I was pretty lucky to be given the opportunity but remained apprehensive about the situation. I didn't want to let anyone down — especially the selectors, who'd shown a lot of faith in me to give me this shot.

Soon we were on a plane to Johannesburg, where the tournament was based. Our first game was against England, at Ellis Park. Which was pretty special — it was only a few years since the All Blacks had played in that torturous World Cup final there. So we were running out onto this historic field, pulling on what felt like an All Blacks jersey, with the silver fern on it. All kitted out in adidas gear.

We felt like we just grew another arm and a leg representing New Zealand. And because we were playing with such high-quality players, all we had to worry about was doing our jobs. I'd never run with a team that strong before, and continued to thrive being surrounded by players of that calibre. I was able to focus more on the intricacies of my own game, to be more strategic in my decision-making, and trust that those around me would always carry their end.

I started against England, and played well. The team was completely dominant — we breezed through round robin play, and soon found ourselves in the semis, where we faced the hosts. That was the first time I got to experience South Africa and just how strong they are when they get on a roll at home. I didn't play at all well in that game. I just felt the pressure and couldn't do anything to shake that awful sinking feeling.

The sensation felt eerily similar to the Christ's College game, where nothing went right. Their players were huge, complete monsters, and we found it difficult to deal with them. I couldn't handle it, and got subbed not long after halftime. Watching helplessly from the bench, I felt awful for playing so poorly in such a critical game. Despite all that, the young Boks only sealed the match with an injury-time penalty.

The atmosphere afterwards was pretty bleak. Still, it was nothing like the abject despair I'd felt after the Christ's College game. It's strange — you'd think the stakes would be higher at a World Cup, with a silver fern on your chest. There's still nothing like schoolboy rugby.

We picked ourselves up for the third-place playoff, where we met Wales again, and beat them easily. I played well, as did the whole team, and we felt some small consolation in closing out the tournament with a performance which better reflected our strength, and how we'd played prior to the semi.

After the game we had a few beers. We'd been good boys right through the tournament — no one drinking much or going out at all. That night we felt we'd earned the right to head out on the town to celebrate and let loose, with the discipline and focus of the event over. We got a few minivans together and went out en masse. It was just the players and security — management stayed back at the hotel.

As a team we'd made the decision to wear our team polos — our armour. We were proud to be representing our country, but also wanted to remove the anxiety of worrying about what to wear. Even though we were in the process of becoming elite sportspeople, we were still just kids in a lot of respects, many of us in our teens, and our confidence on the field wasn't matched in social situations.

We arrived at a dodgy club in the middle of nowhere. I remember finding it a bit weird — after spending all our time up until that point in the rich, secure areas of the city that we ended up somewhere a lot less safe for our one night out. I still don't know how we settled on that particular place, but somehow half the World Cup squads were there, blowing off steam after the tournament.

When we arrived the atmosphere was great, and soon we were on our way to an amazing night. There were lots of shots going down, loud music and low lights. It was exactly what we'd wanted. But at the same time there was a slight edge, too. South Africa was still a pretty divided country racially in some scenarios. I remember being vaguely conscious that certain parts of the crowd might have been disturbed by the Polynesians in our midst. But we didn't worry too much about that — we only had this one night out together, and the group would likely never assemble again, so drinking and carrying on with our mates was the main priority.

After a couple of hours the whole club was heaving. We were raucous, but well-behaved. Then, out of the blue, a voice boomed out over the club's sound system: 'Could all the New Zealanders please leave the premises immediately?' We turned to one another stunned, thinking it was some kind of joke. But the message was repeated, and we began to make our way to the exit. We were confused, and a bit pissed off. We'd been kicked out, as a group, but had no idea why.

We found out as we filed out of the club and saw squad members in black polos starting to scuffle with security around the entrance. Things were getting really heated, and you could tell a fight was probably coming. I didn't like the look of it. With hindsight I should have stayed and tried to cool things down, but if I'm honest, we wanted to keep partying, too. We didn't want to get in trouble, and never imagined that our teammates — big, strong athletes in great condition — couldn't handle themselves against a few security guys. So a couple of us jumped in a car and went to another club. We didn't know it yet, but that one random, somewhat selfish decision might have ended up saving our lives.

As soon as we left things exploded. Players started brawling with the bouncers. But what sent the whole scene over the edge was when reinforcements arrived not long after. Some vans pulled up, and big security types piled out. It became a scene of extreme violence, and guys from both sides were getting seriously beaten up. One of the team laid a couple of guys out, before being overrun. The whole thing had a level of violence way beyond the average pub brawl.

Then gunshots rang out. That seemed to give everyone pause, and our team retreated to the vans. Someone had been pistol-whipped, another had copped a hell of a beating. As the vans tried to leave, the windows were smashed in — our guys were jumping fences, just running for their lives.

A few of us returned to that scene, the immediate aftermath. The club we'd headed to had been shut, so we went back to see what was going on with our teammates. Most of the melee was over by then, but there were still some messed-up people around. A passer-by saw us and recognised our team polos. They yelled at us, 'Get back in your car! Go to your hotel — this place isn't safe!'

We saw Corey Flynn on the phone, talking with Fitzy, checking that the groups were making it back to the hotel. Corey was an incredibly calm head under the circumstances, and had avoided trouble through dumb luck — he'd swapped blazers with a French player, and thus wasn't targeted by the bouncers.

We headed back to the hotel, scared out of our minds, still not quite sure what had happened. We had no idea whether everyone was safe, or what had gone on. When we arrived it was just carnage. There were guys with blood everywhere, guys missing teeth, guys with eggs on their heads, broken noses, black eyes.

These weren't injuries I'd ever seen before — nothing like you'd get on a rugby field, or in a regular fight. It was horrifying. Everyone was terrified, scared for their lives, belatedly realising where they were and how quickly things could escalate. In New Zealand you get in a fight and no one is going to pull a gun on you. We went out a bunch of kids, but came back beaten and bruised, and very aware that South Africa was a very different environment to the one we'd left back home.

We all tried to sleep it off before assembling for a team meeting the next morning. We weren't flying out until the following day. I remember being surprised that management weren't angrier with us. I think deep down they were shocked that things had gotten so far out of control, but that was overpowered by relief that we all made it back alive. Battered, but alive.

Management were trying to get information about what had happened, because they knew New Zealand Rugby were going to ask questions and they'd have to provide a full report. I still don't know if guns were being shot at people, or whether security guards were just shooting in the air to put the shits up them.

It doesn't really matter — the fact that they had guns and were pistol whipping guys and pointing them at us made the situation by far the most serious and intense I'd encounter at any point in my playing career.

The only other incident which was remotely comparable came the following year, on my next trip to South Africa with the Crusaders. We were staying in Cape Town this time, one of the most beautiful cities in the world, and one of the safest places in Africa. We were out having team drinks, getting into a bit of a session, when three of us managed to get lost walking to a nightclub.

I was talking on my phone, straggling about 10 metres behind my friends. They turned a corner up ahead, and there was a brief window when I was alone on this street. Out of nowhere two guys came up, grabbed me and pinned me up against a wall. One of them demanded my phone, but I was a bit drunk and cocky. 'It's alright,' I replied, 'I'm talking on it.'

'Get your gun out and shoot him,' I heard. My blood ran cold. I handed him my phone, put my head down and walked off as quickly as I could, my pulse racing, entirely sobered up. I caught up to my friends and told them what had happened, and we all freaked out and legged it. This was less than a year on from what had happened in Johannesburg. 'I hate this country so much,' I said at the time, and meant it. It was a long while before I warmed to South Africa again. Now, it's one of my favourite countries in the world — it's just one in which you have to be a little more security conscious.

After the brawl outside the club on the Colts tour, we spent a day nursing our wounds and debriefing with management, before we flew back into Auckland. By then the media had got wind of the story, and there was a pack of cameras and reporters waiting in Arrivals. Ironically, all the footage they played afterwards was of Joe Rokocoko being pushed through the airport in a wheelchair. He'd broken his leg on the field, but they didn't let that get in the way of some good, dramatic footage. There was a full-scale inquiry afterwards, and rightly so. The NZRU has taken some serious lessons from the event, and even today use that story to impress upon young touring sides the dangers which exist overseas.

As harrowing as that night was, I look back on it today and feel like we got incredibly lucky. We were young, drunk and in the wrong part of town, and as bad as the night broke, it could so easily have been much, much worse.

4

The Canterbury Dressing-room

I returned from South Africa with a strange combination of feelings bubbling away inside me. On one level I was petrified, still, by the chaos of the incident at the nightclub. But I also had a newfound confidence and optimism about my career and my prospects. I'd played age-grade rugby for my country, performed well enough to start most games, and well enough to think that I was worthy of playing alongside some of the best young rugby talents in the country. I was feeling pretty good about my progress, and looking forward to a break before summer training. Then I got a phone call from Aussie McLean, coach of the Canterbury NPC side. I heard him say that I had been chosen for that year's team.

I couldn't quite process it. I don't know what it's like in other regions, but in Canterbury *that* team is untouchable. We support them with a huge, almost irrational passion. I remember one year in the terraces at Lancaster Park, watching Canterbury hot on attack against Wellington. We turned the ball over, deep in their territory, and Simon Mannix had possession at first-five. Because he was so deep in the in-goal, everyone was throwing Jaffas at him. I'm ashamed to say that I was among them, though none of us got near hitting him. They were all bouncing nearby though, and looking back, it was so disrespectful, so far beyond the way a crowd should behave. But because you're caught up in the mass hysteria it feels normal at the time. We were that kind of crowd, and the Canterbury team just arouses that kind of response in its supporters. And here I was, just turned 20 and being told I was part of that team. One I'd grown up idolising, without ever imagining I would ever pull on its jersey.

The first time I walked into the dressing-room it was with a curious combination of awe and fear. That team was full of players who were already legends within the region. Justin Marshall. Reuben Thorne. Andrew Mehrtens. They were posters on a wall, images on a screen. Huge personalities with incredible records on field. I was just a kid — what could I possibly say to them?

I resolved to keep my head down and my mouth shut, and try to learn as much as I could. I was like a mute that first season, watching what everyone else was doing at training and trying my best to emulate them. I found it hard to quieten down the voice in my head which kept saying: 'What are you doing here? You don't belong.'

When I arrived, most of the biggest names were away with the All Blacks, which made it slightly more low key, though there were still guys like Daryl Gibson in the side. Thanks to the absentees I got some game time, too, which allowed me to bed in a little. We played some lower division sides, which helped, as did playing at 12 as well as 10 — it meant the pressure of piloting the side was alleviated. I came off the bench on debut, against Marlborough, then scored a couple of tries against Mid Canterbury in my first start. They were both Ranfurly Shield games, but on the road.

I played solidly through those opening matches before we

came up against East Coast. They'd done well the year before, narrowly losing the NPC second division final to Hawke's Bay. It was my first game at Jade Stadium. To be honest, though, the great old stadium will always be Lancaster Park to me. I was incredibly nervous running out onto that field, and remained so as the game began. They were into us from the whistle, and the first 20 minutes were hell. I wondered briefly whether we'd even be able to get past them. That's what the Shield does to a team — everyone goes hard at you.

Then, all of a sudden we figured it out, and I ended up scoring a hat-trick. By that stage I knew I could handle myself at that level. But at the same time, I thought it was somewhat meaningless. When Aaron Mauger and Mehrts returned to join Gibson, the midfield was sorted.

You have to understand how huge Mehrtens and Marshall were in Canterbury at the time. They were like gods to us. My only interaction with them had been a couple of years earlier, when the Christchurch Boys' backline was called in to help fill out a video the pair were filming, called *9 and 10*. After it was finished a friend asked Mehrts if he could have his boots. Mehrts replied, 'Yeah, sweet.' Then my mate asked if he could have his socks. So Mehrts takes off his sweaty, smelly socks and hands them over. I was such a fan that I was torn up with envy that it wasn't me holding Mehrts' stinking socks.

That was still my mentality at Canterbury that year — a kid happy just to be in the same room as these guys, never thinking for a moment I deserved to be there. But when Aussie read out the team for the first game with the All Blacks back, there I was, still in the squad. My first game of the NPC first division was against a Wellington team which was just rammed with stars.

Although Tana Umaga and Christian Cullen didn't play that day, Jonah appeared on the wing and one M. Nonu was at centre. I tried to tackle Jonah once at full pace and was blown back two metres. That was my one and only contact with the big man on a field — he was an absolute force of nature. I was grateful I never again had to try to tackle that man.

Every game brought me face to face with guys I'd watched on TV my whole life — a magical time. A year before I'd been playing club rugby colts and working at those weird odd jobs. Now I was playing for Canterbury — earning my living as a rugby player, less than two years out of school. The money was pretty small by today's standards, but for me, living in my garage, paying $80 a week rent, it was huge. You got $400 per game, with a bonus of $200 for a win and $500 for each Ranfurly Shield game. We had the Shield for a good spell that year, so I was getting up to a grand a week at times, plus all the free sponsors' gear which comes with being an NPC player.

As you can imagine, for a 20 year old, now with a significant amount more money than sense, I managed to burn through my pay cheques. Every few weeks I'd buy something new for my garage. I would have had the flashest garage in the city by the year's end: a big double bed, a new stereo, surround sound, a big TV. I completely pimped it out, and still had money left over to shout people drinks whenever we went out.

All over the world, if you want to see how quickly and foolishly a kid can spend, just look for an athlete on their first contract. Given how cautious and investment-oriented I've become over the years, I shudder to think about how quickly I burned through that money. It's something I've thought I might like to do when my playing days are over — educate and advise young players about how to manage their finances and leverage their talent in a way that sets them up for life beyond rugby.

Back then, though, professional rugby was so young that none of that infrastructure existed. I didn't have an agent at that time, and was just happy to be playing at all. I started the season as a fringe player, mostly turning out for Canterbury B or warming the bench, but by the season's end I was getting some good game time. We ended up losing the semi to Auckland, which was gut-wrenching, and Doug Howlett gave me a brutal serve, calling me out as the game wound down. I was a bit scared — nothing like that had ever happened to me before. It's funny — we've become great friends since, and he still apologises to me. I think the emotion got the better of him and I just happened to be the closest guy to him at the time.

Afterwards we did the typical end-of-year blowout party. I was drinking with my idols, guys whose posters still decorated my bedroom back in Southbridge, for days on end. I couldn't have been happier.

I began to lose touch with some of my Southbridge mates. Between the Canterbury team and my uni mates there wasn't much time to spare. I gave them a tonne of free gear that I'd picked up in the various teams I'd turned out for over the year, which was cool. But there was definitely the beginnings of a separation there, which was a little sad, after being so close all those years growing up.

That emotion was completely overtaken by the thrill of being part of this iconic team. Being an NPC player or a Crusader in Christchurch confers a level of local celebrity on you. It's a bit irresistible — you go out wearing your team blazer or tie and it's straight to the front of the line. You don't queue for clubs, or to buy drinks. Once I started appearing regularly on TV, that's when things got really cool — people were always buying me drinks, or having me behind the bar.

There was a rhythm to life through that first season which felt so great. You'd train really hard all week, usually win on Saturday then head out into town, surrounded by these people who are like gods in this city. I wasn't very recognisable at the time, so I got to experience a lot of the fun of proximity to fame without any of the downside.

The team was incredibly hospitable. Even when the All Blacks came back, I was still made to feel welcome. It's such a cliché, but they were like a family. Every team is, but that team in particular was so tight and involving. It's such a key part of Canterbury and Crusaders culture to make every individual feel valued, like they're part of something bigger. We all know that it's only that bond which allows us to ask so much sacrifice and pain of one another out on the field.

After the season I was still basking in the afterglow when I got a phone call from Rob Penney, who'd been my coach at the Academy the previous summer. He told me that Robbie Deans wanted to see me in his office. I didn't know what to feel — whether to be excited, or if I was in trouble. I sat down, and he asked me, very matter-of-factly: 'Do you want to be a Crusader?' It was such an open question that I didn't quite know how to respond. Was he asking me if I had aspirations to one day make the team, or was he asking me to join the squad for the following season?

Either way, the answer was emphatically yes. I told him it had always been a dream of mine to play for the Crusaders. Ever since the game turned professional, they were the Super Rugby team that I supported, the team I watched and loved at Lancaster Park. Of course I'd love to.

He replied, 'That's good, because I want you in the Crusaders squad for the 2003 campaign.' I was overwhelmed, just as I had been so many times over the past year. First the Academy, then the Crusaders Development, then New Zealand Under 21s, then Canterbury. All in less than 12 months. And now this. I sat there, with a big, stupid grin, thinking that was the end of the meeting. But it wasn't. 'Do you think you could start for the Crusaders?' he asked. I replied no, without hesitation. You've got my idol Mehrts and you've got Aaron Mauger, I thought. I'm just expecting to fit in and learn.

He was speaking in a calm, unemotional way, but voicing the most unbelievable ideas. That if I worked hard enough, I could be starting for the Crusaders.

I thought, 'What is he saying?' There was no way I could do it. But at the same time I looked up to this coach so much. He was giving me an enormous opportunity. So I promised myself I'd work harder than I'd ever worked before in my life, to avoid letting him down. There's something about Robbie — he really brings the best out of younger players. Just by giving them that motivation, that vision of what they might become should they put their mind to it. So much of your ambition as a young athlete is governed by the limits of your imagination. It's Robbie's great strength that he finds a way to make those ideas dance in your mind. That helps immeasurably with the volume of hard work you need to push from good to great as an athlete.

As I left the meeting, barely feeling the ground beneath my feet, I still didn't think that I should or could be starting ahead of Mehrts. But I thought that I'd do what Robbie said, and work harder. It seemed ridiculous, particularly given my living situation. The Crusader living in a garage? That didn't sound right. But I'd give it a shot. What did I have to lose?

I was now a professional rugby player. Super Rugby players earned $65,000 a year as a base salary — a vast sum for a small-town boy like me. That came on top of the $10,000 a year base salary I was getting from Canterbury. I signed that deal for three years, which seemed pretty amazing for me at the time. I was still surprised that anyone wanted to pay me for playing the sport I loved. In three years' time, when I was an All Black and was starting to be pretty well known, that $10,000 contract would look like a bargain.

I also didn't have anyone advising me yet. Remember that rugby was still a baby when it came to professionalism. Along with the Canterbury contract, I was also offered a deal to play semi-professionally in Ireland. A friend of Dad's was working over there, and had found some Irish blood which allowed me to turn out for them. Luckily the Canterbury deal was a little closer to home, otherwise who knows what colour jersey I'd have ended up wearing?

While the Super Rugby signing was a huge deal to my family and friends, it didn't rate a mention in the media. I was just one of those fringe players, making up the numbers, on the Super Rugby version of minimum wage. That meant there was nothing to negotiate — you either signed the contract and played, or didn't and watched. And I wanted nothing more than to play.

Even though there was no need to negotiate, it was becoming clear that I might need some help with off-field work. Around this time, after the Canterbury deal, but before the Crusaders, I met with Lou Thompson, a young player agent from a company named GSM — Global Sports Management. Lou met with my parents — he'd actually played against my dad at club level — and seemed genuinely interested in me and my career. He was the first agent I had met, and 13 years on is still one of the guys I trust and respect most in the game. GSM is now known as Essentially, and Lou and his company remain my off-field team.

I feel incredibly fortunate that they found me. When I hear stories about what can go on with other young players, it breaks my heart. It happens less here than overseas, but so many have been ripped off, or signed contracts which turned out to be terrible. Your sporting life cycle is so short that a bad agent can have a huge impact on how the rest of your life plays out. So I was lucky that in Lou Thompson, Dean Hegan, Simon Porter, Warren Alcock and the rest I've found a team who've become great friends as well as partners.

With the contract signed, I threw myself into my work. Starting that December, I began training with Robbie and the rest of the team. It's the last full pre-season I ever had, and I relished it, despite the exhausting, relentless nature of the training. In the past it had been broken up into morning and evening sessions, but now we trained all day. I would barely make it home before collapsing into my bed.

The amount of time I spent sleeping focused my mind towards my living situation. It didn't seem right that a Super Rugby player should be living in a garage. At around the same time, I'd met Honor, and while we weren't together yet, I could tell that she was someone pretty special. And I didn't think she, or any girlfriend, would love the prospect of spending much time in a chilly, damp garage — no matter how much I'd spent sorting it out.

I found a flat, a modern townhouse, with Doug Tausili and Ben Jones, my mates from Christchurch Boys'. A friend from Ellesmere, Nick McKay, and Emma Lawrence, a friend of a friend, rounded out the flat.

I paid $150 for the master bedroom, complete with en suite. It was probably more than I needed, but given the amount of sleep I required post-training, it was good to have a more luxurious home.

We had a lot of fun there, and there was a crew of young rugby players who'd hang out. I met Scott Hamilton at one of the first Crusaders Academy training sessions. It was his debut year as well, and we hit it off. Scott became a fixture on our couch, eventually moving in the following year.

That summer I trained the house down. We'd do three-kilometre runs to test where we were at, and I was always in the top two, just behind Caleb Ralph. Our trainer was a lean machine named Mike Anthony, and Caleb and I were always barely hanging on to him as we smashed out hill sessions and whatever else he decided to throw at us. I found that I loved doing weights, and finished the summer able to bench 140 kilograms, along with squatting some pretty serious numbers. I loved that side of rugby — the discipline and conditioning, and the sense of earning your weekend through sheer hard work.

The weekends were something we all looked forward to, and thanks to my contract we hit town whenever we could. I never even contemplated saving, and just shouted drinks all evening. We'd hit the strip in the central city, back when it was really pumping. Those were incredible times. But as much fun as we had, it was only fun because we'd worked our butts off all week. As December became January the All Blacks drifted back into camp, and we became keenly aware that there were serious games looming, and my first taste of senior international competition as a professional.

We played pre-season games in Greymouth and Nelson, but the most memorable trip was across to Australia, where we faced the Waratahs, up in Newcastle. We stayed in Manly, and the team bonded beautifully. The game went to plan — I played very well in my minutes and came off the field elated, despite having sustained a haematoma at the start of the game. It wasn't very serious, but the doctor told me not to drink. On the bus trip back from Newcastle to Manly I saw the rest of the team having a couple of beers, and I thought I'd just have one — that it couldn't hurt. I didn't think much about it at all.

Then the back-seat crew saw me with my beer. They hauled me down the back to face them. It's one of those things which might seem strange to an outsider, but within sporting sides the bus has a very strict hierarchy to it. It's driven by seniority, and those at the back are responsible for enforcing discipline. This is not negotiable, or something only certain players care about — it's the foundation of the team's structure. So to be called back to face the senior players in my first season was mortifying, particularly on our first trip away for the year.

If there are more frightening sights I've faced than Justin Marshall and Mark Hammett on that evening then I've forgotten them. 'Are you having a beer?' Justin asked.

'I'm only having one.'

'Did you get injured today?'

'I got a haematoma,' I said.

'What did the doctor say? Don't drink,' said Justin.

'I'm only having one,' I repeated, foolishly.

'Right,' said Marshall. 'Chop it.' I sculled it back. 'Chop another one,' I was told. I was racing someone, one of Mehrts or Aaron Mauger, which made it doubly humiliating — being punished by and in front of my heroes. It kept going until I'd had four beers in no time at all. I was half cut and entirely embarrassed. Finally, they let me go back to the front of the bus. I sat, dejected, at the front, thinking about how a week out from my first proper game of Super Rugby I'd jeopardised my recovery and ended up looking a fool to the rest of the team. I made doubly sure to follow doctor's orders from then on.

When people outside of rugby hear about incidents like that — and, believe me, that's mild compared to what went on in the past — they often think it's evidence of rugby's barbaric nature. At times they're right. In the past, sometimes it did go too far, and became unnecessarily violent or rough in its hazing of young players. But personally I think those aspects of team culture and hierarchy are more than compensated for by the good they do.

The breaking down of teams into various committees, and the bonding which occurs among different facets of the organisation, are things many companies could learn from, I feel. Similarly, the team enforcing its own discipline can be a fantastic thing. You realise that it shouldn't be up to management to dictate behavioural standards and protocol. If the whole team is seeking the same result then we should all buy into the disciplines required to achieve it.

It took me a while to shake off that feeling, the shame of having let my team down before I'd even begun to earn my place in it. All week I trained myself to a standstill, as a way of trying to atone for what I'd done. The week ended with the announcement of the team to play the Hurricanes in round one. In my head I had no chance of making the 22 after what had gone on. Even if it wasn't enforced by management, they were surely aware. And, besides, I'd done nothing to deserve it — the best 9, 10 and 12 combination in the world were set and cemented, with Mehrtens in my position, and unquestionably the best player on earth there. That was my mindset when our manager began reading the team-sheet. He went through these familiar names: Number 2 — Mark Hammett, Number 6 — Reuben Thorne. Number 9 — Justin Marshall. Then at number 10 he paused, and said: 'Dan Carter'.

FINAL YEAR DIARY: London, 11 November 2014

Recorded via Skype at the team hotel in London, following the All Blacks' 24–21 victory over England at Twickenham.

Last week was one of those do-or-die matches. The win was all we were after, and we got it. In playoff rugby that is all you need to get through to the next round. Obviously there were parts of our game that we weren't happy with, but overall it was good to come out with a win.

It was excellent preparation in more ways than one. From my experience with World Cup rugby, odd things happen. They come out of the blue. It's not every day you get yellow cards, but yellow cards were happening. We pride ourselves on having one of the best scrums in the world, so to have a penalty try awarded against us for our scrum collapsing was questionable. Particularly right at the end.

Even with Charlie Faumuina's try, when Beauden was just about to take the conversion, they decided to go upstairs and have another look. I was right down there with Beauden running the tee on, and then for that to happen it was quite unusual. The more experiences of that nature you can bank, the better we're prepared for whatever the tournament will throw at us next year. Those memories will serve us well.

I played water boy for the game, which I enjoyed. If I'd had a season full of rugby I probably wouldn't have done so, but I find I learn a lot more out on the field running on the water and kicking tee than I would watching from the stand. It is something I've done a few times now while I've been injured in the last couple of years, and I prefer it over sitting in the stand eating pies.

You do feel part of the game. We're all wired up and there are messages coming from Steve Hansen. The big thing with the coach's message is that you don't actually just run on there and deliver it immediately. You listen to the players' conversations, and more often than not they've already picked it up. On Saturday, I just kept telling Crudes to keep staying flat. Even though their defence was coming up hard and we felt like we were under a lot of pressure, what England want is for you to get deeper, so they can control the tackle line.

Much as I enjoyed playing water boy, I would have loved to have been out there. It is just one of those things. The coaches picked the guys who were selected and once you get over that disappointment you can't be selfish, you have to think about what you can do to help the team get the win.

On Monday we reviewed the game, concentrating on the issues in the first half. But we don't dwell on games; as of today we've completely reviewed and moved on. I'm looking forward to arriving in Edinburgh. I just love the history, the castles, the old cobblestones. One of the first things we'll do is have a stretch tonight watching *Braveheart*.

More than anything else I'm looking forward to is staying in the same time zone. That'll be a relief. We've had something like six different time zones in the last couple of months — Argentina, South Africa, Australia, New Zealand, Chicago, London.

The big thing this week for me personally is the naming of the team. We get told tonight, then it gets released to the media late Wednesday night. As a player you have a bit of an inkling but you never really know. I'd love to start. I haven't started for the All Blacks in a year.

I just want to nail it, as I'm not sure how many more opportunities I'll get, and every game seems hugely significant from here on in.

Auckland, 1 December 2014

Recorded at my home in Auckland after returning from the northern hemisphere tour. The rest of my tour on the field totalled 55 minutes during a scrappy win over Scotland.

I'm just about to sign what is likely to be my last ever rugby contract. I had a hard look at Japan, because I love the country, and competition's easier on the body — plus they only play a 13-game season. But in the end the French contracts were too good to pass up.

It has come down to Toulon and Racing Metro, each of whom has put fantastic deals on the table. The idea of bringing the family to France for a couple of years holds real appeal, too. Above all else, the rugby situation has to be right. With only a couple more years' rugby in me, it's paramount that I play for a club that is moving in the right direction, that has a vision for success in the short term. Both clubs fit that category. So it's the south of France or Paris — a good problem to have. As of now, I'm leaning toward Racing, though, as playing in Paris will make us more connected to the rest of the continent.

I want to get it sorted before Christmas, so we can enjoy the holidays without having the negotiations hanging over me, and get on with planning the move. As much as you like to think you can put these things out of your head, it was very much on my mind on tour. I was in constant contact with Simon Porter at Essentially, my agents, along with my agent in France, Laurent. Ticking away there, all the time.

The tour went south a bit after the England game for me personally. When the team was named for the Scotland game I was gutted. Happy to be starting, but not with the team around me. We were in the conference room, below reception, and he read down the list, justifying each selection. We're allowed, even encouraged, to debate the selections, but in reality only Richie would ever do that. They weren't bad players by any means, but we were so inexperienced, and some were picked out of position. I was hoping to have Aaron Smith inside me, and Sonny Bill on my shoulder, but got neither. It put me in a negative frame of mind.

I got over it, and the team actually trained really well all week. I was given my first 10 jersey in a year. You'd think we'd become numb to the emotion of the occasion, but you never really do.

Closer to the game, there were a few ominous signs. For the captain's run you're supposed to use the match balls — brand-new balls which need to be kicked and passed to lose their shine. But it was obvious we'd somehow been given old balls, and the real ones appeared the following day. That was compounded by the pitch. In Scotland you always worry about the weather, but it had been a beautiful day, so we were certain the pitch would be in good condition.

Wrong. We arrived and it was sodden; I couldn't help but wonder if they'd been watering it all day. It reduces your ability to exploit your skills. It got me into what we call 'red head', distracted by factors beyond my control. We always know things like that will come along, but it was frustrating.

The match never really got going for me. On the day we simply didn't gel for some reason. Maybe it was my lack of familiarity with our running lines, but I was concentrating too hard on the game plan, and lacked the freedom I normally rely on. It really showed in my error rate and decision-making. I was subbed in the fifty-fifth minute. Prior to the match I was told 60 to 80 minutes, all going well. So coming off early, after a very ordinary game to that point, felt like an indictment on my performance. Fair enough — I'd played poorly. But with it went my chance to redeem myself and, so I thought (and so it proved), my chance to push for a place in the Welsh game.

The rest of the tour was coloured by my disappointment in that game. I found the whole All Blacks environment really challenging. I'm not a gamer, and I don't play cards, which are two of the biggest time-fillers on tour. So while many of the young guys were bonding, having fun, I'd just head up to my room and try to plough through some of my emails. Or get sucked into social media. The last couple of years I've really struggled on tour, and have just felt like I was hanging in there until the World Cup. Richie and I spend a lot of time together, and hang out with Conrad, too. But the dynamic lately has felt like the start of school

— trying to find friends. I've lost some of that sense of belonging, and I don't like it.

After the Scotland game, knowing I wasn't playing, it would've been easy to lose my focus and just cruise through the week. But I wanted to lead, and help the team. I was really happy with how I trained. That's something which has come on a lot in the team over the last few years — even if you're not in the side, you're expected to train like you're playing. Had Beauden got injured, I would have been, and the coaches watch how you handle yourself even when you're not playing.

It was a good way to close out the tour, and put me in a positive frame of mind heading into the summer. This is the first injury-free off-season I've had in six or seven years. December is normally a recovery month, or a rehab month, for me. But I'm going to head down to Honor's mum's place in Taupo and train bloody hard. I'll join the Crusaders earlier than usual, on 5 January. It's my last year in New Zealand, and I'm going to make it count.

5
Walking with Giants

Ithought I'd dreamt it. There'd been no prior warning that I'd make the side, let alone start at 10. The remainder of the team went by in a blur, as I struggled to comprehend what had just happened. Then Mehrts walked around, like the perfect team man he is, and shook my hand. 'Congratulations, mate,' he said. 'If there's anything you need from me, just let me know.'

It speaks directly to his character that when a moment like that came, he didn't hesitate — he did the right thing without a second thought. It was a small gesture, in the scheme of things, but it really shows what the culture of the Crusaders is like, the place to which it has evolved over the years. It's been built out of a thousand moments like that, when an individual has been given a choice between giving in to their own feelings or honouring the team. And almost every time, they've chosen the team. I believe it's why the Crusaders have known so much success for so long: we all know we're part of something bigger, and no matter how much we're hurting over a particular decision or situation, we'd never dream of putting our own needs above those of the team.

Back in the dressing-room, I was still reeling. It's impossible to convey the enormity of that decision — you might as well have told me I'd been elected prime minister. This was before rotation, before All Blacks would be eased back into Super Rugby. Mehrts was fit, ready and raring to play. Yet Robbie had picked me over him. I was embarrassed initially. Mehrtens was more than just the incumbent — he was a cult hero in Christchurch. We loved him to a near irrational degree, for his sense of humour, his infectious calm, his outrageous skill, and the way he embodied everything this team and this town aspires to. He was 29, in his prime, and here was this 20 year old, a little punk who barely scraped into the Canterbury team, starting the biggest game of the season. But to his credit, it went beyond the handshake — the remainder of the week he was in my ear, helping me prepare for the game. I will forever be grateful to him for the way he handled himself through that situation. Outside the team, it wasn't nearly so orderly.

Talkback ran hot, and Robbie took a huge amount of criticism for it, which is understandable. The weirdest thing was that I hadn't played much 10 at any serious level. Nearly all my Canterbury rugby had been at 12, and that was clearly where Aussie McLean saw me. In years to come I would grow to love 10, the responsibility and control you have over the game from there. But at the time I had no sense of where I was best deployed, and was simply happy to get a run anywhere.

The whole team was supportive, congratulating me and giving me a fair run. The only guy who didn't seem completely comfortable with the decision was Justin Marshall. Justin's an extremely forthright guy; you won't die wondering how he feels. And he had developed an incredibly tight bond with Mehrts over a full decade playing alongside one another. There's a huge amount of trust that gets built up in the relationship between a halfback and a first-five. A break in that can really destabilise a team. So I can completely understand his reticence — he was sticking up for a mate, and trying to maintain a very successful partnership. It shows his fierce competitiveness, and great loyalty. But it certainly made my job more difficult.

It manifested itself in a few different ways. He would make on-field calls that would normally fall to a 10. He would back himself to make kicks during the run of play in situations where you'd have expected the ball to come back to me to clear. I'm not even certain whether he was aware he was doing it at times. I am sure in his mind he thought it was what was best for the team, that rather than have an untested debutant having too much ball, he'd take over that responsibility. I found it pretty unsettling, though. Add that to the pressure of starting ahead of my idol and I was a mess of nerves heading into the first game.

I don't remember any of my media interviews from that time, which is just as well. I'm not known for my eloquence even now, but back then I could barely get a sentence or two out. I would get so wrapped up in my thoughts that I was persistently conscious of thinking about having to talk, while speaking, but having no idea what was coming out of my mouth. It was such an unnerving situation, finishing televised interviews with no idea what you'd said. I hadn't had any media training, and wouldn't have any until I made the All Blacks — I really hope any footage from that era has been lost, because I must have been such a shambles.

Somehow I made it through the week, with all the attendant pressure, and we stood in the changing room before running out onto the field at Jade Stadium. I was swinging my leg, back and forth, in a kicking motion, without being aware of what I was doing. The team huddle started, and there I was, still swinging away, in a kind of catatonic state. I remember looking up and thinking, 'I should probably go and join the huddle.' I did, and soon we ran out onto the field and kicked off. The first 20 minutes of the game went by in a blur. There were two penalties early on. Easy shots, both. Perfect kicks to settle you down early on.

I missed them both. After shanking the first, I felt pure dread when the second came up in a near-identical spot. I knew I'd miss it. Afterwards you could start to feel the home crowd draw breath, worrying about what this kid was doing out there, how much damage he'd cause before he got subbed. Then Mauger got injured. Mehrts got called on, to a massive, booming ovation. He slotted into 10, and I moved out to 12 to replace Aaron. Mehrts, ever the gentleman, politely asked if I wanted to keep kicking. I practically begged him to take over — I was in a serious panic. At that stage I was on pace to have one of the great disasters on debut.

But Mehrts' arrival seemed to lift all the pressure off. Marshall was happy, because he had *his* 10 back, and the crowd palpably relaxed. I ended up having a great game, scoring two tries and picking up man-of-the-match. It's looked back upon now as a dream debut, which I suppose it was. But the first 20 minutes were pure terror, and were it not for Mehrts' calming influence, it could all have turned out so differently.

After the game I spoke with Ma'a Nonu, who'd also made his Super Rugby debut. I'd met him the previous year, at the Under 21s trial. He hadn't made that team, but was back with a vengeance now. His debut was similar to mine in a way — people were asking who he was, and where he'd come from. It's bittersweet to look back on that game now, a dozen years on, and think about how few of us there are left still playing. Ma'a and I became friends that year, bonding over the shared experiences we went through, and remain close to this day. You tend to get and stay tight with the guys you come in with. That's why whenever I play for the All Blacks it never feels quite right if Richie, or Ma'a, or Conrad, isn't there.

The rest of the campaign was much more manageable. Later in the season Aaron was out for a few weeks. Mehrts naturally slotted in at 10 and I moved out to 12. The three of us grew comfortable playing alongside one another in differing combinations. I played every single game, and I'm not even sure if I ever got subbed. I loved every minute, and felt like I could run forever at that age.

We played well enough to meet the Blues in the final. They were coming to the end of that dominant period they had, and adopted a contrasting style to us. They had pace to burn, with Doug Howlett at fullback, Joe Rokocoko and Rico Gear on the wings and, in Carlos Spencer, an absolute freakish attacker at number 10. It was a brilliant game, and we did enough to put ourselves in a position to win. Hammett scored two unbelievable tries, the first a lineout set piece, the second off a Carlos Spencer knock-on from the kick-off, which was pretty sweet. But they were at home, a packed Eden Park, and came back with Howlett and Daniel Braid crossing. We hit back with a try to Caleb Ralph in the dying minutes, but by then the game was just out of reach. I wasn't happy, but to reach the final in your first campaign was nothing to cry about. Our team was incredibly strong — of our first choice XV, only Brad Thorn and I hadn't yet played internationally — so we felt confident that even if we'd come up short this season, we were well-placed for the future.

That night we went out and had a few beers — nothing too serious, but a good night. The following day was scheduled for a post-season blowout. Something like league's Mad Monday, a way of celebrating the hard work and sacrifice of the season gone by. It started at 3 pm, and was the only thing I had scheduled that day. We were back in Christchurch by then, and I was out with a couple of teammates shopping for fancy dress. You had to go as something which began with the same letter as your surname. So I was looking for cowboy gear — that's as creative as my hangover would allow.

I was dimly aware that the 2003 All Blacks side was announced at midday, but hadn't paid any attention. My thoughts were on having fun with my teammates, so I headed to Camelot Costume Hire on Riccarton Road, renting the stupidest outfit I could find. My phone rang, and it was my old man. I wondered dimly what he might want, and headed outside to take the call.

'Congratulations,' he said.

'For what?' I replied, confused.

'You made the All Blacks!'

I thought he was having me on. The sentence seemed ridiculous. But he'd been listening to the team announcement, and had heard my name called. So that was how I found out I'd been selected. It might seem crazy, in this era, that the team is still named in such a secretive way. But it is — you literally find out by listening to the announcement. As soon as I got off the phone it started blowing up with messages and calls. As with every other selection, it seemed unreal. But this one in particular felt like way too much, way too soon.

What on earth was going on? In less than two years I had advanced from club rugby colts — one of the most marginal levels of rugby's ecosystem — to its pinnacle. It had all happened so quickly. Before I really had a chance to get comfortable at any level, I was on to the next.

My flatmate and I drove back to the house, my head still struggling to process what had happened. When I arrived the phone started ringing. The Crusaders comms people wanted me down to the club headquarters to do some media. It was the last thing I felt like doing, but I dutifully turned out for a 2 pm press session. My hangover was still rattling around, but thankfully Brad Thorn was there to deflect some of the attention. His selection was arguably a bigger deal than my own, given that he'd turned down a spot in the All Blacks in 2001. We had been the last remaining Crusaders starters without an All Blacks jersey. No longer.

Once I'd limped through my media duties I rejoined the team for our session. It was a pretty surreal day. I remember being briefed on what being an All Black entailed, but I just became numb, hearing about my new responsibilities and opportunities. One thing which made me laugh was being told I could go to the local dealer and pick out a Ford. For free. Only a couple of weeks earlier I'd finally gotten tired of driving around Mum and Dad's old Pulsar, which was returned to my folks (it was retired only very recently, with 375,000 km on the clock). I'd gone down to my local Subaru dealer and bought an Impreza WRX, which was the hottest car around at the time. The Kiwi rapper Scribe bought one not long after — it was just something Canterbury boys did when they got their first big cheque.

Three weeks later I was at a Ford dealership, being given the pick of the yard. I chose a Falcon, with only 10 km on the clock, which was cool. For reasons I still can't quite fathom, I picked out a hideous greenish-yellow colour. Lightning Strike, it was called. I drove it home to my flat, feeling completely overwhelmed by what was happening to me. Inside I still felt like the shy country boy from Southbridge. But my life seemed to be stuck on fast-forward.

It was only a few months since I'd turned 21. I had two twenty-firsts — a family-friendly one and one for my mates. The family one happened on a Saturday. We'd played on the Friday night and I booked out Riccarton Racecourse for all my friends and family and had a big party. It was an awesome night, but I remember being frustrated by one thing: the racecourse guys wouldn't let me do a yard glass. It was a hard-and-fast rule. I wasn't going to miss out on that particular rite of passage, though. The following week we had a bye, so I organised a party at our house. There were a couple of us who had turned 21 and hadn't done yardies, and so decided to fix that.

I did mine in 1 minute 15 seconds, and somehow didn't throw up. Afterwards I was a bit drunk and turned into a bit of a show pony. I climbed up on the roof and started sculling cans. I sculled the first one and still didn't throw up. This annoyed me, for some reason — it felt like part of the process. I decided that I wanted to spew off the roof. And on the second I felt it rising. I had a whole yardie inside me, plus the cans, and performed an amazing power chuck off the roof. Everyone on the ground was cheering me on. So juvenile, but so much fun. That's what I remember of my twenty-first — the grungy party the following week, more than the event itself.

We had some pretty good parties around at the house, helped by the fact I was starting to earn a bit of coin. People began to recognise me around town, and I enjoyed that first little bit of fame. I was still lucky enough to be hanging around with friends that knew me before I was in the Crusaders, which helped keep me grounded during a time when it would've been easy to completely lose my head. Your old friends are great like that — keeping watch for the slightest hint of ego, so that they can slash you back down to size.

There was no time to enjoy the afterglow of the selection. Because we'd made the final, camp came straight after our end-of-tournament celebrations. The Crusaders had a huge presence in the squad, which helped ease the transition, but, still, when I walked into All Blacks camp for the first time it was incredibly intimidating for someone so young and so green.

The two major groups in the team were the Crusaders and the Blues. Obviously I was very comfortable with all the Canterbury guys by that point. But the Blues were a different story. Mehrts hadn't been selected, controversially, so this was definitively Carlos Spencer's team. He had been in incredible form that year, and the Blues were champions, so it was well-earned. But going from playing alongside someone as supportive and welcoming as Mehrts to Spencer was quite a shock. He's like me — a naturally shy guy, and we were a little wary of each other back then. It wasn't open animosity — I was so obviously the junior — but it was quite different to the way Mehrts and I had clicked.

I was selected at 12, and at that point was hooked on the position. After my year with Canterbury and then the Crusaders, I felt like this was my spot. There was far less pressure, and you scored more tries — a win-win. 12 felt like a more open position, as we had so many great 10s in New Zealand at the time, from Spencer to Mehrts to Tony Brown. What with it being a World Cup year, everyone was that much more keyed up about job security, so I was happy to stay out of the first-five battle.

We finished up our camp at Mount Maunganui, and within

days England had arrived, as part of their Australasian tour. They were a very strong team, led by the guy who was probably the best first-five in the world at that point, Jonny Wilkinson. I was selected on the bench for the first test in Wellington on 14 June, which was an honour — but also a reflection of my ability to cover two positions. I didn't get on, and we lost. My first game with an All Blacks jersey on my back, and it was a loss to a team to which you really, really don't want to lose. Wilkinson was incredible that night. He was in his prime and tactically out of this world. He kicked us out of the game, scoring all England's 15 points, for a 15–13 result.

Afterwards there was an incredibly dark feeling in the changing room. I wasn't feeling it to the same extent, because I didn't get on, but you could sense the hurt in everyone: from players to coaches to management. That's when I first realised that All Blacks teams just can't lose. Especially not at home. Especially not to England. It was a horrible sensation — dropping our first game of the year, and doing it at home, to England, in a World Cup year.

I looked around the changing room and everyone's head was between their legs. No one spoke, and I kept even quieter than usual. I was paralysed by the silence, and resolved to sit there until someone else made a move. It took 20 aching minutes before the first people started stirring and having quiet conversations, and with that the tension began to ease off. Everyone was just bracing themselves for the press and the public. It's bad after any loss, but we knew that one would be particularly gruelling.

The following day we reviewed the game, an excruciating process, before one of the coaches approached me, and quietly told me I'd be starting the following week. I was incredibly happy.

In an instant any residual disappointment from the game was gone. Even though the rest of the team nursed the loss for days afterwards, I was floating just to know I was playing the following weekend. In a horrible way the loss made it easier, too, because we could hardly do any worse than we'd done in Wellington.

Next up on 23 June we had Wales at Waikato Stadium, a tough but much more manageable assignment. Hamilton's a rugby town, and the whole city was humming. This doesn't always happen in bigger cities, where a test can get a little lost. My parents, aunt and uncle flew up for the occasion, which made it all the more special. Brad Thorn was making his debut, too, and he was carrying some anger about not having gotten on the previous week. The pair of us were seriously up for the game.

I was given my jersey by Leilani Joyce, one of the world's finest squash players of the time, in the early afternoon. I remember racing back to my room and perching on the end of my bed and just gazing at the jersey. It's such a dreamlike situation, your first All Blacks jersey: the whole country grows up wanting to earn one, and here was mine. Stencilled on the sleeve was the date, the location and the opponent.

For some reason I was more relaxed heading into my All Blacks debut than my first Crusaders game. Maybe it was the Mehrts situation, or because we were coming off a loss. But I didn't feel the same burden of expectation, and instead relished all the theatre. The fireworks, the anthems — and the haka. I snuck to the back, as I wasn't very confident. Even though I'd been doing it in the mirror since I was five years old, there's nothing like doing a haka in front of a sold-out stadium to test your technique. Nevertheless, it was an unparalleled thrill; every All Black loves the haka, and knows what it means to the team.

You'd think my memory of my All Blacks debut would be really sharp, but it's anything but. I remember kicking off — then suddenly the match was over. I got to the end and thought, is that it? I was so focused on the moment that I barely registered the wider game itself. Whatever happened, it didn't affect my performance. I scored a try, kicked most of my goals, and ended up with 20 points. A dream debut, with a 55–3 win.

I got my jersey ripped early in the game. That was the early days of the new tight-fitting All Blacks jerseys. So I actually played most of the game with number 26 on my back. Then I was given a replacement after the game. For your first test match you play in one and then you're given another to swap with the opposition, because you never want to swap your very first.

But Steve Hansen was the coach of the Welsh team, and he'd been following my progress, so he made their number 12 give me his jersey without expecting one in return. So I've got my ripped one, which got repaired, my spare one, and my number 26 jersey. They're part of my memorabilia collection at the Southbridge club now — part of a whole walk-in cabinet dedicated to me and Alby Anderson.

We had an after-match function at the back of the casino. My parents were there to see me get my first cap, receiving one alongside a good friend in Brad Thorn. It was just the most amazing night.

I came back to earth the following week. We played France in Christchurch and won narrowly, 31–23, thanks largely to Joe Rokocoko having one of the most extraordinary games a wing has ever had. He scored three tries, and essentially single-handedly saved us.

I think I was about five years old when this studio photograph was taken.

Dad had me kicking as soon as I could walk. Here I am with my mate Sam Manson and my sister Sarah. She'll love me for including this photo.

Playing with my mates and having the time of my life . . . Southbridge Midgets, 1988. I'm at the far right of the back row.

I had three years in the Ellesmere College first XV. I'm first on the left after a match against Temuka High.

Mum and Dad — two of my greatest supporters — on the next-door ground where I used to practise.

Making a rare break during the annual Christchurch Boys' High–Christ's College match in 2000. We lost . . . and the dressing room was a morgue.

A dream debut for the All Blacks against Wales in Hamilton, 2003. I scored a try, kicked most of my goals, and ended up with 20 points.

Proud moment in Hamilton with Mum and Dad after receiving my test cap.

The infamous billboard on the old Copthorne Hotel in Christchurch . . .
I changed my commute to avoid looking at it.

The second test against the Lions in Wellington is now considered my signature game. I scored 33 points, including these two second-half tries. It was a good enough game that, when I missed a kick at goal — my only miss — I remember being particularly disappointed, like I'd messed up my day statistically.

Jimmy Cowan seems pretty happy with the second of my two tries against Wales on the 2005 end-of-year tour. My 26-point haul was a record for an All Black against Wales.

With the Kelvin Tremain Memorial Trophy for New Zealand Player of the Year and the IRB International Player of the Year trophy: 2005 had been a special year.

Rugby World Cup, 2007. Top: Making a point to Smithy and Ted prior to our ill-fated quarter-final at Cardiff. Middle: Frustration sets in as we struggle against the French. Above: I had braced myself for the onslaught after returning to Christchurch . . . instead the fans turned out to show their support and loyalty.

The final match of 2010, against Wales at Cardiff. Top: Kicking a penalty goal to break Jonny Wilkinson's world test points scoring record. Middle: The big screen at Millennium Stadium acknowledges the feat. Above: Celebrating victory and the All Blacks' third grand slam in six years.

Going into the Tri-Nations we felt incredibly insecure as a result of the loss to England, and the near miss against France. It was a truncated tournament, thanks to the World Cup, but we came in with real intensity — with something to prove. That manifested itself in two of the most brutal and comprehensive wins of my career. We put 50 points each on South Africa and Australia in consecutive weekends, both at their fortress-like home grounds of Loftus Versfeld and Telstra Stadium.

That got our wind back, and while the next two games were far closer, we still did enough to win both the Bledisloe and Tri-Nations — the perfect way to close out an otherwise problematic build-up to the World Cup.

Within the team we felt confident, and I was still fresh off the boat and just happy to be there. But unbeknown to me, the side was experiencing some growing pains because of the transition from amateurism to the professional era, which would become apparent before the tournament was finished. In time they would lead to a cultural sea-change which still echoes in the side today.

None of us knew that at the time, and we commenced the final stretch of pre-Cup preparations in earnest. After the Tri-Nations there was a month's break, during which a series of camps were held around the country. Each one was capped with a Possibles-Probables game of escalating duration. These were the closest thing to a real match we'd get ahead of the tournament, and even by the normal standards of such games they were particularly difficult. I was on the Possibles, a group of young guys with nothing to lose — we went really hard to try and make an impression on the coaches.

The final matchup went for 60 minutes, with Steve Walsh brought in to ref, to try and provide as close a simulation as possible of a real test. He and Carlos never got on at the best of times, and Walsh ended up sending him off for too much chat, which says all you need to know about how niggly those games got. I knew I hadn't done enough to change the starting line-up, but I enjoyed the battle regardless.

Once the camps were over we flew across to the tournament. I was still essentially a passenger, still watching and learning. But I could sense how much it meant to the senior players in particular, how excited they were to approach the tournament. When we arrived, though, much of that excitement disappeared. We were based in Melbourne, an AFL-mad city where you could easily have been unaware the Cup was even happening.

That was vividly illustrated to us one evening, when a group of us were in a taxi on our way to dinner. The driver asked us what we did. I told him we were rugby players, in Australia for the World Cup. He had no clue that there was a World Cup on — or even what rugby was. He kept going on about the Melbourne Storm. It was a little deflating.

We stayed in Melbourne for almost the entire tournament, only leaving for a couple of days when we had games in other cities. The thinking was that we'd be well-insulated from the hype, and better able to focus as a result. It was a nice idea, but I'm not sure if it had the desired result. We were housed in apartments away from the city, and started to get seriously bored.

That wasn't the only thing which was wearing on us. There was a team song which we had been singing all season. At first it got you excited, but by the end it had lost all its meaning. As a team, we thrived on new experiences and challenges. Unfortunately there weren't a lot of those, with the way the '03 tournament was organised.

On the field, things were more exciting. I had entered the

tournament just making up the numbers, behind Tana, Aaron and Carlos in the competition for the first- and second-five positions. But an injury to Aaron meant I played three games through the pool stages, and I was enjoying the game time immensely.

Aaron was fit again by the time the quarter-final came around, so I returned to the bench. This felt like the start of the tournament proper, and we played brilliantly in beating South Africa. There was a lot of adrenalin around afterwards, as we headed back to the hotel. I assumed we'd have a couple of drinks and call it a night. That wasn't the way it played out.

We ended up having a little court session in the team room, and a group of us went out on the town afterwards. At the time, while I enjoyed the night out, I remember wondering what the hell we were up to. I was just a young fella, so I wasn't going to question it. It wasn't a huge night, and we scrubbed up fine. But it's not something which I could ever conceive of happening mid-tournament today. It was another piece of evidence, perhaps, of the level of confidence and relaxation within the side. We simply hadn't been put under much pressure throughout the year, and subconsciously that starts to affect you as a team.

After the win over the Boks we finally said goodbye to Melbourne for good, packed and relocated to Sydney for the semi against Australia. Suddenly the hype arrived, and we were absolutely aware that not only was the World Cup on, but that it was reaching its conclusion. We were stoked. We'd put 50 points on the Aussies in Sydney a few months before, and had been killing most teams. We had been playing an exciting, overwhelmingly attacking style of rugby, which had been working in our favour all year. We had every reason to think we could handle Australia.

If we'd known to look, there were little signs that it was going to be tougher than we thought. Most pertinently, Tana was out of the tournament. He was immense, one of the real leaders of the team. Leon MacDonald, who hadn't played centre all year, was filling in, and kicking goals over Carlos. Nothing seemed to matter though — we had huge self-belief.

We started the game well, and were putting them under real pressure. I watched the game for the first time in years recently, and was struck by how much ball we had, how attacking our style was. But Stirling Mortlock scored an intercept try against the run of play, which felt like a 14-point swing. A couple of subsequent penalties meant that Australia were playing at home, in a World Cup semi, with scoreboard pressure on their side. They tackled incredibly well, and I watched, increasingly tense and despondent, as they took out a deserved win, and ended our hopes in the tournament.

In the sheds afterwards the silence was prolonged and heavy. I saw the hurt on players' faces, and belatedly realised exactly what the World Cup meant. It was that precise moment which made me determined to be there for the next one. I almost think of myself as starting my preparation that day, knowing that I'd be in my prime come 2007, and desperately wanting to go into the same situation and find a way to create a different outcome.

6

Road To Nowhere

After the pain of the World Cup semi-final loss against Australia in Sydney, we had to pick ourselves up to play France in the most pointless game of all — the playoff for third and fourth. I only got on after an injury, and while the game didn't matter, I was happy to get a run, and a convincing win, 40–13.

After the tournament we were given the option of flying home, or staying in Sydney to see some sights. The majority of the team returned to New Zealand, but a group of us young guys decided to stick around. It was 2003, and 50 Cent's 'Get Rich Or Die Tryin' had come out at the start of the year. I loved the album, and there was a group of four of us who called ourselves the P.I.M.P.s, after the song. Ma'a, Ben Atiga, Joe Rokocoko and myself.

We went out the night before the final, still sore about the loss to Australia, and felt like we should have been playing the following night, not watching the Cup be decided on television. We headed toward Cargo Bar, in Darling Harbour. When we got there the place was packed, and we went in, wondering what had drawn such a huge crowd. Once we got inside it was revealed: Prince Harry was standing there, having a big night out.

Eventually we went across to chat to him. He was pretty pleased with how the tournament was going, and for some reason decided that he wanted us to kiss the rose on his England jersey. That was definitely not going to happen. It was a pretty surreal scene — this prince, out on the beers, trying to get us to bow down to the English rose. But the moment passed, and we ended up having a good time. Particularly Caleb Ralph, who got chatting with Zara Phillips, Harry's cousin, and dated her for a while afterwards.

The following day we watched the final — at a bar. That wasn't how we'd pictured it when we'd flown over. It was a fun weekend, but tinged with regret at what might have been. I flew back to Christchurch determined that we'd learn from the defeat, and I'd play a more meaningful role next time around.

2003 had already been an incredible year — but more was to come. That summer was when Honor and I first started spending time together, and our relationship began. We were both young, ambitious athletes — she would make her New Zealand debut the following year — and I think that was part of why we clicked, and stayed together through all the stresses of our careers. Being with someone who truly understands the pressures and rhythms of top-level sport, and can relate to the highs and lows, has made each of us so much stronger. So while I didn't yet know how important our relationship was going to be, I knew that she was special, and what we had was rare. And as my career took off over the coming years, so our relationship grew and solidified.

After the tournament, the old coaches were gone, and in some ways the modern All Blacks were born. With Graham Henry and his assistants came an understanding that the new regime would make changes to imprint their own style on the team.

Being such a junior member of the side, a lot of that either went over my head, or I ducked to avoid it. I was still really shy in group situations, and didn't feel I had remotely earned the right to speak up about how the team was run. I was 21 and still lucky to be in any team I played for, as far as I was concerned. I might have had certain elite rugby skills by that stage, but by no means did I have enough elite rugby experience to comment, let alone the confidence to do so, even if I had.

So 2004 dawned with me grateful to be back in the Crusaders environment, one with none of the complexity of the All Blacks at that time. Rather than the doubt which I experienced going in on debut, the previous season's form meant I felt I belonged in the side, and thus enjoyed the pre-season that much more. We had such a strong squad that year — largely unchanged from the previous year — and I felt very, very good about our chances.

I also felt like my own status within the side had begun to shift. No longer would I have to prove myself each time we played — senior players had a good handle on my capabilities, and their growing confidence in me nourished my game.

With that prominence came new opportunity off the field. To this point my attitude towards sponsorships would have been 'Where do I sign?' It just blew me away that people would offer me something free. But I'd only had a couple of deals up until then, neither of them particularly important. The first was with Nike, who sponsored Canterbury in 2002. The extent of the deal was: 'Here's some free clothing and a few pairs of boots; now you're a Nike athlete.' Looking back, I should've shopped around, and certainly not signed for any length of time. But I was just happy to be there, and signed off without even putting the deal in front of anyone. With so many things back then I just smiled, shook hands and agreed. Which makes me all the more grateful that the first agents to come in front of me were Lou Thompson and

Dean Hegan, and not some of the less competent player reps who do the rounds.

When I made the All Blacks at the end of the previous year they had an override clause, which meant I was back in adidas. That suited me, as I'd been wearing adidas prior to joining Canterbury, from my time with the New Zealand unders, and genuinely preferred their boots. Going into 2004 I thought I'd have to be back in Nike, but Andrew Gaze, a Kiwi who ran international sponsorships for adidas, had seen something in me that previous season. He approached my new agents about getting me an individual contract with the company internationally. This was pretty serious, as it meant being paid to wear their clothes and footwear, and being promoted all over the world. Most All Blacks are simply covered by the NZRU deal, which doesn't bring any additional financial support. This put me in rare company — only Doug Howlett, Richie and Jonah were on international deals.

Prior to the adidas deal, my biggest sponsorship was with a toy company. It was in the middle of 2003, just after I first made the All Blacks, and the ad involved me and Steve Devine. The object was called the 'Vortex Mega Howler', a NERF toy, and the concept called for an established All Black and an up-and-comer. Apparently one of the women at Hasbro liked the look of me — I wasn't prominent enough at the time to get those kind of deals on merit. But I was young and happy to be asked.

We tossed this thing back and forth for an afternoon, and they made a TV commercial around it. The funny thing is, like the Canterbury NPC contract, it ended up working out really well for Hasbro. The deal allowed them to play the ad for three seasons — 2003 through 2005 — which were pretty good ones for me on the field. So the ad kept coming back to haunt me — every season it would pop up: 'Hey Steve — catch this!' 'Wow — great throw, Dan.' I had won a Super Rugby title, become the regular All Blacks first-five, won the 2005 IRB World Player of the Year, and the ad kept coming around. My teammates loved to give me shit about it, and I'd beg Dean, my agent, to get it off air. But there was nothing we could do. Still, it was a good lesson in how to structure deals in future, particularly in regard to paying attention to term.

It wasn't my only learning experience. After signing the adidas deal, I gave all my old Nike gear to Dad. He loved it — the first free gear he'd had in 50-odd years of rugby. Then a shot of him in Nike clothes made the paper, which didn't impress adidas.

After the adidas and Vortex deals I thought I was beginning to get a handle on the commercial side of things, and enjoying the extra bit of cash that came along. But in truth I knew nothing, which would be proven by the next deal which presented itself in the middle of the year. One which would be embarrassing, ground-breaking, lucrative and, for better and worse, define me for years to come.

The model booker Sara Tetro approached me directly in 2004, saying that Jockey wanted to shoot me in their underwear. They'd gone to Richie first apparently, but that had been a pretty short conversation. I was heading the same way. Then my sponsorship agent Dean Hegan got wind of the deal, so we started to discuss it. There was something about it I found a bit exciting. Mainly that Sara ran a modelling agency, which made it seem more glamorous than it might otherwise have been. So we had a meeting. I was still probably only talking for the sake of talking, not because I intended to do anything about it. But then she put the figure in front of me. And it was big — at least compared to how much I'd been getting, and how little work was involved.

I was still torn, and talking to a few people about it. One of them was Steve Hansen, a new assistant to the All Blacks. He might seem like an odd guy to approach on something like this, but I was so young and so confused that I'd have talked to anyone. He asked me how much they were offering. I told him, and he said, 'Well, go back and ask them for three times as much. If they say no, you're sweet, you don't have to do it. But if they say yes, you're rich.'

It was great advice, and exactly what I did. Jockey were understandably a bit upset. Who did I think I was? Which it wasn't about at all — it was more a recognition of just how little I wanted to wander round in my undies in front of a camera. I thought that was the end of the story. But the very next day they came back and agreed to meet the price. You'd think I'd have been pleased at such a big cheque, but it was the opposite. All I could think about was having to tell my parents.

Only the money kept me from backing out entirely. Eventually the big day came. I was following a Jockey Australia ambassador at the shoot. She was just finishing up when I arrived, and made the whole thing look so easy. Sara knew how nervous I was and completely cleared the set, so it was just me, the photographer and a couple of assistants. I took forever to come out of the changing room for the first time — they probably wondered if I'd escaped. But the photographer was brilliant, and before I knew it we were wrapped.

That was only the beginning of the drama. The billboards were up within weeks, in all the test match cities. I walked into the All Blacks team room on one occasion and someone had put a poster up on the whiteboard. I tore it down, burning with embarrassment. To this day I don't know who put it up. But if I had to guess, I'd go with Justin Marshall. The Crusaders team had a culture of practical jokes back then, and Justin was an absolute master. There were holes cut in socks, shirts dyed pink, flip-flops sliced up — nothing was safe. So the poster's appearance was to be expected really.

And anyway, I was hardly blameless when it came to practical jokes. One of my favourites came early in my career. The Crusaders were staying in Johannesburg, with most of our rooms in a row on a single corridor. We were deep into the Super Rugby season, and some of that road boredom was setting in. One evening I was hanging out with Aaron, and I got dressed in full compression skins, and told them I was a superhero, out to take down the whole forward pack. Aaron bought in, and got into his skins too. Then we started our mission.

The first door we came to was that of Brad Thorn and Greg Somerville — two of the biggest, toughest guys in the squad. We threw ourselves at them, and started wrestling with all our might. From memory, Greg didn't love the idea, but Thorny was more than game. We came off second best, unsurprisingly, but I think he was impressed we were willing to have a crack. We worked our way down the hall, causing chaos, but apart from Brad we pretty much dominated the rest of the pack, from memory. It was a lot of fun, and typical of the kind of boredom-busting prank that will occasionally rear up on tour. Whenever they arrived, I'd always be keen.

The Jockey deal opened me up to all kinds of jokes from my teammates over the years — though now half the team's in the campaign. This is a big change: back then All Blacks just didn't do that kind of thing — not because they didn't want to, but because the opportunity simply didn't exist. Apart from Jonah's various deals, and Carlos with Toffee Pops, there were virtually no individual All Blacks endorsements. The Jockey deal would come to be seen as opening the door on what is now an important income stream for players.

I didn't enjoy the notoriety one bit. Mum was horrified, and I literally changed my commute in Christchurch to avoid having to look at the billboard. But I'm glad I stuck it out. It's become the base of my commercial relationships, and was responsible for changing the value of endorsements, and the way brands saw rugby players, which has had a positive impact on the whole sport. It also helped me get over my fear of cameras at a young age, which would prove very useful in years to come.

The Jockey sponsorship really has become a big part of my life, and helped set me up for my career post-rugby in a way which wouldn't have been possible in the amateur era. Even today, at 33, I've stayed with Jockey — I'm still an ambassador.

Everything else has flowed from there, including some which have had real prominence internationally. Adidas and MasterCard have used me internationally, and Gillette booked me for a global campaign alongside Tiger Woods and Roger Federer. It ended up falling over, but the process of negotiating at that level was an education in itself.

My commercial experience has also helped me leverage my profile for charities, Canteen in particular. When I was first starting out in the Crusaders, a pair of young fans with cancer came to every practice. I struck up a friendship with them, and was devastated when they died. I found out that they'd been taken to the sessions by Canteen, and decided to work with the organisation however I could, and have found it the most affecting and satisfying work of my career. It's very different work to the commercial side, but each nourishes the other, one teaching skills and giving profile that I can exploit for both myself and for others in much greater need.

I'm incredibly fortunate to have lived through this era, but I also feel like I've helped shape it in some way. Somewhat surprisingly, despite being a country boy, I found myself enjoying figuring out how to navigate this new world. What I've found is that often it comes down to amplifying existing NZRU contracts. Which is great for guys like me and Richie. But I do feel for some younger All Blacks, or guys who play less high-profile positions. The sheer number of sponsors that the NZRU signs on, across so many different areas, means players' ability to maximise their incomes is quite limited. I've been so fortunate having such a long career, and one with some prominence. For more fringe All Blacks, the window is shorter and smaller, and after I retire I'd love to be able to help with advice or opportunities to better equip them for life after rugby.

The adidas deal was part of what made the summer of 2003–2004 more relaxing than the previous two. I was finally starting to become comfortable with my position in rugby's ecosystem, to understand that I was there on merit and this life wasn't likely to be yanked away from me any minute. I'd barely had pause to breathe since making the Under 21s two years earlier, and had played a tonne of games through that period — more than anyone would be allowed now, in all likelihood. It had done wonders for my game, but I was due a break to refresh, to think about what I'd accomplished, and where I'd like to push on to in the coming year. I spent the summer reconnecting with family and old friends I'd lost touch with. We had some good times, but always in the back of my mind was the idea that in 2004 I wanted to grow, rather than standing pat.

This was driven home by a media interview in the pre-season. One of the *Press* reporters persistently asked me about second-year syndrome. It wasn't a term I'd heard before, but the guy was so dogged that it felt less a possibility than an inevitability. Like a disease or illness I was destined to catch. He talked about the amount of time my opponents would spend analysing my game, and how they'd have worked out my tricks. In a funny way it made me more determined than ever to be different, and to prove to those waiting for me to fail or fall back that I would do the opposite.

To a certain extent he was right. Coaches and opponents do study your game. They'll know that you're defensively stronger on a particular shoulder. I'll even hear them on the field, saying, 'Watch his left-foot step,' 'Watch his right-hand feed.' Those are go-to moves for me, and I'd find myself getting annoyed — 'That's my secret!' But it's inevitable. We're on TV, for all the world to see, slow down and pick apart. That interview made me realise I had to keep evolving, to work hard to be more elusive and unpredictable.

That's something all players do, but one thing I've paid a lot of attention to is less obvious, and came from Wayne Smith. He's a coach I consider one of the true geniuses of the game. It was around 2004 or 2005 that he told me to not just work on my weaknesses, but my strengths, too. That just because someone knows something is coming, doesn't mean they can stop it. So if you have a strong left-foot step, double down on that and make it that much faster. If you're a good tackler, work hard to become a great one. It's something I've always kept in mind — the power of improving elements of your game you already rely on.

Knowing that there was a contingent expecting me to find the second year far tougher than my first made me determined to enter the season in perfect condition. I retreated to my work ethic, that Canterbury mentality: 'hard work conquers all'. So if I was pushing a specific weight last year, then I'd need to do 10 per cent more this year. If I was running a particular time, I needed to be 10 seconds faster. I had to kick more balls, run more laps, lift more weights and generally destroy myself in the pre-season to make doubly sure I would avoid losing momentum.

It wasn't just physical, either. I knew that my first year I'd been quiet to a fault, especially for someone playing in a backline position which requires some leadership. And while part of that came from wanting to watch and learn, to earn respect rather than demand it, I knew that it also came down to shyness, and being naturally deferential. It was simple: if I wanted to continue to grow as a player I would need to find my voice on the field.

It took a while, but eventually it came. I think now it's an area the academies really stress with young players: the need to speak and communicate well. For the most part that's a great thing, as you have guys coming into the top rugby environments with no hesitation about speaking up, even to some of the most senior members of the squad. They can bring new insight into what can be settled patterns of thinking. But it can also cross the line into cockiness. Sometimes you see them challenging a captain before they've begun to earn their place in the side, in a way which would have been completely unthinkable 10 or 15 years ago. But for the most part we have more debate over game plans and strategy than at any time in the past, and that's a very good thing.

Once again I came into the Super season playing at 12, arriving with a head of steam. It was a dream season: my body felt great, and I missed just one game. Inside me in the backline was a different story. Aaron Mauger started the first two games at 10 with Mehrts relegated to the subs' bench. Later, Cam McIntyre battled Mehrts for the position. There was destabilising flux at first-five, but I felt very secure at 12.

The drama was unfortunate. Mehrts was never anything less than a gentleman to me, for which I'll be forever grateful. But his relationship with Robbie really deteriorated as the season progressed. It was sad to watch, Mehrts being pushed out of a team which was his heart and soul. And Robbie unable to cope with a senior player's needs in the same way he could brilliantly nurture his young talent. It really was unfortunate. I think Robbie is probably the best coach of young players you could hope to find. He sees talent early and nurtures it as well as anyone. But once that talent gets older, and develops their own voice, he can be a little inflexible, unable to adapt the relationship to reflect the player's evolved skill-set and perspective.

Despite the personnel issues we were still a spectacular team, with talent right across the park. We made the final and faced the Brumbies, who were exceptional around that time. In the final Cam started, with me and Aaron around him at second-five and centre. And we got absolutely drilled. We were just over-awed by the occasion, and completely lost our composure. Within the first quarter of the match they'd scored five tries. We were down 33–0, and the match looked like it was already over. To his credit, Robbie took drastic action, and put Mehrts on for McIntyre.

What followed was one of the greatest comebacks I've ever been involved in. We scored two tries before the break to go in at

33–14 with the faintest glimmer of hope. That promptly dimmed when they scored near the start of the second half. We battled hard, despite the margin, and ended up losing a very entertaining final 47–38. The first 20 minutes aside, we dominated the game, but it was simply too far gone by then. What I'll always remember is Mehrts' performance. He wasn't in his best shape, and had endured a pretty troubled season. But you saw all his poise, his intellect and his tactical skill in that last 60 minutes, and what a true champion he was.

For any other franchise, two straight trips to the final would probably have been cause for celebration, and enough to get the coach a new contract. In Canterbury and with the Crusaders, our standards are so high that we were crushed. The mentality is such that we demand more from our team than that. I didn't quite appreciate that the first two years. I was still young, and subconsciously I still felt this was someone else's team. That it wasn't to my credit if we won, nor my fault if we lost. But by the year's end I was starting to understand what it was to be a Crusader, to adopt that rugged mentality.

Guys such as Reuben Thorne, Justin Marshall, Greg Somerville, Aaron Mauger and, increasingly even then, Richie — they had such a fierceness about them. A hardness. They almost seemed to relish the game getting tough, and have a level of self-belief that no matter how daunting the situation we could still pull it out. So, despite the team having just missed in both those finals, I believed in those guys and that team, and wanted very badly to join that group and embody the same attitude and ethic.

Coming out of Super Rugby I knew the All Blacks team was imminent, and after the way I'd played that season I was confident

I'd get picked. I was named Super Rugby Player of the Year, and had collected over 200 points to be the competition's top scorer. I thought there was a good chance that I'd start and, sure enough, I was named at 12 in the Probables side to play the Possibles at Eden Park.

That kind of game has gone out of fashion now but that year it had a real edge to it. The Possibles were very strong — I was up against Sam Tuitupou, who had been outstanding all year. Our opponents were all trying to steal the jerseys off our back. It was really close at the end when they were penalised. Even though the etiquette is to ignore penalties in those games, we wanted to win, so elected to kick for goal. I put it over from 40 metres to seal the game.

It was a very physical way to start the international season, but we needed it. Our first opponents were England, fresh off their World Cup win, and without doubt the standard by which all other sides would be measured. These were our first games under the new coaching regime, though, so there was a sense of optimism through the camp, and a hunger derived from the knowledge we'd lost when it mattered at the last World Cup.

This was my first contact with Graham Henry and, if I'm honest, I was shit-scared of him. I'd never met him before, but watching his interviews and seeing the way he handled himself, he looked a real hard bugger. You could tell he'd been a headmaster, let's put it that way. But after I'd gotten over my initial fear, I found the change of coaching personnel refreshing. With Robbie so integral to Mitchell's set-up there hadn't been a big difference stylistically between the Crusaders and the All Blacks. Henry was a good guy to be scared of — if you got out of line, you'd hear about it. He's old-school like that. But between him, Steve Hansen and Wayne Smith there was a new set of voices and perspectives coming through, and as a young guy who was still learning every day, I revelled in it.

Henry turned out to be slightly different to what I'd assumed. At times he'd be as serious and awe-inspiring a guy as you'd ever meet. At others he'd surprise you with practical jokes or unexpected flashes of humour. Beyond Graham, Wayne Smith was someone I really bonded with. He's very analytical and structured, which took a while to absorb, but was a marked and welcome contrast to the more free-flowing, instinctive style of Robbie. Prior to that regime, I'd never spent time on computers. I hated it at first, the repetition of the video. And not whole games — very specific and finely cut sections of play. It was broken down into pieces so small you wondered whether there was any real use to them. Now I see that Smithy was way ahead of his time.

We went in to the England series determined to atone for the previous year, and did so pretty comprehensively. I kicked incredibly well, missing only once as we swept them in the two-test series. Although it did little to make us forget the lows of the World Cup, it still felt good heading into the Tri-Nations, which we'd won the previous year.

The tournament began reasonably well, with tight wins over Australia and South Africa in July. But in August things started to turn. We lost a close game to Australia in Sydney, during which we failed to score a try. I'd been playing fairly well, but rolled an ankle and hobbled through until just after halftime, at which point I checked out of the game for good. Carlos was pulled as well, so the second half finished with Mehrts and Sam Tuitupou at first- and second-five — quite a different side and style. The changes made no difference — we lost 23–18.

Heading into the final game against South Africa I was

desperate to play. I had hated watching us lose to Australia, and thought the injury was marginal enough that I should at the very least be given the chance to prove my fitness. I was starting to feel comfortable in the team. But my mood changed when the team was read out for the weekend. I was furious when I was omitted — it was the last game for some weeks, and we still had a real shot at winning the competition. I didn't feel like I was being given a decent chance to prove my fitness.

I responded in a very immature way, typical of a 22 year old. I drank, pretty heavily, for most of the week. Me and the rest of the DDs (Dirty Dirties — rugby slang for non-playing reserves) would have a couple at the hotel, then head out to bars and have a fair few more. It was just considered normal back then, but would never happen today. Nowadays everyone has to be ready to play. And if you're injured then you're rehabbing, and likely not drinking at all.

But those of us who weren't playing were just having a good time. We were out until two or three in the morning on the Wednesday or Thursday before a test. We weren't thinking about how we could help the guys who were playing. Instead, we were just concentrating on enjoying ourselves, and not so subtly saying to the coaches and management that if we weren't playing then we would do whatever the hell we wanted.

It wasn't out of the ordinary. Those coaches had played and coached most of their lives in the amateur era, when tours and standards were very different to today. So had some of the senior members of our squad. There are things you can demand of a salaried professional that you cannot ask of an amateur who is taking time out from work and family to be there.

The social side of the sport was a definite attraction for

players back in the day, as it remains. But there was a period of adjustment, whereby some of us professionals were wanting to have our salaries, but keep our amateur-style socialising, too. The coaches didn't seem particularly worried. But it certainly didn't help, and may have contributed in some small way to what happened on the field.

Which was a bloodbath. South Africa ran rampant, putting 40 points on us at Ellis Park in what remains one of the most lacklustre All Blacks performances during my time with the team. Centre Marius Joubert scored a hat-trick, and Percy Montgomery was kicking goals from all over the field. It was dismal, and rather than the sadness or anguish which normally accompanies a loss, there was an anger — a much uglier emotion — in the air.

That night we had a court session. These exist to air any grievances in a controlled way, and are mostly light-hearted team-bonding exercises. It's a mock judicial scenario, in which minor infractions are described and a few beers are drunk as sentences for 'crimes'. We all get a bit pissed and everyone goes to bed happy. A court session is supposed to be fun, and for the most part they are. Even though there are punishments dished out, they almost function like a reward at the end of a season or a tour.

This one was very different. It happened in a small, drab conference room at our hotel. The mood wasn't great to begin with, with the loss still hanging in the air, and swiftly got pretty dark. Players were angry, and the kind of accusations flying and sentences imposed were so much harsher than usual.

Instead of beer, it was spirits being doled out. People were absolutely hammered, throwing up everywhere. It just got completely out of control. We didn't look like the world-class sports team we aspired to be. We looked like a stag do gone wrong.

I felt it particularly acutely, as I had to apologise to the whole team on behalf of the DDs. Graham had found out we'd been going harder than we should have, and it was felt we needed to own it in front of the group. As a young guy, and a shy one at that, I found it intensely humiliating. All the DDs felt terrible, like we'd devalued the jersey, and bore responsibility for the nature of the loss. The whole team ended up getting into it — from doctors, to management, to coaches. And rather than a few hours, it went on the whole night. Even when I left for the airport the following afternoon, some of the guys were still on it.

I've never been part of a more raw and ragged court session. You could sense it was not sitting at all well with some people. Wayne Smith in particular seemed appalled at the state of us. You could sense him thinking: 'What the hell is this team?' Afterwards, I think he was ready to walk away. When we woke up the following morning — or afternoon in some cases — we all knew that what had happened wasn't right. That something had to give for us to become the kind of team we aspired to be. And to ensure a night like this never happened again.

FINAL YEAR DIARY: Christchurch, 26 January 2015

Recorded at my apartment at the Clearwater Resort in Christchurch, during Crusaders pre-season.

I signed with Racing in mid-December, and haven't regretted it for a moment since. Honor and I are so excited about moving to Paris, and our children learning French. It helped set the mood for a brilliant summer.

My training in Taupo went really well. The nerve issue in my leg seems to have calmed down, and being away from the distractions of Auckland meant I was able to focus on conditioning in a way I haven't been able to for years. Nic Gill, the All Blacks' trainer, put together a series of different workouts for me, and life down there got a nice rhythm going. I'd wake up, have breakfast with the family, and spend time with Honor and Marco. Then around mid-morning I'd head down to Owen Delany Park and run through my workouts.

Sometimes Honor and Marco would come with me, and play while I went through my exercises, with Marco competing against me for the last few. I'd end each day with a series of kicks at goal. It all helped me feel a growing sense of confidence in my body that I hadn't felt in years.

Afterwards I'd break for lunch, then go to the gym, followed by some off-feet conditioning in the pool or on the Wattbike. Then I'd often go paddle-boarding, which I love, out on the great lake. It was a perfect combination of relaxing time with the family, and good, hard pre-season work. Christchurch has been a continuation of the theme, minus the family time. With Honor getting pregnant with baby number two it's meant I couldn't be there to help her as much as I'd like, but it has its advantages when it comes to preparation. While I'm down here there's nothing much else to do but train. Getting this length of pre-season with the Crusaders also feels like a gift. It's been years and years since I was able to integrate with the team this early.

I'm starting to really enjoy being a senior member of the team, and being able to take on some of the associated responsibilities. This week a reporter asked us about rumours we'd be playing a game in Fiji. It felt like some people in management liked the idea of it, but we travel so much that it seemed like a real player welfare issue to me. In the past I'd have grumbled privately, but ducked the question. This time round I felt comfortable owning the issue in front of the media. At this point in my career, what have I got to lose?

Christchurch, 15 February 2015
Recorded via Skype at Clearwater Resort following a season-opening loss to the Rebels, 10–20 at AMI Stadium.

I've got the family down, which has been good, particularly after the ugly result. I don't know where it came from; we'd had a really good week of preparation. I thought everything was feeling really good, but then nothing flowed out there.

What made it worse was coming away hobbling again.

The scary thing is that it's right in the same spot as I had nerve troubles last year. I still can't walk properly today. There is definitely something going on in my leg in that area.

I played a couple of pre-season games and had been running freely. I remember warming up before the game and realising it was the best I'd felt for a couple of years. I had no niggles and my whole body felt good. Everything seemed to be on track for the season. Now I've just got a bit of a hurdle to get over.

It was pretty traumatic. That might be a strong word, but I was just starting to get my confidence back and then my first competition game back I get a whack, and it brings back all those memories. I'm just trying to stay positive and hopefully it will settle down over the next couple of days.

The match was just as bad. It was one of those average games where I didn't have many opportunities. The Rebels' defence was excellent, the way they rushed up on us. I wish our forwards would just fire up. When they got desperate at the end of the game they started playing really well. But even in the pre-season it was the same thing — we'd be getting hammered, then out of halftime we'd finally start playing with some spark.

The challenge is finding that desperation right from the first whistle. We're just not getting that. I'm so used to having a forward pack that dominates, and getting ball on a plate going forward. That never came, and I couldn't really do a lot unfortunately, so I felt like I was playing within myself a bit. I'm sure things will improve, but between that and the flare-up I'm not feeling great at the moment.

Christchurch, 22 February 2015

Recorded via Skype at Clearwater Resort. Crusaders defeat the Highlanders 26–20, but I missed the game with what felt like a recurrence of last winter's leg injury.

The last week has been pretty tough. I don't think I've had a week like this, where I've been talked about in such a negative way before. I haven't really read too much in the media, but when all your friends start texting you and telling you not to worry about what the papers are saying, it's hard to avoid the sentiment. Your friends and coaches are all of a sudden asking if you're alright, so it becomes pretty real. It was only round two of the competition, and I've only played half a dozen games in the last 14 or 15 months. I'm not sure if they're expecting miracles. So that's what makes me frustrated. Having another injury like this, minor as it is, you do get that self-doubt and the lack of trust in your body again.

What has helped me through it was a catch-up I had with Wayne Smith during the week. We met for lunch after training, at Mesh, a café near our training ground which is always full of Crusaders and coaches. I haven't worked with Smithy since 2011, since the World Cup. He is probably the coach that I hold in the highest regard; I think he's the best coach in the world, in terms of the detail in which he analyses the game. I worked pretty closely with him for many years at All Blacks level, before he went and started with the Chiefs.

Now he's back on the All Blacks coaching staff, and he was down in Christchurch working with the Crusaders coaches. He reached out to me, wanting to catch up and have lunch. He pointed out a couple of really simple things he thought had been going wrong with my game. The level of preparation he goes to is inspiring; he'd made up a video of some of the more memorable moments throughout my career. He pulled out a laptop there in the café and walked me through his observations. There was some footage of the Lions game, some footage of Crusaders games. He points out that at my best I play with real freedom. I'm making line breaks. I'm fending. I'm physical.

He thought my problem at the moment, what was making me sluggish, was that I'm over-thinking things. I'm trying to control the game and always looking for space to set other people up, whereas in my early years I played with complete freedom. He pointed out a couple of little things in particular. I had a really strong fend and sidestep, which I just haven't used for the last couple of years, because I've been more into the mindset of wanting to direct the team around the field. It seemed so clear what I needed to do, after speaking with him. I was rejuvenated by the chat, and really excited about getting back to training with new focuses.

7

Triumph and
Near Disaster

Court sessions are part of rugby's fabric. Like mauls or scrums, outsiders might scratch their heads at them, but those within know what's going on — and why they matter. They remain a huge part of rugby culture, particularly at club level. I personally have participated in dozens of courts, often leading the charge. We used to have them regularly at all levels, right the way up to the All Blacks. It was part of a wider culture which had hung around from the amateur era. During my early days a keg was often rolled into the sheds after a game, and no one allowed to leave until it was empty. This was seen as a reward for our combined efforts through the week.

That would never happen nowadays. There's a higher scrutiny, an expectation of performance, and a degree of medical understanding which simply didn't exist when I first became a professional. On the rare occasions we have a court today it's much more controlled, and our whole approach to alcohol has changed, particularly at All Blacks level. That evolution has its origins in that one dark night, on a tour of South Africa in 2004.

It took the Johannesburg court to make both the players and

the new coaching staff certain about the need for change within the team. The new coaches, rather than make wholesale changes immediately, watched the way we operated for a while first. That was absolutely the right thing to do — we would rightly have reacted negatively if a group of outsiders with little knowledge of our internal culture started trying to tell us what we were doing wrong. Because, World Cups aside, the All Blacks were still an incredibly successful team by world standards — the best in the world, no question. The problem was that we had developed a habit of approaching the World Cup like it was just another tournament, when it wasn't. Other teams were treating it differently and beating us consistently. But figuring out how to rewire the circuitry of a machine as large and complex as the All Blacks requires some knowledge of how it operates.

That's what Graham, Wayne and Steve set about acquiring through 2004. The survey culminated in the ugliness of that court session in Johannesburg. Afterwards, we flew home, nursing hangovers and lingering resentments. But while most of us moved on, the coaching staff set to work on a plan to rebuild this team. They didn't do it alone. Senior players were intimately involved in the decision-making process, which gave us all a sense of ownership of the outcome.

The first major signal that something had changed came when the squad was announced for the end-of-year tour to the northern hemisphere. There were major changes — a selectorial night of the long knives. Some key players who'd been a big part of the team for years had vanished. Others whose All Blacks careers were meant to be over were suddenly back in the frame. Among those who'd disappeared were the two brilliant first-fives who'd been at the centre of a debate which had divided the country for many years: Carlos Spencer and Andrew Mehrtens. Selected instead were me, Luke McAlister and Aaron Mauger, all three of us able to play both first- and second-five. It was made clear to me, though, that I was picked as the primary 10.

It was a huge show of faith, saying to me and to New Zealand that I was the first-five of the future. I appreciated the gesture, but felt it had come around — like everything in my career seemed to — very quickly. I had grown comfortable at second-five, and thought I'd found a permanent home there. Now I was being asked to drive the game plan, help run the team and be the vocal leader of the backline. I had never had a playbook before, never paid much attention to set pieces. Now, I would have to know the moves and call them based on what I was seeing out there on the field. I'd played almost all my professional rugby at 12 and, when Luke was injured before the first match, I was virtually alone at 10, with four games to prove myself. As usual, my response was first fear, then determination. I respected the hell out of the coaches, and felt like I owed it to them to give it my best.

Just as my role evolved within the team, other returning players helped change the chemistry, too. Most notably Norm Maxwell and Anton Oliver: two tough, spirited forwards with long All Blacks careers which were commonly thought to be behind them. Obviously it meant a lot to all of us to be selected for the team. But for us young guys there was a limit to how much we could value the jersey — it was those who had worn it and lost it who really knew what it was worth. We had that graphically illustrated to us in the hotel, ahead of the first test against Italy. Norm and Anton were openly weeping, overcome with emotion at being given their jerseys again, after spending long periods on the outer. No one in the room will have failed to appreciate the significance of that moment, nor will they ever forget it.

That game was my first start as an All Blacks first-five. I was incredibly nervous beforehand, particularly given how my Crusaders debut at 10 had played out. There was so much more to keep in your head. But very early on I set up Conrad Smith for a good try, in what was his All Blacks debut. I remember thinking afterwards, as we celebrated, 'This is awesome — I love playing 10.'

That feeling never really left. It helped that just as I was learning this new position, the All Blacks were building a new culture. There was a spirit of rebirth throughout the squad, which meant we were all more open than usual to learning and growing. Because it wasn't just about moving on from court sessions; it was about looking deep into the history of this team, what it had done and what it meant, and finding ways that we could write our own chapters to that story. Respecting and acknowledging the history, without feeling constrained by it.

A lot of that was driven by Tana Umaga, who I thought of very highly as a leader and a man. We had been captained by Reuben before then, who was in that traditional stoic mould — he didn't say a lot, but when he did, you listened. I really rated Reuben — he was the epitome of the Crusaders man in his work ethic, enjoying a beer and always putting the team first. When Tana superseded him as captain at the start of 2004 he brought a different approach to his leadership. It was as much cultural as anything else, with his Samoan ancestry dictating his style to an extent. He was almost like a god to the Island boys, but then that was true for most of us. It certainly was for me.

Tana had a presence about him which was just so powerful: that rare type of man who made you want to lay everything on the line, because you watched the way he always, always put the team at the heart of every decision. That wasn't just on the field — he really held the line for his players in the commercial arena, too. There'd be situations with sponsors where you were drained and getting nowhere, after a long day's shooting. He'd walk in and just pull us all out. That might have made life difficult for the NZRU — we're certainly a bit more accommodating today — but it sent the most powerful message to us as a team, to always put rugby and player welfare first.

We loved him for that. So whatever he did, you followed, knowing it was the right thing. It was through this period that Richie was beginning to get a bit more prominent, too, becoming part of the leadership group. He made his debut as captain against Wales, leading a very young All Blacks side to a narrow but exhilarating win. From that day on, despite his youth, we knew he was captain in waiting. We've become close friends over the years, and my leadership role has grown out of wanting to support him — you see how much he sacrifices for his teams, and want to do what you can to help. But it took me years to imagine myself as a leader, whereas he was born to it. What impressed me was the way he stepped into that role so easily against Wales — he was leading players in their late twenties and thirties, and commanding their respect. Nothing changed about his demeanour — he was still just the same old guy that I'd known for the last couple of years.

I often hear talk about Colin Meads or Michael Jones, but I never got a chance to play with those guys. Maybe it's me being biased toward my own experience, but I think Richie's better than anything we've ever seen before. No one else in world rugby has stayed at the highest level for so long. Even the best guys will have a few great years then come down. It's natural — you get injured, or go missing for a couple of years. I certainly have, more than once. But Richie has been the best player in the world for well over a decade and the record goes to show that. It's just freakish. It was 2004 when we first started to see that side of him. We were so fortunate, through that period, to have those two incredible leaders within the side, and I'm sure he learned a lot from Tana, who had the vision for so much of this new All Blacks culture.

This era also gave birth to our beloved 'Kapa O Pango' — a new haka for a new team — and the start of a period where we valued the haka highly. Not that we hadn't in the past, but it was more a method of firing you up than something from which you drew strength and pride. Derek Lardelli, the composer of 'Kapa O Pango', came in to teach us the meaning behind the haka, so we could bring that out through our performance. He taught us how we were bringing the spirits up through the ground, the energy that we absorbed, the meaning of pukana — the eye dilation. The first time we tried out the haka after that lesson was in Italy, and we all felt different — like the true nature of the action was present in us on field.

On the tour we started to talk so much more about the All Blacks legacy. About how it was our job not just to play for the All Blacks, but to add to that legacy. You had to leave the jersey in a better place than you found it. That was your aim. It made being an All Black so much more meaningful. When I think about the modern All Blacks, what we strive for, the standards we set ourselves — so much of that grew out of that tour and the conversations we had with one another.

As much as it was exciting, with this new team and new values, it was hard, too. No Carlos or Mehrts for me to lean back on, and a group of youngsters who were forced to shoulder major responsibilities without the mentoring and support of older players, which might have happened in a more orderly transition. We all knew, though, right from the start, that it was the right thing to do. The 2004 northern hemisphere tour stands out in my memory as the most critical period in the evolution of the modern All Blacks.

Despite the turmoil and ugliness of 2004 at times, thanks to that tour there was an optimism in the camp as we came into 2005. That was partly due to the new values the coaching staff and senior leaders had inculcated, but mostly driven by the looming Lions tour. They come around so infrequently that it's easy to miss their significance. The last time they had visited rugby had been an amateur sport — I was 11 years old, and only dimly aware of the visit, and what it meant. It's only as you get older that you start to appreciate the significance of the event, which is directly derived from its scarcity. Whole careers can occur without experiencing a Lions test, and they have a sense of history that goes right back to the dawn of rugby in New Zealand in the nineteenth century.

It wasn't until 2004 that I started to appreciate that, when the world champion English side toured to open the international season. Among the English players, fans and press the tour was seen as little more than a reconnaissance mission for the Lions series to come the next year. As a young All Black, hearing about the team for the first time, you started to get a sense of what it really meant. International rugby is a relatively limited game. We play the same two or three teams a number of times during the New Zealand winter, and the same half dozen at the end. So, to have a brand-new team appear on the horizon made us very motivated going into the new year.

It also focused my mind. On the previous northern hemisphere tour I'd finally started to feel comfortable in the All Blacks environment, to have a sense of belonging. That allowed me to set concrete goals for the first time since high school, covering what I'd like to achieve. I knew that the only way I could guarantee a place in the side to play the Lions was to dominate Super Rugby. And we did, winning the competition for the first time since I'd joined in 2003. For the first time I played the bulk of the competition at 10, and was again nominated for Super Rugby Player of the Year. I was now feeling more than comfortable with the responsibility and control of the new position, and looking forward to transferring that to the All Blacks.

The first game of the international season was against Fiji, who we cleaned up 91–0. Sitiveni Sivivatu had a ball, scoring four tries on debut. Then the Lions arrived, and with them the biggest contingent of fans I've seen outside the World Cup. The first test was in Christchurch, and walking into the Square that week you'd have thought it was their home game. They just took over the central city, which meant the atmosphere was as electric as I've ever felt going into a test. When we arrive at a stadium ahead of the game it's normally a quarter full, and pretty quiet. This time I put my kit bag down and headed out and was shocked to see it already packed, an hour out from kick-off. We were so up for the game, ready to put on a show for the crowd.

Then the Christchurch weather closed in, just in time for kick-off. It grew bitterly cold, with rain and sleet going sideways — some of the worst conditions I've had to play through. It was frustrating, because we were way up for the game. Their team was outstanding — so good that Jonny Wilkinson, who'd led England to the World Cup in 2003, was shunted out to 12 to make way for

Stephen Jones. All we wanted was to test ourselves against them. It wasn't going to happen. I managed to slot a couple of penalties, and make a break, but we were all so limited by the weather. At halftime I had to stand with my fingers under the hot tap for 10 minutes just to thaw them out and try to get some feeling back.

The second half was no better. We won, 21–3, and played well, given the circumstances, but the weather ensured there was no chance of us showing the kind of running rugby we had wanted to exhibit. Instead the game is remembered mainly for Tana and Keven Mealamu's tackle on Brian O'Driscoll which put him out of the tour. Because the match was otherwise somewhat colourless, it became the dominant storyline, and Tana in particular was hung out to dry. Within our camp, though, it became a source of strength. He was our leader, and a guy who inspired awe among our team, so we rallied around him that week. We didn't talk about it much formally as a wider group, but between players when we met socially there was little else discussed. Thankfully Tana was cleared by the judiciary, and we approached Wellington with an edge. We knew they'd come at us, but were quietly confident we could absorb it.

Once again the stadium was extraordinary, in full song well ahead of kick-off. Our fans took it as a good-natured challenge, and responded with songs and chants of their own. It was one of the best home crowds of my career. We really fed off the atmosphere going into the game. As predicted, they threw themselves into us from the first whistle, and scored within the first five minutes. We seemed flat, and found it difficult to respond. That changed around 15 minutes in, when our forwards seemed to lift palpably, as if they sensed the Lions had exhausted themselves a little with their opening thrust. That's all you need as a first-five — from then on it felt like I had the ball on a string, and all the time in the world to make decisions.

As the game wore on I knew I was performing well, but it felt like it was driven by the whole team's strength. I had no sense that it was particularly out of the ordinary. I was conscious, though, that there was a flow to the game which I hadn't experienced much before, and that almost everything I tried was coming off. Breaking the line felt effortless, passes perfect, tackles solid. It was a good enough game that, when I missed a kick at goal — my only miss of the day — I remember being particularly disappointed, like I'd messed up my day statistically. Right near the end I was tackled and did my AC joint. It was the seventy-eighth minute, so I thought I'd take the shot at goal anyway. It sailed over from the sideline. I watched it go, then went off to have the injury attended to. Thankfully, the game was so comfortably in hand that there was no need for a replacement. We'd already emptied the subs' bench and we played the last couple of minutes with 14.

After the game I was told to go and do media. That wasn't an unusual situation — a few players do it, and it's often first-fives who are requested. But when I arrived they were asking questions which implied something out of the ordinary had happened. They told me I'd scored 33 points in our 48–18 win, which sure sounded like a lot — before then I hadn't been aware of my own tally. That was my first inkling that it had been a particularly significant game. I returned to the changing room afterwards, and turned on my phone. Back then Ma'a and I had a little competition between the two of us, to see who got the most texts after games. We used it as a way of measuring who'd played better. Nowadays I'd be happy to get two or three, but back then you'd get 10 or even 20 if you'd had a seriously big game.

I turned on my phone, and it just kept vibrating. I think the final number was in the seventies. They were all the same: 'best game ever', 'greatest game' — that kind of thing. That was when I sat back and thought about it, and started to realise what had happened. (The thing was, for all the praise that was being heaped on me, my shoulder was still wrecked. So while the rest of the team celebrated the series win, I sat with medical staff and had my injury assessed. I didn't even have a drink.)

It's now considered my signature game, one which cemented me as the 'best first-five in the world', and all kinds of other superlatives besides. I read that stuff in the days to come, and enjoyed it in the way that everyone enjoys being praised. But I didn't take it in. To me it was too much — it was just one game, and only my sixth time starting at 10 for the All Blacks. The big thing for me was that it had happened against the Lions. To perform like that against such a strong team meant something, in a way that it wouldn't had it been against a second-tier nation.

Regardless of my own conception of the performance, it resonated within the team and beyond. It seemed to mark a transition for me, from being a junior member of the squad to one whose opinions were sought out and valued. Sponsors had noticed, too, and I suddenly found myself far more in demand from a commercial perspective. The media seemed to go into a frenzy about my performance, and I couldn't resist reading all the pieces which were published about it. It was pretty seductive, to read all those hyperbolic words about yourself. Especially when coupled with all my friends and teammates echoing it, I found it difficult to avoid letting it go to my head a little.

I was so engulfed in all of that I started to think I was a bit invincible. It probably wasn't helped by the fact I was rehabbing my shoulder, so didn't get sucked back into the grind of training and playing right away. It didn't take long to get that mood smacked right out of me.

We played South Africa and got beaten in Cape Town, 22–16. It knocked my confidence, though at the same time I didn't go right back to square one and start doubting myself. Those experiences seem to come along when you need them, and got me back to those fundamental questions: What are your goals? What are you trying to get out of each game? It was a bad game for the team, but good for me in the long run.

We managed to finish the home season off strongly, and won the Tri-Nations. I played well enough, despite being injured again and missing one match in particular which I'd been anticipating for a while. When we met South Africa again at home in Dunedin, we debuted the new haka, 'Kapa O Pango'. I'd been a part of its development, and wished I could have been out there, performing it for the first time. But it was inspiring sitting there watching from the stands too, and feeling like I'd played a role in creating something historic.

The last remaining task for the year was our northern hemisphere tour. These are always the highlight of the year, and the most difficult tasks, playing less familiar opposition while away from home for such a long period of time. In 2005 the expectations felt heightened on a number of levels. Firstly, it was a chance at a grand slam — games against all four 'home nations' — my first as an All Black. Secondly, the reasonably emphatic victory over the Lions meant all the home sides were wanting to avenge the defeat, particularly Ireland, who were still in full fury over the O'Driscoll tackle. And, lastly, the press were talking me up as the best player in world rugby, which meant there was an unbelievable level of pressure to perform. No matter how much I tried to put that stuff out of my head, it was hard to entirely escape it.

Ahead of the tour we assembled at the Heritage Hotel in Auckland. Before we flew out we went to Eden Park to try to clear our heads and focus on the enormity of the task ahead. To us a grand slam tour was similar to a Lions tour — the opportunity didn't come around often, and the feat had only ever been achieved once before by the All Blacks. That meeting at Eden Park was something the management team arranged, part of their newfound emphasis on valuing the jersey and taking pride in what we were doing, the legacy we were drawing on and building. It really focused our minds on the challenge and opportunity which awaited us. But as much as I thought my head was focused on the task ahead of us, the tour would prove that I still had some growing up to do, as shown by one last big slip-up.

Wales were our first opponents. We landed on a Friday, a week ahead of the first test on 5 November. We trained on the Saturday, but had Sunday off, so went out on the Saturday night as a team for a few beers. I was feeling pretty good at that point. At 23, I was the unquestioned first-five for the best rugby team in the world. Over the previous 12 months I'd won my first Super Rugby title, had what was being called a perfect game against the Lions, and won the Tri-Nations. I was routinely being called one of the best players in the world. And I liked a beer.

That night we went out, and when the bars closed headed back to the hotel to keep drinking. About 5 am there was a hardcore group of us still left: Piri, Jimmy Cowan, Aaron Mauger, Leon MacDonald, Jason Eaton and me. One of us — I can't remember who — had the bright idea of going to London in a taxi. We got obsessed with the idea of going to The Church, the London pub which became a New Zealand institution. It only opens for four hours, from midday on a Sunday, and is filled with Aussies, Kiwis and South Africans. It closed recently, which is probably a good thing for touring sports teams. But while it was open they delivered very lowbrow fun, with sawdust on the floor, drinking games on stage and six-packs of Foster's over the bar. All our London mates went there regularly, and a bunch of us had been there after the previous tour and had a ball. Hitting The Church is a great way to cap off a successful tour, but a ridiculous way to begin one.

Obviously we weren't thinking clearly, but the idea was infectious, and we eventually found a cabbie mad enough to take us. We gave him £300, grabbed some mix CDs and a box of beers and were soon speeding towards London. The sun came up, and we quickly got through our beers. Slowly the first shards of doubt started to enter our heads. Maybe this wasn't the greatest idea we'd ever had? Still, we were in too deep to turn back.

We entered the city around 8.30 am, and the driver was soon profoundly lost. Being Welsh, he wasn't overly familiar with London. The only place we could find was a hairdresser, which was randomly open before 9 am on a Sunday. A couple of us went in there to try to rustle up another cab, while the remainder went next door to eat some Subway. We were still trying to push through encroaching sobriety and make it to midday, but it was an uphill battle by then.

Eventually we found a cabbie who knew where The Church was, and he dropped us there at 10 am. We were four hours into our odyssey, but still two hours ahead of doors opening. A security guard told us to head to a McDonald's round the corner.

We trooped in, ordered our food and sat down to eat it when the penny finally dropped. 'What the f . . . are we doing in London?' asked Aaron. 'We've got to get out of here.' He was right. We instantly realised what fools we'd been, and completely panicked.

In the mad rush to get back to Wales, we split into two groups. Our group aimed for the train, while the others were set on getting another cab. Our group made it to Paddington Station at 11.55 am, just in time for the midday train to Cardiff. Our elation at getting there in time turned to despair when we saw an enormous line for tickets. Just as we were about to trudge off and try to figure out a plan B, we saw the rest of the guys at the front of the line. Somehow we got the tickets and scrambled on board, just as the doors were closing. But after the adrenalin of making the train, reality bit again. We sat, heads down, wondering what the hell had gotten into us. Worse was to come. I'd had my SIM card in Leon's phone, texting my London friends to meet us at The Church. But when he put his in again, it started to vibrate with texts from our manager, Darren Shand. 'Where are you guys?' 'Are you in London?' We knew then the game was up. There was no escaping this — we were just going to have to wear it.

Eventually the train got back to Cardiff and we taxied back to the hotel. We snuck back to our rooms, and stole a couple of hours' sleep, before being awoken by a text about a team meeting that evening. We knew we'd been caught, and had no choice but to face what was coming.

The timing couldn't have been worse. We'd violated all the team's principles, everything we'd created from that year before. We weren't living the All Blacks values, and we'd let our teammates down badly. It was just an awful decision. When we arrived at the meeting we looked around and it was just players, no coaches or management. This was what the new era was about — imposing discipline on ourselves. Which made it so much worse — failing your friends, your peers.

Tana absolutely ripped into us. 'That's not good enough,' he said. 'You should be sent home.' Jason Eaton hadn't even played a test, hadn't even played Super Rugby. Tana really got stuck into him, asking him who he thought he was, pissing on this amazing environment. Same with Leon and Aaron, who were part of the leadership group, who were meant to impose discipline, not need it. Piri, Jimmy and I were lucky in a way, caught in between. It was an absolutely brutal drilling, and as low as I'd felt as an All Black.

The following week was awful. Every night I went and saw mental skills coach Gilbert Enoka, trying to avoid drifting into black thoughts. He was invaluable at times like that, when you were vulnerable and away from home. But aside from getting a barrelling from Tana, that was the end of it. I think everyone knew that we'd heard the message. Our effort at training showed how sorry we were.

The only way out of it was work. We trained like dogs, buckling down and working harder than ever. When match day came I was more nervous than usual. I was just so keen to have a great game to blast away those bad thoughts. Before then I'd only ever had good press, and had started to feel a little untouchable. The trip to London ended that in a hurry.

Thankfully, the game went brilliantly. I scored two tries and kicked a pile of goals, and became the All Blacks' record points scorer for a single game against Wales in a 41–3 victory. It was a long-standing record, which had belonged to the great Canterbury fullback, Fergie McCormick. Mehrts, who had also scored heavily against Wales a few years earlier, sent me a typically smart-arsed text of congratulations.

The rest of the tour went much more smoothly. We comfortably beat Ireland, 45–7, then won a tight game against England 23–19, and I was named man-of-the-match. The last game of the tour was against Scotland, for a 29–10 win. A number of the first team and I had the game off. I remember being surprised that Tana was playing, given that he'd had a few tough ones leading into it. It became clear why he'd turned out in the dressing-room afterwards, when he announced his retirement out of the blue.

It was a shocking moment. No one saw it coming, and he'd told no one except management. Afterwards, we didn't breathe a word, and it didn't come out until the following year. Most retirements nowadays are so managed, almost choreographed, but it really speaks to Tana's values and priorities that he did it with so little ceremony, telling his teammates and coaches directly, before anyone else. I don't think we'll ever see his like again.

After the tour there was one last event to attend. I was nominated for the IRB World Player of the Year. The event was in Paris. I was excited just to be nominated, at 23. Then I won. It felt like the culmination of a crazy few years, all capped off by being named the best rugby player in the world. There had been some rough moments at times, but that night flushed them all way. All I could do was sit there, thousands of miles from Southbridge, and let it wash over me.

8

World Cup Dreaming

After having such an extraordinary year in 2005, I finally felt I belonged on the world stage. I was determined to prove it was no fluke — to back it up with another strong year. The Crusaders' Super Rugby campaign went brilliantly, with us losing only once on the way to the playoffs, ensuring we'd be at Jade Stadium throughout. We took care of the Bulls comfortably in the semi, before winning a second consecutive title in a tense game over a very strong Hurricanes team. The game will forever be remembered as the match in the mist. The strange, thick sea fog rolled in about an hour before kick-off and just as mysteriously vanished not long after the game. How I managed to put the ball between the posts that night is beyond me.

When the All Blacks assembled we approached the games knowing it was our last full season ahead of the World Cup. We'd deliberately scheduled a pair of games against France at the end of the season, knowing the trouble we'd had with them in the past, and that they'd be hosting the tournament and final. We were taking those games very seriously and, to a certain extent, treating the Tri-Nations as a build-up to both the northern tour, and the World Cup the following year.

One of my clearest memories from that year is a kick up in

Pretoria, on the Highveld. We had a penalty on halftime, well inside our half. I was shaping to kick it into touch to end the half when Luke McAlister, who was playing outside me, said, 'Have a shot!' I looked down field. It was 62 metres, on the angle, and my first instinct was 'bugger that'. But as it was halftime I decided to give it a crack. The crowd were chatting and laughing, thinking there was no chance. But I gave it a heave and over it went — the longest kick of my career.

The following week's game was at Rustenburg, so we stayed at Sun City, which is a beautiful place. While we'd already won the Tri-Nations by that point, there was another incentive for the game: the record for most consecutive test wins. We'd won 15 on the trot — the record stood at 17 — and we were in pretty incredible form. But instead of embracing the challenge it represented, and the opportunity to make history, we never mentioned it at all. It was like we shied away from it, not just in public, but as a team.

Today's All Blacks would never operate like that. We actively seek huge challenges, and embrace the chance to break records. It's an evolution in our mindset, to try and be the best team in any sport on the planet. To be that we'll have to work incredibly hard. Records and World Cups are hard marks to achieve, and don't come along every couple of years. To break them or win them you have to do something extraordinary, and not treat them like they're just another game.

In 2006 we didn't even discuss the record, and had a relaxed week in the sun heading into the final game. Somehow it became a holiday. We were staying at an amazing resort, and playing at a fairly ordinary venue, out of the city. And because the Tri-Nations was already taken care of, subconsciously we lost focus.

Our training and preparation suffered, and we enjoyed all the comforts of the resort in a way we never would have had the series been on the line. We were playing golf, hitting the casino and spending a lot of time by the pool. None of which is bad in isolation. But to do all that without a focus tends to let your mind drift.

The game ended up being very close. We were leading for much of the way, but they seemed to sense we were there for the taking, and sent wave after wave at us. We still had the lead until the final moment when Rodney So'oialo gave away a penalty, which handed the game to them. He was hurting afterwards, but we should never have got into that kind of position.

The end-of-year-tour provided redemption, in a series of fairly comprehensive victories, including an emphatic 47–3 defeat of France. But the frustration of the Rustenburg loss lingered, and still aggravates me to this day.

Still, it was ultimately a blip in an otherwise dominant season.

That summer I couldn't have been in better shape, physically or mentally. The previous couple of years had seen me grow from a fringe All Black to owning my position, and I felt in peak condition as we headed into a World Cup year. While during the previous tournament I was making up the numbers, and watched in a slightly detached way as our tournament fell apart, this time I felt like this was my team. I had immense confidence in our set-up, from coaches to training staff to players. Most of all, I had confidence in myself — I was in form, in shape, and at the perfect point in my career arc. This was my time to shine, my moment, a chance to prove myself not on a world stage — I felt I'd done that — but at a unique and special tournament.

As the year began, you could feel both the hum of anticipation but also apprehension from the public. We had lost four World Cups in a row, so both media and the public worried about how that would affect the team. Personally, I didn't feel a huge amount of pressure based on our run of poor performances at the tournament. To the public that might seem odd, given how distant 1987 was. But the majority of our team had played in one World Cup, if that, and we didn't feel like we were responsible for the failures in prior tournaments. Which is a good thing, because there's pressure enough at a World Cup without weighing the losses of your predecessors, too.

Despite that, I knew this year, and this tournament, was different. As a result, I made the decision at the start of the year to try to push on into new realms of conditioning and focus. Part of that involved giving up drinking, to try to become the complete professional athlete. And, apart from a couple of beers after the Super Rugby final, I kept to it. My thinking was that it would help me reach a new level, take away a distraction and build me up into a rugby machine. In time, I would learn that humans don't respond well to being treated like machines. But, as 2007 began, I felt great about the decision.

This was the year of the now infamous 'conditioning window'. So instead of starting Super Rugby training with the Crusaders, the other Canterbury All Blacks and I were conditioning separately. It felt strange, to be physically separated from your teammates, as they worked towards a goal we all shared, but the strategy sounded solid, so we didn't question it. I barely touched a rugby ball at first. Instead there were long gym sessions, with lots of fitness and speed work. I was feeling fantastic physically, and agreed with the principles which were driving this different approach. It was a very long season, so it seemed logical to build slowly and deliberately.

When we finally integrated with the Crusaders in late March, though, something was missing. By then the season was more than a month old, and the wider group had been training for four months. The usual feeling of unity and purpose was absent, and there was a bit of an us-and-them sense within the camp. It was a really weird dynamic, the strangest I would ever encounter in the normally rock-solid Crusaders environment. But because I was feeling good, and focused on the big prize at the end of the year, I didn't give it too much thought. I look back and shudder a bit, because that's so far from where I like to be as a Crusader and a teammate.

Despite the disjointed dynamics, we scraped through to the semis, in our usual style. Once there we faced the Bulls in Pretoria. It's a real cauldron up there, and you can only give yourself a shot if you're entirely committed. We weren't, and they exposed us. It bothers me still, because we'd come off two consecutive wins with essentially the same team, and we had a terrific chance to emulate the great Crusaders side of the late '90s and win three consecutive Super Rugby titles. That would have been a real milestone for our team. But even when we lost I wasn't too fussed. Subconsciously I wasn't as engaged with the Crusaders campaign. I was just waiting to get into camp with the All Blacks.

There was a similar motivational issue with the Tri-Nations and the Bledisloe. Winning them had become a bit routine, and coupled with the immense anticipation for the World Cup it really felt like no one cared too much: from our opponents, to our coaches to the public. They only really mattered as signposts to where we were headed. The older I get, the more this situation bothers me — when games become routine or diminished.

Especially the Bledisloe. It has a history to it, which the Tri-Nations lacks. I remember the first time I won it, in my debut season as an All Black in '03. The Aussies had held it for years prior to that victory, and I saw how much it meant to the more senior players, given the number of agonising and dramatic losses we'd experienced in the late '90s and early 2000s. The Eales penalty. Gregan's tackle. It's also an amazing trophy to drink out of, which is a small but tangible part of the motivation. It's massive, and gets filled up and passed around the changing sheds after we win it.

The Tri-Nations? It's nice to win, but the years just blend together. We did well despite our ambivalence, only losing to Australia, in front of a huge crowd at the MCG, and closing out with big wins over South Africa and the Aussies. With that over with we flew to Corsica to begin our preparation for the World Cup. The plan was to go somewhere warm, relaxed and secluded to help us get over our jetlag and acclimatise. All the media came and stayed with us, in this beautiful spot, with incredible beaches and perfect weather.

Then something strange and frustrating happened. The media got stuck into us — I never could figure out why. The line seemed to be: 'Who do these guys think they are?' The stories were completely outlandish: me wandering round with my shirt off, with a room full of Moët, the team just sunbathing and having a good time. As if we were living a glamorous lifestyle. The intimation was that we weren't taking the Cup seriously, and were slacking off. When in fact we weren't training much for medical reasons — because we were getting over jetlag.

It annoyed me, given the amount of thought and care which

had gone into the season, but we couldn't dwell on that. Next we flew to Marseille and did some promotional work before the tournament started. The best part was a session with the French footballer Zinedine Zidane, then one of the biggest stars in sports. He and I took turns kicking balls at a goal out over the water, which was a pinch yourself moment.

Afterwards there was hilarity during a question-and-answer session Zinedine did with the rest of the All Blacks. The first hand which shot up was that of Sitiveni Sivivatu. His question was a total clanger: 'How much do you make?' Zinedine handled it well, to his credit, saying 'far too much', or words to that effect. We gave Siti hell for it afterwards.

Then it was into the Cup proper. First up: Italy. We played brilliantly in that win — Richie scored twice in the first 10 minutes, and we put over 70 points on them, for a 76–14 finish. Obviously they're not a first tier nation, but they've come on a lot over the past decade. Then came Portugal, a game I skipped, but the team took care of them 108–13. The last big game was against Scotland, who were in a pretty deep hole at the time. I returned, and while we played poorly, we still beat them 40–0.

Afterwards we were given a couple of days off to refresh. In a tournament of that length it's important to not be solely focused on rugby the whole time — you just lose focus and get bored. I was lucky — a group of my high-school mates were touring Europe on the cheap, following the All Blacks. So whenever we'd have a break I'd go and find them, sunning themselves on a beach, and get updated on their stories. So I had a good escape valve.

For the rest of us, the break was a necessary refresher within a long tournament. At the same time, though, it did feel a bit weird to splinter off into different groups rather than doing something as a team. The current All Blacks team would never do that, but I don't view it as a poor decision. It was, like so much we went through, a learning experience for players and management.

We needed the break. It had been a long season, and we were in the midst of a long tournament. Some guys met up with their partners or had downtime with family, but a group of us decided to go to Monaco. Byron Kelleher knew an ex-Welsh player named Mark Thomas who'd somehow ended up on the Monaco bobsled team. He hooked us up with a house there. It was Byron, Richie, Luke McAlister, Nick Evans, Doug Howlett, Brendon Leonard and myself. We flew out, got tuxedos and had a magic couple of days.

Mark turned out to be really good friends with Prince Albert. He was away, but we hung around with his wife, Princess Caroline, living a crazy lifestyle, surrounded by famous people. We were treated like royalty — probably because we were hanging out *with* royalty. We went to the casino and were given free chips. They showed us a poker table where the minimum bet was a million euro. I was just in awe of the wealth, but quite self-conscious, too — it was just so far from who I was, and what we were there for. Thinking back on that mad weekend, we were incredibly lucky the media didn't find out, because it would've looked pretty bad. And, if I'm honest, we did get caught up in the moment a bit. At times we probably forgot that we were actually in France for a World Cup.

Following the break, the team reassembled in Aix-en-Provence to prepare for our final pool game against Romania. We knew we had to go to Wales for the quarter-final, but the games beyond there would be in Paris. There was a lot of talk about the last two weeks of the tournament, the logistics of moving to Wales then back again, and so on. That should have been a red flag, that things had been going a little too well for us, and we were starting to make assumptions about how the remaining games would play out.

Worse was to come. In the first training session after the break, I felt my calf go early on, and stopped training immediately. I knew it wasn't really serious, but I didn't want to risk it. The following morning it was sore to walk on, so we made the call to pull me out of the Romania game.

I was really unhappy about missing the game. I'd only played an hour or so against Italy, along with a ropey game against Scotland, which meant I was heading into the quarter-final seriously underdone. The calf was slow to come right, and I was kept out of training the whole week leading into the quarter-final. I just watched, and rehabbed and hoped it would come right. It really added to my anxiety, not being able to kick a ball. I was walking through the kicking motion, visualising kicks, which was better than nothing, but certainly not what I wanted heading into such a huge game. Even during the captain's run I was at half pace. I felt like on balance it would be fine, but that was more hope than confidence.

Game day came. We'd played France twice on the previous northern hemisphere tour. We beat the hell out of them in a sensational performance at Lyon, although they did provide a far sterner test in Paris a week later. Earlier in the '07 season, France brought a depleted side to New Zealand — the tour clashed with the concluding stages of their Top 14 competition — and we put 100 points on them across two tests.

A few hours before we were due to run out, word filtered out that Australia had lost their quarter-final against England in

Marseille. It was extraordinary news, and electrified the team. We couldn't believe it — we had considered them our biggest competition, yet they'd faltered at the quarter-final. Everything was looking so good.

As soon as we got out there, though, something felt off. The way the French advanced on us during the haka definitely caught us by surprise, and the first half was much more of a grind than we had expected. We were up at the break, and not playing too badly, but it was a closer game than we'd have liked, and they were a very different team to the one we'd been beating so comfortably over the past year.

It wasn't long after the half that I felt my calf give out. I could barely walk on it, let alone run. I knew in my heart that it was probably the end of my World Cup. I limped off and told our medical staff it had gone. Not long after there was a picture of me taken which was printed everywhere, looking utterly broken. It accurately summed up my feelings at the time. I just had nothing left. There were a couple of factors playing into that. One was that I knew the injury was serious enough to have me out of the tournament. The second was the game itself. Things were deteriorating before my eyes.

We weren't playing the game we'd practised. The French had grown an arm and a leg, and the crowd was rising behind them. Nick Evans limped off with about 10 minutes to go, so we were down to Luke McAlister, a third-choice first-five, without much experience running the team. We hadn't selected Doug Howlett or Aaron Mauger, two guys who'd been stalwarts of the side for years. I understood why ahead of the game, but as it tightened up towards the end I wished we'd had more cool-headed experience out there.

Even with 20 minutes to go I felt like there was an inevitability about the result. My dream, the one I'd worked so hard for, made so many sacrifices for, was disintegrating in front of me, both on a personal and a team level. When Yannick Jauzion scored with just under 10 minutes on the clock, making the score 20–18 to France, a feeling of dread started to rise within me. I think I already knew the game was gone. And so it proved.

After the final whistle blew we assembled in one of the bleakest dressing-rooms of my career. We'd lost in the quarter-final of a tournament we were heavily favoured to win. It was only natural that there'd be anger and despair, manifesting itself in different ways throughout the squad. I retreated into myself, feeling blank incomprehension.

I got quiet and distant, unable to process the situation. After a while we bussed back to our hotel. We were staying at a golf resort, out of the city. By this stage everyone was drinking, and starting to let it all out. I didn't want any part of that — I got off the bus and headed straight to my room. I just didn't want to be around anyone. I didn't sleep, of course, and didn't try. I literally sat and stared at the ceiling for three straight hours, cursing my injury and trying to figure out what on earth had happened.

At 5 am I had a knock at my door. It was Ali Williams and Chris Masoe. They said what I needed to hear, which was to pull my head in, that I wasn't achieving anything by sitting up here and feeling sorry for myself. They were right, of course. At first I wouldn't give in; told them to piss off and leave me alone. But they wouldn't take no for an answer, and insisted I come and socialise with the team.

Eventually I grumpily agreed. Downstairs it was chaos. Everyone was letting their hair down, all responding differently to the stress. There were guys in tears, having heart-to-hearts. Other guys had guitars out or were singing, looking like they were having a good time. Most of the guys were very emotional. It was a pretty highly charged scene. Still, as messed up as it was, I was glad I joined them. It's important a team stays together, win or lose, and there was some small comfort to be around my teammates.

The hardest thing was having to spend another night in Cardiff before we could figure out what to do next. No one had planned for this, even at a contingency level. We were meant to be on a plane to Paris, not heading home to New Zealand. So management were scrambling to organise flights and connections. Ideally we'd have gone home in one group, but that proved impossible given the size of the touring party.

It meant we had another big night in Cardiff. This became an open session in the conference room, during which anyone could say whatever they wanted without recrimination. A lot came out. Some guys were extremely despondent, others almost defiant in the face of it all: 'I don't want to be in any other circle than this one here' was a common sentiment. It was particularly poignant knowing that a number of guys had likely played their last game for the team.

Then we all got on a bus to London. I had been sober all year, remember, so was really feeling the hangover. Looking back now, I think it was a mistake to give up the booze for the year, odd as that sounds. It became 'rugby, rugby, rugby', when, instead, as athletes and people we need the opportunity to kick back and let our minds go elsewhere. Everyone's different, and while having a couple of beers helps me relax, it doesn't work for others. But my abstinence meant that when the pressure really went on, the game felt like the only thing that mattered. That mentality didn't do me any good — if the game's all that matters, how do you reconcile that with a loss?

When we got to London we started to go our separate ways. I was lucky to make it onto the first plane back. The second group stayed on, and ended up getting into a bit of trouble. They combined with the Aussies, who were staying at the same hotel and feeling the same way. It got a little toxic, predictably. Luckily for me, by then I was on a plane, and mentally preparing for the reaction of the press and the public.

The worst part was that as I was flying out, my family was flying in. Mum, Dad and my sister had planned to come for the semi and the final. They were up in the air when it happened, and had no choice but to continue with the trip. They ended up having a couple of weeks in Paris, and had an alright time. But Dad sold his tickets, and I missed catching up with my sister, who I hadn't seen for a few years, as she'd been living in Canada.

Before the World Cup I'd joked that if we didn't win, I wasn't coming home. I said I'd grow a beard and become a fisherman in the south of France. Then we lost in the quarter-final! I sat on the plane and it was all I could think about, how awful it would be to confront the public. I flew home via Tokyo, to Christchurch. When I came through the gates, the airport was packed with people. I braced myself for the onslaught. They had a right to be angry, and I expected to get it in the neck. I could live with that — we had let them down on the biggest stage.

It never came. Instead people were slapping me on the back. You could see they were hurting, just like we were. But they were there to show their support and loyalty, even at that darkest hour. It was unbelievable, and gives me goose bumps to this day, just thinking about it.

There was some negative stuff, mostly in the media. But over the weeks to come I was consistently surprised and gratified by the reaction of our supporters. The comments were incredible. 'Thanks for the last three years'; 'I can't imagine how you guys are feeling right now'; 'Hard luck — we're feeling for you'. It took a good month to get out of the black hole the loss put us in. But it would've been a lot longer if it wasn't for the support of our fans.

FINAL YEAR DIARY: Christchurch, 21 May 2015

Phone call recorded at Christchurch Airport as I wait to fly to Sydney for a game against the NSW Waratahs. It's essentially a must-win if the Crusaders are to make the playoffs. I missed a few games with the continuation of a leg injury, and, most importantly, my son Fox was born.

For the first few rounds I was not in a good space mentally: 'Here we go, back to where I was last year.' Thankfully it came back alright. I was lacking my speed and bounce, and it was troubling me all the way through until three or four weeks ago. I came off the bench against the Highlanders in early April, but only played 20 minutes until I got a whack on it again. I started to feel really low about that time, but mercifully it actually bounced back reasonably well after the game. The next few weeks we had a win over the Blues and losses to the Hurricanes and Chiefs. I was just playing crap rugby, as all I could think about was my leg. I had no confidence at all — it was starting to really do my head in.

That's why I haven't been kicking for the last month. It's my plant foot and all my weight goes through that part of the leg when I'm kicking. It got so bad that I'd subconsciously changed my kicking motion, which is where all my accuracy comes from.

I kicked really poorly against the Chiefs, and only noticed on reviewing video that I'd changed my motion. Normally I'd plant when I was going to kick on my right foot and land back on my right foot after contact with the ball.

But on review I noticed that I wasn't kicking through on my right foot any more; I was planting my foot and landing on my left. I was hiding and protecting my right leg.

It was getting out of hand, and with the bye a few weeks away I had a chance to try to fix it. I got in contact with the All Blacks physio to put a plan in place. It centred on taking the load off my leg and doing a lot of rehab to try to get it right. And it worked; it has finally settled down. Even though I wasn't kicking in the last couple of games, it's been so much better playing without having to think about my leg. It's still not 100 per cent and I'm not sure if it ever will be. But maybe this is the new normal?

The other major change has been the birth of Fox, my second son. I went over to South Africa and returned early to be around for the birth — that all worked out well. I got to be there for the delivery, something I didn't want to miss after experiencing it the first time with Marco. I wondered in advance if it would be just as emotional. We were certainly a lot more relaxed this time around — but as soon as he arrived, all those feelings came flooding back again.

I was around for the whole first week. I got to spend some time with them and look after Marco as much as possible, but soon I had to head back to Christchurch, leaving poor Honor to deal with caring for the two of them by herself. It was really hard, leaving her this time. I'm actually really struggling this year with being away from the family down in Christchurch — feeling helpless, wishing I could do more. When it was just Honor and me it was easy. At the back of our minds, we know that this time next year we'll be together as a family in Paris, and I'll be around a lot more.

In the broader context of New Zealand rugby, my leg coming right has coincided with a string of injuries to other first-fives. During the opening of the Super Rugby season, Aaron Cruden was playing really well, as were Beaudy Barrett and Sladey. There was a lot of competition, and it felt like any one of those guys could step into that position and do well.

I was a bit frustrated, playing 12 while they all got to show what they could do at 10. And a small part of me was cruising a little. I almost felt like the All Blacks didn't need me any more as those young guys were all so good. Barrett's been there for a couple of years, but Cruden has been around a long time. He took his chances last year and it felt like the guy could step up and run a team. Now, with him injured — and probably out of the Cup — it's really weird, but I've got the hunger and drive back, knowing that the team might need me after all.

That said, there are mixed emotions, because I hadn't been playing first-five regularly for the Crusaders, so it's going to be tough for me to show what I can do. Will the coaches be able to pick me at first-five when I haven't played there all year?

I do get frustrated. We have these sayings at the Crusaders — pillars which make up what it means to be a Crusaders man. One of them is 'putting your ego on a hook'. I know that this is the best thing for the team, and the way Sladey's playing, I can't doubt that. But I thought maybe I might get a bit of a run at first-five, especially with Izzy out injured for over a month, and Sladey able to cover fullback.

I probably wouldn't care so much if I'd played a lot of

rugby in the last two years, but the fact I haven't means I can't help but wish I was playing in my preferred position. I say to the media that it doesn't really matter. That we're both ball players and they're support positions. But there's a lot more contact, I'm making a lot more tackles. I'm having to clear out a lot more rucks, I'm taking the ball to contact to try and get us over the gain line.

By contrast when you're at first-five you get to pick and choose your moments. You see a weakness and you go, taking the ball to the line on your terms. In the midfield you're used to trying to get over the gain line and there's a lot more physicality. I enjoy that, but I do miss directing the team around a little more and having that control. Now that Crudes and Beaudy are injured, it only increases my desire to exert that in a game. Unfortunately, for the time being, I'm at 12, and just have to accept that.

Auckland, 3 June 2015

Recorded at home in Auckland. In the previous weeks the Crusaders had essentially ended their season with a loss to the Waratahs, then played the Hurricanes, with me playing my first game at 10 in months.

We had the completely wrong game plan against the Waratahs. It felt like we'd been playing some good rugby until that point, but they took us apart. That's been the story of our season. We'll beat a team by 40 or 50 points and then lose the next game, which is exactly what happened. We were coming in off a high against the Reds, a pretty emotional week with our last game in Christchurch, but somehow we just didn't prepare right for Sydney.

Afterwards I was gutted. I've never missed the playoffs. In my last year I wanted to finish on a high, and we weren't going to do that. But the following day I started to see the upside: a window in such a busy year during which I can actually spend some time with my family, work on some conditioning, work on some of my niggles and go into All Blacks camp from day one. So: bitterly disappointed, but in the bigger picture it wasn't all bad.

The next week we played the Hurricanes. Sladey had been injured, one of a number of key players to go down that week: Kieran Reid, Sam Whitelock, Wyatt Crockett. It felt like it was just Richie and me, the old guys, leading a very young side. We enjoyed that part of the preparation. Richie was captaining the side again, and I was back at 10. When we spoke during the week, we chatted about how important it was for us to really lead that week.

It felt good. There was a bit of a siege mentality, too, because we were playing against the Hurricanes, who were top of the table and had only dropped one game all season, while we were getting bagged by the media after missing the playoffs. I absolutely loved the week because when everyone is writing you off, you're playing with nothing to lose.

That game went brilliantly, and a lot of people who'd doubted my ability to play at the top level any more were saying I was back. I didn't feel like it was fair to have been written off without a chance to play 10, so this felt like vindication in some ways.

At this point there's still a mathematical chance of us making the playoffs, but after the Waratahs game I just ruled that out. I wanted to concentrate on the fact I've got three weeks left being a Crusader. So I want to make the most of it. We talked about it as a team, about finishing the season with pride. I want that to be my main focus over the next few weeks: savouring my last moments as a Crusader. That and finding a house in Paris, which is proving harder than we thought.

The other inspiring part of the last few weeks was an All Blacks leadership meeting in Wellington. Sometimes I have doubts about wanting to play at the highest level, then one of those meetings will snap me right out of that mindset. I flew into Wellington on a Sunday after a game. But after being among the other leaders of the All Blacks, and the coaches, I came out so pumped.

We met across from the airport at the golf club. I literally flew in, walked across the carpark, had a meeting for four hours and flew back. All the All Blacks leaders were there: Kevvy Mealamu, Conrad, Ma'a, Ben Smith, Richie, Reado, Sam Cane, Brodie Retallick and myself. There were also the All Blacks coaches — Wayne Smith, Steve Hansen and Ian Foster — trainer Nic Gill, Darren Shand, the manager and then Ceri Evans and Gilbert Enoka, the mental skills coaches.

We were focused on finding what is going to drive us this year. We've come up with some really inspiring goals and concepts, and I'm excited to rejoin that environment. But before then I want to really relish these final few weeks in red and black.

9

Learning Business the Hard Way

Through the middle of the 2000s I had grown very comfortable and confident on field. But off it I was still mostly an average 20-something, making good and bad decisions and trying to find my way in the world. Rugby had been very good to me financially. It's a tough game, one which breaks far more dreams than it makes. But if you're one of the lucky ones who makes the All Blacks and sticks around a while you can end up doing very well for yourself, earning what a lawyer or banker might not make until well into their thirties or forties. Unfortunately you're earning it in your twenties, before you have the life experience to know what to do with it.

The public and media can lose sight of this — how young we are when all that arrives. Particularly when we screw up, say the wrong thing or do something silly on social media. I'm grateful that wasn't around early in my career. But all that stuff is just noise. The real area we can struggle with is investment, financial planning and saving. It comes down to the right structures. When Rupert Murdoch made rugby professional overnight in the mid-'90s, the game had to scramble to pivot from a century-old amateur approach to professionalism in a matter of months. In many ways it's a miracle we're as organised and orderly as we are, given that in professional terms we still haven't celebrated our twenty-first.

My generation were among the first to be able to view rugby as a viable career path, and the last to have grown up alongside men who'd played in the amateur era. In many ways that was a privilege that today's generation have missed out on — the culture of amateurism was different, and in many ways a lot more fun. But it did mean that a lot of what we needed both as organisations and individuals simply wasn't there. I rate my agents at Essentially very highly; they're some of the smartest and most creative people in the rugby business. But they have had to learn by doing, figuring out the needs of their clients as they go along.

To the public, the investment I'm mostly known for is, ironically, one into which I never actually intended to put money. But because it was so widely covered, and in a glamorous industry, it's commonly thought of as my big play as an investor. It's nothing of the sort — that would be Arvida, a far less well-known and much more successful venture. But the story of GAS is worth telling, because it illustrates the hazards that exist for us as rugby players, of getting involved in ventures without fully understanding their complexity and particularly the risk involved.

Despite being a country boy, I've grown to love fashion. It started in 2004, on that first European tour. I was walking the streets of Paris, just enjoying the history and vibrancy of the city, when I came across a Louis Vuitton store. Ordinarily back then I'd have found it too intimidating, but for some reason I was in a confident mood, and walked in.

Security eyed me warily, and I could feel them judging me for wandering in wearing jeans and flip-flops. I think that's what made me determined to show them I wasn't who I appeared to be. I wanted to prove my worth by buying something. I ended up picking out a beautiful designer jacket. I've still got it, and wear it to this day. It cost a packet, more than my dad would have spent on clothes in years, probably. But it was worth it, both for the wear I've got out of it, and the looks on the security guards' faces. After that I was hooked, and became more and more interested in that world. It was that experience which made me so open to the GAS opportunity when it came along.

I met Rhys and Lucy through a friend. They'd been searching for a good label to bring into New Zealand, and came across GAS, a premium Italian streetwear label. I hadn't heard of it, but liked what I saw, and got caught up in the idea. I ran it past my accountant, he crunched a few numbers, and gave it a cautious thumbs up. Part of what made it easy to get involved was the dollar requirement: zero. My stake would come from my name and image, which seemed like a pretty good deal. Even so, it was a big unknown. In hindsight, I didn't give it enough due diligence, but Rhys really sold it to me. That, added to my not having to invest any money, made it pretty easy to say yes. They just wanted to use my profile to help sell the business. Where was the harm in that?

We opened in Christchurch first, in a new development called SOL Square. It's sad — the area was hard hit by the earthquake, and even today you can see a GAS billboard above the now-shuttered shop. The rentals were really cheap at the time, helping it feel low risk. I loved the process, and got involved in picking the ranges, which was a lot of fun. You're predicting trends, shopping 18 months in advance. It was mostly out of lookbooks, but once I went to Italy after an end-of-year tour to do it in person. It was mentally taxing, and a long way outside my core experience, but I loved going through the process. It was so different to my day-to-day life as a professional athlete.

Something I didn't have an understanding of was the mark-ups and margins. With what we were paying to GAS, we needed to sell jeans for $250 to $300. Shirts were over $150. There just aren't that many New Zealand men who are willing to spend that kind of money on clothes. But I just left the business side to my partners. Their backgrounds were in engineering and retail, respectively, so it seemed reasonable.

At first, GAS did well. We had a good opening, and were ticking along and not losing money. In hindsight I wish we'd just stayed in Christchurch and been content to remain a small business. But we took a store on Mercer Street, around Lambton Quay in Wellington. Suddenly we were paying prime retail rent, before we'd really established ourselves. It wasn't just the rent, either — the stores had to have that premium, European look. And while GAS helped out with some of the fit-out costs, they were still very expensive exercises.

Even though the rents were costly, I didn't worry about that stuff at the time. I was still caught up in the feel-good element. The brand felt like a hit and was attracting a lot of positive media coverage. GAS was expanding and it seemed fair to assume it would continue to. It was also a lot of fun. Rhys and I would go down to SOL Square and work behind the counter on a Friday, and there was a great energy around the business.

Then financial crisis started to bite, and the kind of discretionary income people have to spend on high-end clothes dried up. We started to have to pay for the clothes up front, before they'd be shipped, which put pressure on Rhys and the accounts, and he asked if I could invest some money. I put in a little, not a huge amount, but something. Rhys was working incredible hours, still at his engineering company, but running the business, too. I felt like I had to help him out, even though it was a ways off the original terms of the agreement.

That was when we were approached by Cameron Brewer. He was head of the Newmarket Business Association, and pitched us the idea of coming to Auckland. He said we needed to be there, that it was New Zealand's fashion capital. We hadn't thought about expanding into Auckland, but it was a seductive idea. And even though the Global Financial Crisis was rising, we thought that a store in Auckland might turn it around for us.

We had a great opening and tremendous publicity. But after a few months — when it became clear the GFC wasn't a blip, but the new normal — it started to die away. I found it incredibly stressful, watching it get stretched to breaking point, desperately wanting the brand to work but not having the experience or time to make that happen. The worst part was that we'd had to put down personal guarantees to get the leases in Auckland and Wellington. So even though I hadn't put money into the business, suddenly I was on the hook for hugely expensive commercial retail sites, with lengthy leases.

At that point I got my accountants and lawyers involved to assess the situation. They pointed out that the only way to keep the business operating was to continue to keep reinvesting until it turned around. The worrying element was that there was no guarantee that would ever happen. And from my position I had very little control of the business. After a lot of back and forth, and a significant amount of stress and pain, we made the decision to wind up the business. We got some short-term sublessees into the stores, which was important, but at a much lower rent than we had committed to. At the time it was near impossible to lease commercial retail, so we were lucky in a way to even get tenants. So for the next couple of years we were all continuing to top up the rent of stores we no longer occupied. It was a painful period for all of us.

When I entered into the venture, I never contemplated what would happen if it went south. The media loves a good fail story, and because of my involvement it got so much more coverage than it would have had it been just an ordinary retail failure. I found that really difficult to take. Up until that point I'd had almost entirely positive coverage, on and off the field. But now my name was constantly in the press, associated with an entity over which I really didn't have any day-to-day control.

It became a tremendous learning experience, both as an investor and about the dangers of being publicly associated with a business. In the end it was probably more my decision to shut it down. I felt awful for Rhys, because the type of workhorse character he is, he would've done anything to save it. But the advice I was given was that it would continue to demand money with no end in sight. Maybe that was a selfish way of looking at it, but at the same time I needed to concentrate on my rugby, and the original pitch was of an investment which would trade off my name, and not my capital.

Since then I've had dozens of opportunities come my way, some of which I've taken up. I think what I've learned from the way GAS ended was to look for those which involve people with a proven record in an industry. If they've done something over and over, and been successful, then they're much more likely to be able to do it again. Whereas with GAS, none of us had any real experience in managing a retail business. So if we were going to make it, even if things got tough, we were going to fluke it. And there are not many flukes in business.

Despite the failure of GAS, I still loved business, and still liked the idea of leveraging my profile. A couple of years later Ali Williams, Richie and I were talking about wanting to give back to the community. We set up Water For Everyone on the principle that a certain percentage of every bottle sold goes to charity. Similarly to GAS, we probably started out with a little too much ambition. We also tried salads, and milk, but dealing with supermarkets was incredibly tough, and the margins are very slim on products like that. So we reverted to just the water side, and the charity — which recently changed its name to iSport, to focus on youth sport — has given over $200,000 to various causes.

GAS and For Everyone were learning experiences, and very public ones. But my first real investment was much less public, though hopefully it will prove far more successful in the long run. It came about through Grant Adamson, an old Canterbury rugby man and private banker, who kept an eye on guys like Richie and me as we were coming up in our early twenties. He knew instinctively that the dynamic I described above would be operating: young men earning good money, without a clue what to do with it. He and a group of investors had realised early that with an ageing population would come a long-running, near insatiable demand for retirement villages. And that could be a strong, sustainable investment opportunity.

Richie and I, along with a few other players, ended up putting money into a pool which would purchase individual retirement villages as their owners came ready to sell, or were given the opportunity to cash out. It's a form of group consolidation which has happened throughout any number of industries over the past few years: everything from dentistry to radio has witnessed the phenomenon. Grant knew that there was an opportunity to build a portfolio of retirement villages which might one day be combined into a large group, with all the economies of scale that implies, and that it could prove a great investment, particularly for young guys like us.

We kept topping up the investment over the years, as new villages came up for sale, and it would sit quietly in the back of my mind, giving me a sense of security around my financial planning. Flash forward a dozen years to mid-December 2014 and I found myself on the seventh floor of Zurich House. It's a state-of-the-art building in downtown Auckland, with expansive views across the waterfront. The room was full of men and women in sharp business suits, knocking back champagne at 10 in the morning. I was in a conference room of NZX, the New Zealand stock exchange, where I'd been asked to ring the bell to ceremonially commence trading for the day. At 10.30 am one new company would be listed on the New Zealand stock exchange.

Its name was Arvida, the group which held those retirement villages we started buying way back when. There was a real poignancy to the moment, as Grant had passed away not long before. Everyone in the room knew it was largely his vision and drive which had brought us to that moment, so his presence was very much there with us. Soon a countdown was chanted: 10, 9, 8, 7, 6, 5, 4, 3, 2, 1 . . . Clang! And with that the company was listed. It was such a privilege and thrill to ring the bell, and the culmination of a long, mostly quiet, but very satisfying investment experience. One which taught all of us a lot about where our money should go, and what we should look for when assessing opportunities.

The huge gulf in outcome between GAS and Arvida is a big part of what has me interested in helping athletes out after my rugby days are over. There are a lot of players out there who are quite naive financially, just as I was. We get an opportunity put in front of us, and our first instinct is to say yes.

Rugby rewards, even demands, risk-taking to an extent. The sport is full of adrenalin, and you look for experiences off the field which create a similar response and really excite you. And business can be exciting. But, like sport, it is also brutal. Without some experience behind you, you risk falling over when times are hard and many more people fail than succeed. I would love to share some of my experiences, or even use some of my contacts, with young players getting their start in professional sports. I wished I'd talked to more people with experience in the fashion industry to help me make a decision on GAS. I might still have given it a go, but I would have been entering that world with a far more clear-eyed view of the very real risks involved, and not just the far less likely reward.

While that outcome was unfortunate, it wasn't the end of the world for me, thanks in part to my luck in meeting Grant, who helped mentor me financially over the years. But too many other young players, who might not have such long careers, don't meet a guy like that. Instead they're vulnerable to making one bad investment decision and losing the largest chunk of their capital. That forces them to keep playing long after their bodies have given out, or leaves them starting from scratch — or even debt-ridden — in their early thirties. That just doesn't seem right.

10

Bitter-sweet Sabbatical

I ended the 2007 World Cup wounded mentally and physically, and wanting badly to escape the weight of what had happened. While the constant commiseration from the public was well-intended, and initially genuinely gratifying, I felt like a fraud accepting it. I knew deep down that we had failed, and couldn't stop thinking about how good it would have been to bring the Cup back, and see those faces had we won it. But I also wanted to get away from New Zealand, and be a regular guy, rather than an All Black.

Honor had planned to come over for the final stages of the World Cup, but cancelled when we lost. We still wanted to travel, so one morning I woke up and said to her, 'Let's book a holiday.'

We went travelling for a month, back to Europe and the Middle East, just exploring. We went to Barcelona and saw some of Spain, then through Northern Italy, stopping at Lake Como, Milan and Venice. Eventually we arrived in Treviso, where we spent time with John Kirwan, who was coaching Italy at the time. While there I visited the GAS factory, which was a fascinating experience, seeing where the clothing was made and designed. We had some time in London and Dubai, and a brilliant week in the Maldives, just chilling — two young people, completely anonymous.

It had to end, and we flew home to New Zealand in early December. Honor was moving up to Auckland early the following year, after getting a really good job in marketing at DB. The idea of us living in different cities wasn't appealing, so I decided to join her. It didn't make a huge difference to us day to day, as I was on the road or in Christchurch so much. But it did make me wonder whether I should explore the possibility of playing somewhere else. I'd had some offers from overseas, and looked reasonably hard at them, though more as a thought experiment than anything too serious.

That's part of what prompted us to come up with the sabbatical concept. I just needed a different challenge, and I guess I wanted to push the boundaries a little. The Essentially guys did an outstanding job there with the negotiation. It was conducted simultaneously with Richie's, to maximise leverage, so we ended up getting a good contract, but also the innovation of the sabbatical clause, so I could get a new challenge and experience life playing overseas.

After I moved to Auckland I thought I needed to test the Crusaders people a little. I said to Warren Alcock, who runs contracts for Essentially, 'Go and hit up the Blues and see if they're keen.' They came back with a ridiculously good offer. I wasn't really interested in playing for anyone else, but wanting to send a message to the Crusaders, who took pride in paying their players the least. The attitude seems to be that they want you to play there for something beyond money. And you do — but you also don't want to feel like they exploit you or your attachment to the jersey in the process.

There was another dynamic at play, too. It was Robbie Deans' last year as Crusaders coach, and he knew he'd be either coaching the All Blacks or off overseas after that. So he was desperate to retain me, and try and win one last title. That appealed to me too. But the scale of the Blues' offer did give me pause.

To their credit, the Crusaders responded by putting together a good package, and let me commute back and forth, so I could still live with Honor in Auckland. I'd play on a Saturday and go home Sunday. There was a day return for training on Tuesday. Wednesday was a rest day, then I'd be back for Thursday through Saturday. It was tough, but in the end I'm glad I stayed a Crusader. I still can't imagine what it would've been like to play against my old team.

Two other things helped sway me back to Canterbury. Firstly, the leak of my negotiations with the Blues. I know it didn't come from Essentially, and I can't stand leaks, particularly in situations as sensitive as a contract negotiation. That directly led to the second thing, which might have really made the difference. After the leak my Nana called me. She was very upset, and begging me not to play for Auckland. They're a pretty parochial bunch down there, and she got me thinking about all the thousands of Canterbury people I'd be disappointing by leaving. That, probably more than anything else, led to me re-signing.

The Blues' case wasn't helped by my impressions of the city when I first moved there. I took Doug Howlett's old house when he moved to Ireland after the World Cup. It was flatting, but in a beautiful, five-bedroom house. I hated the city at first (sorry, Aucklanders!). The people were so much less friendly, the traffic was awful, there was too much going on — I just couldn't stand it, for two straight years at least. The only thing the city had in its favour was that Honor was there.

The commute was hard. My body took a beating — it's not

designed to go way up in the air, then train an hour or so later — and I ended up having to fly down the night before trainings. But I'm glad I did, because we won the competition in 2008, a fitting way to send off Robbie Deans. He'd been a brilliant coach, one of the best I'd ever played for, and we wanted to get that last title for him. I just wish he didn't have to go to coach Australia. That didn't sit right with me.

At the same time, I understood why he had to go. There was that huge national division after the World Cup about whether Graham Henry and his guys should be reappointed or not. I was truly undecided. I had so much respect for each of them, and certainly didn't think Graham deserved to be fired for that quarter-final loss. We were consulted about the decision — I had conversations with Steve Tew and Jock Hobbs on the subject, during which I spoke highly of both Graham and Robbie. In the end I was somewhat surprised that Graham Henry got reappointed, because it seemed to be how we did things — if you lost, you were fired. But he kept his job, and it proved the right decision.

I think that was borne out by more than just the World Cup win in 2011. If you look at the shift that's happened with this team since 2004, the 2007 loss looks like a minor blip compared to everything else which has gone on. Henry, Hansen and Smith are an incredible trio. From what I've heard, the three of them turned up and made a fantastic presentation, showing what they'd do if reappointed. Whereas Robbie, perhaps rightly, expected that with his record and the World Cup performance, he'd be appointed as of right. I feel bad that it didn't turn out that way, but grew so much under Henry and his team that I wouldn't change a thing.

Winning our third Super Rugby title in four years was a great way to purge some of the bad feelings which came out of the World Cup. It was a specific goal with a finite time horizon, thanks to Robbie's leaving. But the same couldn't be said for the Tri-Nations. I understand that it's an important part of the revenue package which underpins rugby in the southern hemisphere. And it has been enlivened somewhat more recently by the addition of Argentina to the schedule. But for both players and fans fatigue does set in.

Even as I write this, I'm struggling to distinguish between different campaigns, and in the aftermath of a World Cup, when you play such a variety of teams in a short space of time, the familiarity of the Tri-Nations can become pretty wearying. Doubly so given that it comes straight out of a Super Rugby tournament which features much the same players and locations. I feel very differently about the end-of-year tours. Even though we're mostly playing the same five or six teams, they're one-off tests, in huge international stadiums, with vibrant cultures and crowds around us.

This effect was particularly acute in 2008. We won our ninth title, despite losing twice, and no one was particularly excited by it. Throughout the tournament and the tour which followed my mind was firmly on Perpignan. It's funny, my overseas sabbatical was often characterised as a naked cash grab, but that really doesn't accurately represent its meaning. Because obviously, if it was all about money, every All Black would leave for Europe and never return in their mid-twenties. We don't, because the team really does matter. I took the first sabbatical because I really was getting bored of playing the same opponents, and genuinely wanted to refresh by playing against different opposition, with different styles, in different tournaments.

As a result, once I made the decision to sign with Perpignan in mid-'08, I was counting down the days. After the northern hemisphere tour ended there was a commercial window before my NZRU commitments were up. I stayed on in Milan for a few days, working with adidas on some promotional events. They had around 10 of us All Blacks paired up with the AC Milan soccer team. We were given a complete tour of their facilities, which were just outstanding, particularly by comparison to the bare bones Crusaders and Canterbury set-up. I did some kicking stuff with the great Brazilian playmaker Kaka, a competition with soccer and rugby balls, trying to bend the ball into the goal from different angles. It was another one of those pinch yourself moments.

It was interesting, though — the moment the event ended the AC Milan guys couldn't get out of there fast enough. The carpark was filled with exotic cars, and within minutes they were all gone. Zeljko Kalac, their back-up goalkeeper, stayed behind. He was an Australian, and was stoked to see us. He explained the team culture in football, or the lack of it. According to him there's very little interaction beyond training — it's just every man for himself. You come in, you work, you leave. It made me appreciate what we have in New Zealand, the bonds of friendship I've forged in the Crusaders and All Blacks.

Not long after, I went down to Perpignan to join the team. It wasn't my first time in the region, so I had a sense of what it would be like. A few months earlier I'd had a break while injured, and flown in to sign the contract. Thousands of people turned up to the stadium — just to welcome me. I walked out to these booming cheers, and people chanting my name. All thousands of miles away from Southbridge. It was, to this day, the most overwhelming reception I've ever had as an individual.

When I pulled up to the stadium for my first training session there was a cauldron of people to negotiate. It was emblematic of the passion of the French people — they're so much more open with their emotions across all facets of life. We think our crowds are loud, but they're nothing compared to European fans.

It carried across to the players, too. In the changing rooms, ahead of our first game, the forwards went to the showers and started yelling at each other. They were head-butting, slapping each other in the face, working up into a frenzy. I couldn't relate to it — that kind of behaviour was just so far from my realm of experience in rugby. My focus was on fitting in, and just being a good team man.

The club and the captain wanted me at the centre of attention, though, so it was an awkward little dance. The captain wanted me to run out first. I was adamant I wouldn't, but he pushed me out in the end. The crowd were completely out of their minds in that game. We faced the Leicester Tigers, with Aaron Mauger playing second-five and Scott Hamilton on the wing. It was great to get a win in first up — you always love beating your mates. It was a major learning experience: a completely different style of rugby, and I loved the challenge of absorbing a new set of moves and structures.

I was out of my comfort zone, which was what I'd been seeking. But it was tough, too, particularly the language barrier. I came into the team with no French, and the coach had almost no English. My first training session was a video review ahead of the Leicester game. It came following a big week of promotion for the All Blacks, culminating in a few drinks with the boys to celebrate the end of the season. The video session consisted of an hour going through the game in intricate detail — all in French. At some point I must have dozed off, and awoke to someone tapping me awake, with the whole team looking at me. I was so embarrassed. One of the South Africans then translated what the coach had been saying. It took him all of 30 seconds. It seemed a little backwards to spend so long grinding the point out, but that's just the way they did things over there.

I had a couple of weeks to settle into my house before Honor arrived to spend the Christmas and New Year period with me. I played a second game, and had one more game to get through in early January before a break we had scheduled. In our last training session before the holiday, on Christmas Eve, my left Achilles tendon started getting a little tight, but as I had just arrived at the club I didn't want to cause trouble, so trained through it. I figured the holiday period would allow it to settle down. Honor and I went across to Marrakesh in Morocco. It was 20 degrees, a nice escape from the French winter, and only a three-hour flight away. But what we were both seeking was the feel of the New Zealand summer holiday season. So heading to a country which doesn't celebrate Christmas wasn't ideal. We enjoyed the trip, but were a little sad, missing our families, and conscious that we only had a brief time together due to Honor's hockey commitments.

When I returned for the next game, in early January, my Achilles was still sore. I still played but I had to come off at halftime. I'd aggravated it, so sat out the next couple of weeks to try to get it to settle down. All the while I was conscious that I was only there for a short period of time, and wanted to play as much as possible.

The game I was targeting was a huge match against Stade

Français at a sold-out Stade de France, in front of 80,000. Honor was flying out that night, and actually had to leave just before the end of the game. I was desperate to get on the field. Coach asked if I was ready to play, and I told him I was, even though the Achilles was still bloody sore. I warmed up, and despite some pain, I decided to push through. I took some painkillers and anti-inflammatories and hoped for the best. It was an amazing scene. Because club rugby is generally not big enough to sell out the stadium on its own, they built a huge show around the game. So it felt like half the crowd were there for the game, and the rest for the spectacle. They had a lion — a real, live lion — emerging from a giant rugby ball float, and topless women, with just a little star over their nipples. The contrast with New Zealand's match presentation was pretty stark.

Luckily, the game lived up to the opening. It was incredibly close throughout, and probably the best I ever played for Perpignan. My Achilles felt pretty good in the first half. The scores were level near the end, when we were awarded a penalty about 55 metres out. I'd been kicking the whole game, but that was beyond my range. They had a guy who could kick it a long way, so he took the shot. It missed. Stade Français gratefully received it and you'd have expected them to just kick the ball out, as it was the eighty-fourth minute. I probably shouldn't have played the full 80, with my Achilles in that condition. Stade Français sent it back to us, and the ball was passed to me. I took it to the line, and just as I was powering up to go into contact I felt a pain in my leg. As I went to ground, I looked behind me, thinking I'd been kicked — that's what it felt like.

But there was no one there. I realised right away that it was my Achilles. There was a scuffle above me, but I just lay on the ground, knowing there was something seriously wrong. They did the squeeze test on my calf, and there was nothing. It was just dead.

The worst part was that Honor had headed to the airport with 10 minutes to play to catch her flight. She called me from Dubai, and wanted to come back, but I told her I'd be okay. I went and saw some specialists at the Paris Saint-Germain soccer club, and spoke with Deb Robinson, the All Blacks doctor. She wanted to be kept in the loop, but the language barrier made it tough — was it a full or partial tear? I still didn't really know. But it had implications for the All Blacks, in terms of their planning for the year. It was initially reported as a partial tear, but turned out to be a full. I was doubly distraught, for both myself, and everyone at Perpignan.

Regardless, I had to organise surgery, away from my usual contacts. I initially got in touch with Bruce Twaddle and Barry Tietjens, leading orthopaedic surgeons in Auckland. They found me a surgeon in Lyon. After the op, I was in traction, recovering in Perpignan. I was lonely, and depressed, not only injured, but away from friends and family.

A guy named Benoit Brazès took me under his wing. He had a media role with Perpignan, but was so much more than that — a club stalwart, son and grandson of Perpignan players. He'd die for the club if they asked. He ended up travelling with me to Lyon, helping with the language, keeping me company — he'd do anything for me. The other players would give him shit, but it was a godsend to me at the time. We'd have long conversations about rugby, and in time he opened up that when the new president took over the club, he asked Benoit who they should target. He'd said: 'Dan Carter'. So he was the whole reason I was there, really.

Benoit was typical of the whole organisation, the whole town. While France is a soccer-mad country, in the south around Perpignan rugby is number one. They're as passionate as we are, but hadn't won a title since the '60s. So when I'd gone there they'd all rallied around me, as if I would bring them that long sought-after title. Then I get invalided out after only five games. Irrational as it sounds, I felt incredibly guilty. But I was determined to try to repay the club and its fans. As soon as I was allowed out of hospital I went and did a signing session as a way of trying to repay the club. It lasted hours, and the fans were brilliant. It was almost the opposite of my perception — they saw my injury as shedding blood for the jersey, as some kind of testament to my devotion. In reality it was just a freak injury, which could have happened at any point in my career. But they seemed to view me as almost heroic, for having sustained such a serious injury in Perpignan colours.

I found out not long after that, thanks to my injury, it was insurance paying me out, rather than the club. That got rid of most of the guilt, and I decided to hang around the club anyway. The NZRU wanted me to come home and rehab with them, but I felt a loyalty to Perpignan now, so wanted to stay and see out the season. Honor was still six weeks away from returning, so three of my best friends came over to stay and help me live: Mark Murdoch (Mank), Nick McKay (Mazda) and James Young (Youngie) who I knew from Ellesmere College or my days around the university. They are a fun bunch, so we went pretty hard. But they also helped with my rehab. I needed blood-thinning injections every day, to help my circulation. The nurse taught us to do it, so my friends took turns jabbing me in the tummy. It was a little bizarre, but it worked.

Those weeks were like the TV show *Entourage*, except with a moon-boot. We toured and partied our way through the area — I went clubbing on crutches. We had a great weekend in Barcelona, and saw their football team play in front of 100,000 people. Mank and I share a birthday, so we celebrated that together. It was a fun few weeks.

After my gang left, Mum and Dad came over. We did more sightseeing, travelling around France. Then Honor returned, just as I got out of the moon-boot. I was essentially learning to walk again. The Achilles was so tight that my foot was pointing straight down. I didn't fully trust the local medics, just because it was so crucial to my career and livelihood. So I paid the All Blacks physio Pete Gallagher to come over, out of my own pocket. We worked out twice a day, in water and on land, and he basically taught me how to walk again. He created an incredibly detailed rehab plan, and gave me my confidence back in my body.

Honor stayed for a month, during which we'd travel through the week, then watch the team play on weekends. A strange thing started to happen during a run of road games — we went on a winning streak. French teams really emphasise home games, and worry less about road games. But we really stressed the importance of away games that year, and it paid off. We blew out of the European Cup, which turned out to be no bad thing, as we could concentrate on Top 14, which is a huge competition in France. We made the quarters, then the semis, then the final. There was an amazing feeling around the club — they hadn't won a title for more than 50 years, but were now one win away. I was in Paris for the whole week leading into the final. I leaned on contacts I had with Moët and adidas to get tickets to the 2009 French Open, and got to see Roger Federer on his way to finally winning the French.

I'm a bit of a Fed fan, so that was a great experience.

We were playing Clermont in the final, a perennially strong French club. I sat in the stands in my Perpignan number ones. Thousands of our supporters had made the journey up, and it was electrifying to see the stands full of Perpignan and Clermont colours. It was at Stade de France again, a neutral ground, so there was no hometown advantage.

And we won. Despite my only having played five games, I still felt a part of it. The reaction was incredible, and I instantly understood how much this trophy — the famed le Bouclier de Brennus — means to French rugby. Much more than the European championship, because of its history.

We flew back with the trophy, and had a parade through the city centre. It reminded me of early Crusaders days, when fans would be hanging out windows on Colombo Street to see the Super Rugby trophy. The streets were covered in flags, and the event culminated in a ceremony during which each player was introduced to huge cheers. My turn came, and the guys ripped my shirt off, which was mortifying.

The next day we continued to celebrate at a bar owned by a former player. At one point I walked outside and was spotted by some construction workers in the street outside, who turned out to be huge rugby fans. They convinced me to swap my Perpignan gear for their hi-vis vests, which is why there are a few videos of me floating around in the aftermath of our claiming le Bouclier, unaccountably dressed like a road worker, dancing on the bar.

The next two to three days were spent celebrating. When it started to die down I gingerly dragged my hangover onto a plane and slept the whole way home.

FINAL YEAR DIARY: Auckland, 6 July 2015

Recorded during All Blacks camp in the lobby of the Heritage Hotel, hours before we flew out to Apia for our first ever test in the Islands.

My Crusaders career is officially over. We missed the playoffs for the first time in the 12 seasons I played for the franchise, yet I'll remember this season with real pride. Mostly because of how we finished it. In the last three weeks we beat the Hurricanes, Blues and Brumbies by good margins, and took some real satisfaction out of the way we closed out the season. The last few days I was very conscious that it was all coming to an end. After the final game against the Brumbies, Richie and I were presented our jerseys by Stephen Larkham and George Gregan, two guys against whom we've played a number of memorable games. Then we flew home for a special event in Christchurch to farewell the five guys who were leaving the team. Families were invited, so Mum and Dad were also there to share the moment.

All week, even though it had been emotional, I had kept it together. I was sad I was leaving, but I felt fine. My attitude was that it was the end of one era, but also the start of a new one. Then Andy Ellis got up and made a speech, and he played a video of my Crusaders career. I was watching it, finding it pretty affecting. Wyatt Crockett was standing alongside me. He nudged me and whispered, 'Are you going to tear up mate?' I laughed and told him I was alright. And

I thought I was. Then I got up to speak to the group and just lost it. Just absolutely lost it. I felt a real deep sadness for this moment, knowing I'd never wear a Crusaders jersey again.

I couldn't get any words out. I just teared up and spluttered my way through a speech thanking people. I can't even really remember what I said. I think I said that it was nice for some of the younger players to see how much it means to be a Crusader, but that isn't what I was thinking. I was actually overwhelmed with gratitude for the time I'd had. The fact it had lasted so long. I limped through the speech and sat down, then Richie had the same sequence. He didn't quite tear up, though, and kept it together a little better than I did.

I was slightly embarrassed afterwards. I rang Honor, who was up in Auckland with the children, and told her I'd made a complete fool of myself and cried in front of the whole team. She was really supportive and it meant a lot to be able to talk with her straight away. I had a good couple of days with the team afterwards, through the end-of-year festivities. With that I effectively said my goodbyes to Christchurch.

A month before there was another, much more shocking and tragic, goodbye. I was in Auckland with the Crusaders, and had driven back to the Crown Plaza after a kicking session at Eden Park. I parked, and walked up to my room, where Nafi Tuitavake, my roommate, was waiting. 'You heard about Jerry?' he said. No, I thought. 'Have you not heard?' he said. And my heart just sank. I thought the worst immediately. I heard Nafi say, 'He was in a car crash. He's dead.' I was lost for words, just devastated.

You just don't expect this kind of thing from the people who you play with. You hear of ex-All Blacks passing away, you're sad, but it's so different when it's actually someone that you call a friend and you played with. This was around 5.30 pm and I was hanging out to watch the news to get some more information. I went to the team room and I saw Aaron Mauger and Richie. We just started sharing stories — JC stories — straight away. It was quite cool. The first thing you do is share your sadness with people who are in the same position, grieving a mate. We just started to reflect on the guy's incredible character.

Aaron talked about the first time he played against Jerry. I think it might have even been at school. He was this huge, amazing athlete, so much bigger and stronger than everyone else. He was in line for the captaincy of the New Zealand Schools team, but the coach must have seen him having a drink or smoking, and they didn't pick him for the team. Obviously they'll have regretted that because of what he achieved later on.

Throughout his career he was his own man. You'd hear stories about him playing for the Hurricanes on a Friday then club rugby on a Saturday or league on a Sunday. No one loved the game as much as him.

My first experience with him was a few weeks before the first All Blacks game of 2003. I had heard a few stories about what a staunch guy he was, and was a little bit scared of him, to be honest. I was at a bar with a few of my mates — non-rugby mates — and he saw me and called me over. I went, nervously. This was one of the first All Blacks camps I'd been to. 'Are you drinking?' he asked. 'I'm just having a couple with my friends,' I said.

He then lined up eight vodka shots. I was freaking out. 'Four each,' he said. 'Let's go.' I looked a bit worried. 'You do four, and I'll do four, then I'll leave you alone for the rest of your career.'

I put on a brave face, tried not to throw up, and necked them all. He patted me on the back and said, 'You're a good man.' And I just wandered back to my mates. It was almost like he was trying to work out what kind of person I was. After that moment I seemed to have earned his respect, and we became really good friends.

We sat next to each other on the bus for years. One of the first things he did was teach me his signature. On the bus you get passed a lot of pieces of memorabilia to sign, and if Jerry couldn't be bothered, he just got me to sign them.

But behind all the staunchness there was a huge heart. I knew that he always had my back in any situation. Often on the field, as a 10, you're targeted by the opposition, trying to shake you off your game. I always felt that bit more relaxed if that happened when Jerry was playing, knowing he'd be the first guy to stick up for me. He just wouldn't take shit from anyone.

It was so tragic that it happened at a time in his life when he seemed so happy, seemed to have found peace. All day leading into the Blues game on Saturday I couldn't stop thinking about him. I was incredibly grateful, a few days later, that I was able to attend his funeral. It was a real celebration of his life. You got a sense of how many people he'd touched, particularly around his community in Porirua.

The week after I was in All Blacks camp. Even deep into my career, I still forget what a step up it is. You've got the best coaching, the best nutrition, the best medical team — it's all there, and just makes it so much easier to perform. And I'm finally here in good shape. The last few years I haven't been able to do the annual fitness test due to injuries, which has gotten me some stick from a few of the boys. But I did it this year, and went okay. Fourth in a running test called the bronco, which I was pretty happy with, at my age. Most of all I'm excited about playing in the first test of the year, up in Samoa — and starting at 10.

11

The All Blacks Falter and Recover

I arrived back from Perpignan into an awkward part of the season. Super Rugby was just reaching its climax, but I was still rehabbing, and didn't want to distract the Canterbury side from their focus. But the Air New Zealand Cup was in preseason, still a while away from the campaign proper. That left club rugby, which was probably about the right level for a guy like me, returning from a serious injury.

Despite being Southbridge born and bred, at that point I'd never played a game of senior club rugby for them. Midgets and junior grades, sure, but then I played colts and senior grade for High School Old Boys. This meant I was about to play my first game of senior club rugby for Southbridge at the ripe old age of 27. And while I loved my time at High School Old Boys, the chance to play for Southbridge was one I thought might never come again. The club has so much meaning for my family and me that it was never in doubt: I would turn out for Southbridge Seniors. Finally.

My debut was against Hornby. The suburb is the first set of traffic lights when you hit Christchurch — so what were they doing in the Ellesmere competition? It's actually a big rugby league community, which takes a lot of their young talent, so the Hornby side struggled in the Christchurch club scene. They transferred to Ellesmere to get a break. It was an away game for Southbridge, and despite the club's administrator's trying hard to negotiate its return to our town, Hornby refused to budge. Good move, too — they did their best bar takings in years that night.

I trained with the Southbridge boys Tuesday and Thursday, as club footy demands, and was given my Southbridge kit. This was a very meaningful moment, knowing that Dad and so many other family members had worn it over the years. But it was also a little daunting. Club rugby's no joke, and I was very early in my comeback. I'd done some speed work, but didn't have my acceleration back, so was a little apprehensive about what I'd find in the heat of the game.

After the whistle blew it didn't take long to realise I was a target. I'd pass the ball and have to sidestep the next two tacklers flying by late. It would make a club rugby guy's career if he could tell his mates that he smashed me. In truth I'd been half expecting it.

Despite the uncertainty over my fitness, one thing I thought I could rely on was my boot. I'd even gone the extra mile to make sure kicking the ball was as familiar as possible. With club rugby you use whatever ball is available, but ahead of the game I'd gone past Canterbury to get a set of four new Gilbert balls. What could go wrong?

A lot, it turned out. The first kick of the game was just to the side of the posts — a sitter. I was sure I'd nailed it, but with the short club posts it was hard to tell. Either way, the touch judge's flags stayed down. Things fell apart from there — I ended up missing my first four kicks! I was in danger of going through

22.02.2011. The effects of the 2011 Christchurch earthquake are clearly visible right outside my house in Shirley. Above: Liquefaction on my front lawn. Below: The little bridge at the start of our right-of-way sags dejectedly.

I felt a pop from within, and collapsed to the ground, screaming in agony. The ball dribbled 10 metres in front of me, and I lay there, crumpled in a heap. My World Cup dream was over . . . again.

With Israel Dagg, Jerome Kaino, Andy Ellis, Mils Muliaina and Kieran Read after the RWC final in 2011. I was so happy for my teammates, for the coaches, for the whole country.

Wedding day, 9 December 2011. Above: Honor and I pose with the bridal party. Below: With Mum, Dad and my sister Sarah.

Leaving Westpac Stadium
in Wellington after a special
presentation following my 100th
Super Rugby match in April 2012.

With the Bledisloe Cup after our
22–0 victory over Australia at
Eden Park in 2012.

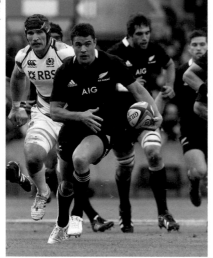

Attacking against Scotland on the
northern hemisphere tour in 2012.
I still regard this as one of my best
matches in the black jersey.

With Nana Carter and the IRB Player
of the Year trophy at the end of 2012.

My 100th test match, vs England at Twickenham, 2013.
Top: A pair of the special adidas limited-edition commemorative
boots. I couldn't wait to wear them. Middle: Liam Messam pulls me
up by the jersey during the haka. It was a huge mark of respect and
I was almost overcome by the moment. Bottom: After the match
with fellow members of the 100 club, Woody, Richie and Kevvy.

Final farewells at Christchurch, 2015. Above: With Richie after the Crusaders'
win over the Reds and, below, after the All Blacks' test against Argentina.

Laying on the pass for Dane Coles to score a long-range try against Australia in the Bledisloe Cup decider at Eden Park, 2015.

Conrad Smith, me, Ma'a Nonu, Keven Mealamu, Richie McCaw and Tony Woodcock pose for the last time together with the Bledisloe Cup, Eden Park, 2015. We had accumulated almost 700 test caps between us.

Dropped goal in the 70th minute of the 2015 World Cup final. I rode it all the way to the posts.

The image that had been in my mind's eye for years: with Richie and the boys, and the greatest prize in world rugby.

the whole game without scoring, until I snuck through for a try near the end. I sprinted extra hard to make sure I scored under the posts, as by that time my kicking had become a running joke. After I made the conversion I got a sarcastic standing ovation from the crowd on my jog back to the half.

It took me a long time to live it down. Even when I played again for Southbridge in 2014, during another post-sabbatical rehab, they kept reminding me of my performance. 'Hold on, I know your kicking stats for Southbridge, mate. I think I'll take the kicks this week.' I had to beg to take them, and felt real pressure after the debacle at Hornby.

After the Hornby match there was one more ritual to be completed. I had played about 60 tests for the All Blacks by then, but I was still a rookie in Southbridge's eyes. I had to go through the traditional club rugby initiation. Hard work — but afterwards I was finally a true Southbridge clubman.

I didn't have long to enjoy the club rugby lifestyle. The following week I turned out for Canterbury, and not long after found myself in Sydney, lining up a penalty in the Bledisloe Cup. Two minutes to go and two points adrift of the Wallabies. I struck it well, and we won the game. It was such an incredible feeling, especially in my first All Blacks game in almost a year.

I couldn't help but reflect on the contrast — a few weeks earlier I'd been spraying the ball all over the park on a suburban ground in Hornby. Now I had nailed a match-winning kick in front of a packed house in Sydney. It reminded me how much I loved the All Blacks environment, and had missed the pressure of those moments.

As good as the Australia game was, it didn't reflect reality for the All Blacks at the time. South Africa were in dominating form, and had twice convincingly beaten us in the lead-up. After the Australia game we played the Boks one more time, on a cool, clear night in Hamilton. Same result — a close but still decisive loss. Losing three times in a single year to the same opponent wasn't something I'd ever experienced previously, and prompted a lot of soul searching within the team.

As a leadership group we discussed the losses extensively ahead of the northern tour that year. We were concerned that we'd become too tight, too fixated on the coach's instructions, to the detriment of our ability to think and respond freely within the flow of the game. We lost our number-one ranking. This was shocking to us at the time, but helped galvanise the team ahead of the tour, which ended up being one of the most satisfying we'd had in a long while. The best game came in Marseille. We played in white and took apart a very good French side 39–12. I felt back to my best, and the team reinvigorated as we headed into 2010.

The year prior to a World Cup can be difficult. Your mind is so focused on what's to come that it's easy to find yourself less than enthusiastic about the routine of the year. Familiarity can breed, if not contempt, then a certain amount of boredom. In 2010 it was different, at least at a Super Rugby level, because it was my first year under Todd Blackadder as coach. I'd only ever played for Robbie at Super level prior to that. He'd been part of the All Blacks coaching set-up as well, so the prospect of experiencing an entirely different staff with their own ideas and processes was exciting. And he was incredibly respected within Canterbury.

When you think of the Crusaders, and Crusaders men, three key people spring to mind: Reuben Thorne, Richie McCaw and

Todd Blackadder; and Todd was the first — the guy that created the Crusaders culture from the very beginnings of the team. To play for him, a new coach and legendary figure, was just the kind of fresh challenge I've always sought in my career.

The season went well enough, and we flew to South Africa to face the Bulls in the semi-finals. But because the soccer World Cup was on, we were displaced from many of the traditional rugby stadiums over there. So instead of playing at Loftus, we were in Soweto. I'd only been once before, during that ill-fated Colts trip a decade earlier, and had found it a very affecting place. Very run-down, with the effects of poverty and homelessness everywhere you looked.

I thought it would be an interesting place to play. Many of the locals have really got in behind the Crusaders and New Zealand rugby in the past. So in the back of my mind I wondered whether it might play to our advantage. As soon as kick-off came I realised I was dead wrong. Nothing was going to stop the Bulls that day. They got that big South African pack rolling, and seemed completely unbeatable. Everything we tried fell apart in the face of their dominance. We were never in the game, and lost by 15 points.

Heading into the All Blacks environment, there was an edge to the Tri-Nations. Losing three consecutive games — and the world number-one ranking — to South Africa was not sitting well with any of us. We won our opening trio of games handily, over Ireland and Wales, before steeling ourselves to face South Africa again at Eden Park.

We came out like men possessed. We wanted that number-one ranking back, and to show them we wouldn't be intimidated. Our forwards were as punishing as I've ever seen them, inflicting some viciously dominant tackles. South Africa pride themselves on their physicality, and rightly so. But on that night we were on another level.

After a number of years of emphasising other competitions or milestones over the Tri-Nations, we had a renewed focus on that competition in 2010. That went doubly so for me. Despite my achievements across my career to that point, I had never felt I'd been able to truly leave an imprint upon an entire Tri-Nations. I had a number of conversations with Gilbert Enoka, and we came up with an aspiration to be the best first-five in the competition. Having those kinds of specific and contained goals helps focus my mind.

One game in particular showed a real hardness from the All Blacks. We were playing at the new soccer stadium in Soweto, and South Africa were leading in the closing minutes of a game which had real meaning for them, thanks to it being John Smit's 100th as a Springbok. Towards the end of the game, he had a hold of Ma'a by his boot. Ma'a slipped it off, made a break and set up Izzy Dagg to score and steal the game. I felt terrible for John, missing a tackle in front of a packed stadium to lose the game. But it was a brilliant, hold-your-nerve win, one of a number we'd complete over the coming years, in what would start to become a signature of this current All Blacks team. Following that, we went through the competition unbeaten, which was hugely validating after the doubts and losses of the previous year.

After the Tri-Nations there was a clear month or so before we headed away on the end-of-year tour, and I had something big planned. After the final game in South Africa, I'd woken up in my hotel room and thought: I want to marry Honor. As soon as the thought had taken hold, it just seemed like the most natural thing in the world. I couldn't understand why I'd taken so long — she was the person I wanted to be with for the rest of my life. So I set about preparing to propose.

As usual, rugby got in the way. Before I could start, I needed surgery on my ankle, a clear-out of bone fragments. I flew straight to Christchurch to have the surgery, thus missing the Bledisloe Cup game in Sydney. The timeframe was tight if I wanted to be ready for the end-of-year tour. I was scheduled to fly back to Auckland the following day, but made a detour through Blenheim without Honor knowing, so I could ask her father Jimma for his approval.

He picked me up from the airport, and we went out to lunch. I was incredibly nervous, and he probably wondered what the hell I was doing there, alone, making this unscheduled visit. Eventually I got around to asking the question, and soon we were drinking champagne to toast the occasion.

Having gained her father's approval, I set about trying to find the opportunity to propose. Between her hockey career and full-time marketing role and my rugby commitments it can be hard to try to schedule any decent period of time for us together. It was about a month until our schedules matched up, and I was able to book a weekend in Queenstown. But once I had that locked in, I still had one more thing to accomplish — getting Honor's mother's permission. She'd come up for a hockey tournament, and had been staying with us, but I'd kept putting it off and missing opportunities. I was seriously nervous, and running out of time.

One night her mother Maling and I were having dinner together, just the two of us. It was the perfect opportunity, but I couldn't get the words out. In time she headed up the stairs to bed, and I blurted out, 'I've got something to ask you.' She turned, looking worried, and asked what she'd done. I spilled my plans, and she was first relieved, then very happy.

With the parents on side, my next task was to get Honor to Queenstown without her knowing what I had planned. I cooked up a story about needing to go down there for a Rexona sponsorship commitment with some prize winners. That kind of thing happened all the time, so it was the perfect cover. I told her that they'd offered to fly her down for the weekend too, which seemed plausible, so we flew down in early October.

I had a friend down there helping me plan it all. I wanted to fly her to a secluded lake in a helicopter and propose there, but had a back-up plan in case the weather fell apart.

The day came, 9 October 2010. I woke up early, and looked out at a grey and drizzly sky. This wasn't what I wanted. I had a good plan B, but was desperate to do the deed by the lake. All morning I furtively looked out at the clouds, and was relieved to see the sky finally clear in time. I snuck away and spoke to the pilot, who gave me the all clear. It was time for the second part of my subterfuge. I pretended to get another phone call from Rexona, saying that the chopper they had for prize winners was free for an hour ahead of the meet-and-greet. Did we want to use it, I asked Honor, trying desperately to appear casual.

'Nah, not really,' came her reply. Disaster! I played it cool and we went for coffee, where I managed to persuade her to go along. We arrived at the helicopter, and the pilot was a family friend of hers — Louisa 'Choppy' Patterson — which I used as cover to justify why I'd been so keen to get her along. We tiki-toured around the district, before eventually arriving at Lake Luna, a private lake on a farm, with a fishing hut alongside it. Choppy dropped us there, with a picnic basket, then said she'd leave us alone to eat. Only Honor wouldn't let her leave! She insisted on her staying and enjoying a meal with us. I was standing behind Honor with eyes like saucers, mouthing at Choppy to make an excuse. Luckily, she thought on her feet, and said she needed to find the farmer and ensure we had permission to land there. Honor bought it, and let her go.

As the helicopter flew off and finally left us alone, I realised that despite all this planning, I had no idea what I was going to say. Any thoughts I had about taking my time to come up with a speech were dashed when Honor opened the picnic hamper and saw a bottle of champagne. She turned to me and said, 'Wow — champagne at 11 in the morning?' I got a sinking feeling, certain she would guess, and proceeded to make a complete hash of the moment.

I grabbed the ring from my jacket pocket and threw it towards her to catch. Then I tried to get down on one knee, but discovered my jeans were too tight. I was stuttering and mumbling my way through, inverting her surname and middle name. It was an absolute shocker — I'd planned everything perfectly, but somehow neglected to think about what I'd do and say to actually verbally propose. When the moment came I choked more comprehensively than I ever had on a sports field. Thankfully, she said yes, which was a huge relief. But a couple of minutes later she made me do it again — properly this time.

Presently Choppy turned up and whisked us back to the hotel, where Honor's parents and mine were waiting — I'd organised for them to be flown in while we were away — and we ended up having a fantastic weekend. I'm still proud of all the intricate plotting I did to get her to that location. But I'd advise those planning their own proposals to practise the speech itself with as much attention to detail as organising the actual occasion.

Soon enough we were headed back to Auckland, and not long after I was flying off on tour, leaving Honor to plan our wedding. It felt so great to have that period over with — as much fun as it had been, I'd never been so nervous in my life. Playing rugby in packed stadiums again felt like a relief.

The end-of-year tour began with a strange game against Australia in Hong Kong. It was a Bledisloe game, but we'd already secured the Cup by then, so it felt like a festival event: in this unfamiliar location, with nothing really riding on it. Playing in a part of the world where rugby isn't so important somehow made it feel less genuine. We lost the game, and with it the opportunity to challenge the record for consecutive test wins by a tier-one nation. Stalled again on 15 — three short of the magical 18. We got close three times throughout my career, and each time we've dropped it near the line. I played the first hour, then Beaver came on for the last 20 minutes. They snuck a win at the end, with James O'Connor converting to get them across the line, which was frustrating. But my main memory was of watching the way they celebrated afterwards — like they'd just won the World Cup. We would use their reaction as motivation whenever we met them the following year.

After the game Richie gave us a bit of a rev-up. He talked about how much this tour meant, given what was coming the following year. He gathered the team and told us we were all staying in that night. That might not seem that big a deal, but we were in Hong Kong, a city we never visit, and a few guys were pretty disappointed. Richie didn't care — the decision set the tone for the tour. We were there to do a job, not have a holiday, and had to take it seriously.

That mentality steeled us for the games to come — the third grand slam of my career. It was a fitting end to the year, with only a single loss blotting an otherwise perfect preparation for 2011, the home World Cup which loomed as the most important of any of our lives. But before we got there, nature would intervene in the most cataclysmic way.

12

February 22, 2011

I'd not long finished training when it came. I had hung around afterwards, lingering on my warm-down — it takes longer when you're my age. Many of the other players were already off eating lunch or at home. I was walking through the warren of changing sheds and meeting rooms underneath the stadium at Rugby Park. As I left the dressing-rooms, just having finished my shower, the ground beneath us began to shake with an unbelievable violence.

The bare concrete-block walls had nothing to grasp for support, so I was thrown about helplessly as the earth buckled and heaved. It seemed to last forever, the shaking, accompanied by a monstrous sound. There were great booms, with no specific location, coming up from the ground. The building was shrieking as it flexed, and everything in the stand rattled and rang as it was tossed around. I couldn't imagine how the building could withstand those forces. It was horrible, knowing that if it had come a couple of seconds later I'd be on the grass, shaking but safe, instead of stuck in here.

Those of us still in the changing room let instinct take over, and tried to run through the waves out onto the field. We had just made it out when, as suddenly as it came, it wound down.

I was bruised, and scared, but breathing. The stand had survived. I picked myself up, shaking from the adrenalin, and ran out onto the field. Everyone congregated there: the players who'd stayed on, and the coaching and administrative staff who filtered down from the offices. We were all in complete shock. Even those who'd experienced the September quake had no idea how to process this one; it was obvious that it was on a different scale entirely. We assessed injuries, but thankfully no one was seriously hurt. Most were like me — grazes on knees or elbows from trying to stay upright.

After a few minutes a member of management told us to go home and check on our families. My memories of that period immediately afterwards are just fragments — sharp but dislocated and impossible to reassemble coherently. I walked out to my car, parked in a nearby suburban street, in a daze. I drove mindlessly, unable to absorb what had happened, and what it meant.

Honor was up in Auckland, thankfully, so my first thoughts were for my sister, who was living with me at my place in Shirley. I tried to call home, but communications were patchy.

As I travelled these familiar streets a lot of filthy, sandy water started to flow up from the ground. I know now that the mud is the result of liquefaction, as shaking reduces soil to a fluid state, and it was something we would be dealing with for months. But back then I had no idea what it was, what it meant, and it made an already frightening time that much more eerie.

I had the radio on from the drive in, without really noticing. Everyone was reporting on the earthquake, even pop stations like ZM had stopped the music and just tried to grapple with the event. Soon after I left I got a call from Lou, one of my agents at Essentially in Auckland. I was surprised that the phone was working, and he stayed on the line for most of the drive. I couldn't absorb anything he was saying — and somehow didn't think to tell him about the earthquake. I mostly sat, mute, listening to him talk about business, grateful for the sound of another voice — though one completely oblivious to what had happened.

The scene was devastating — everywhere you looked was a familiar landmark, distorted or broken. I already had a horrible feeling in my stomach, knowing that if the situation was this bad out here in the suburbs then the city would be a wreck.

I drove very cautiously, aware that aftershocks could come at any time. Soon the roads began to fill with people trying to get to their loved ones, and what was normally a 10-minute cruise to my house took three-quarters of an hour, as traffic lights were out and the road torn up. As I drove along I saw people flowing out of their homes into the street, looking around at the flooding and devastation, beginning to absorb the scale of what had just happened. They were in tears, breaking down — the emotion of the event evident everywhere.

It's so strange how different people respond to this kind of trauma. Most people I saw were in tears, but I remained mostly numb. In games sometimes, I have to fight the instinct to freeze, or withdraw into myself. It's something I've learned to control over time. But this was obviously infinitely more serious than anything I'd encountered on a field, and I remained in that frozen state the whole way home.

Eventually I made it to my home in Shirley. It had been the first house I bought, in 2005, down a quiet, wooded street. There were so many memories in the house. The first time Honor and I lived together, our first taste of domesticity, and a few great parties, too. But it had also been where my sister was living during the first quake. That one came in the night. She was living alone, and it rattled the house so hard that she climbed into a wardrobe and waited two hours before coming out.

There's a small bridge over a creek which leads down a right-of-way to a group of five houses. As I turned into our street it was obvious that the bridge wasn't passable. It had sustained damage in the quake, and sagged dejectedly to one side. I parked on the street, jumped the creek, and ran down the drive. I was so relieved to see my sister standing outside the house, and our neighbours out in their garden, too.

As neighbours, we weren't particularly close prior to the quakes. But something about the experience, this shattering event that we all lived through, meant that all across the city a sense of community welled up. In the weeks and months to come we'd be present in one another's lives in a way we never would have before the quakes. That afternoon we ate an early makeshift dinner together with our neighbours, before my sister and I decided to head out to Mum and Dad's place in Southbridge.

It was about 6 pm when we left. It didn't feel like we had any option. There was no water, no electricity — nothing. It didn't seem like there was anything to be gained by staying there for the night, and cleaning up was too enormous a task to contemplate at that moment. I had to head into the house to pack a few things, which was unsettling, as we knew it was damaged and were aware another aftershock might come at any moment. We grabbed sleeping bags, water, just the rudiments of survival. We were heading out to Southbridge without knowing what we'd find. But we knew the quakes were centred close to the city, so Mum and Dad's place was likely to be relatively safe.

The drive out took two hours. Traffic was backed up in every direction: it felt like everyone was fleeing the city. We sat in silence for the most part, listening to the radio, still in shock. In those early hours there was so little information — no casualty toll, no evacuation plan, no real idea of what had happened.

We eventually made it out of the city and across the plains to Southbridge. It was such a relief, but tempered by finding out that Dad had headed the other way, into the heart of the city. As a volunteer firefighter he was called up to head into central Christchurch to help wherever he could. Those guys — the police, firefighters, the army — they're such heroes, doing something so selfless at a time when the vast majority of us were just worrying about ourselves and our loved ones. Thankfully, he returned later that night, so we knew we were all safe.

I finally spoke to Honor, who was probably more shaken than I was — unable to get hold of me, fearing the worst. It was one of the realities of the way we were living, her in Auckland, me in Christchurch for much of the week. Much as I was grateful she was safe in Auckland, the period during and after the quake made the distance particularly difficult to tolerate.

That night we watched the news for hours on end. Seeing the images of what had happened to the iconic parts of Christchurch made it horrifyingly real. Afterwards, though, I still managed to sleep soundly. It's a talent of mine: no matter what the situation, I can always sleep. Even after an earthquake.

The following day I headed back into the city. A bunch of my mates from Southbridge came with me. It tells you a lot about the town and the guys I grew up with that they would do that. We all brought tools, wheelbarrows and began the clean-up. We started from our house, at the back of the right-of-way, and worked our way forward through the neighbours' properties.

While there was some structural damage, our houses were newer and well-made, so it was almost all about the liquefaction, which had oozed into our homes and gardens. For eight hours a day we shovelled, wheeled and dumped it out onto the road.

On Thursday, less than 48 hours after the quake, I took a brief break from the clean-up. The Crusaders held a team meeting to discuss how we would respond to this extraordinary situation. The crux of it was that, natural disaster or not, we had a game that weekend, and needed to decide whether we would play. The team began the conversation roughly divided down the middle.

I wasn't. I didn't feel in the right headspace to think about rugby, and while I would have played had we swung that way, it wasn't my preference by any means. The other side were led by Andy Ellis. He's a real tough nut, and will probably be the mayor of the city one day. He's one of the most loved and loyal Cantabrians — a real champion of the city.

Andy just wanted to do it for the people. He'll do anything for the team, and he's such a tough bugger that he wanted the win, even in this raw, emotional time. I admired his conviction, but didn't share it. It felt too soon, and in the end the majority arrived in the same position. So we didn't play the Hurricanes that weekend. They just called it a draw.

That gave us an extra week to plan. We were keenly aware of what the team meant to the city at all times, especially at that moment. We used that week as Crusaders to go out into the community and help with the clean-up. It was the right thing to do, and it felt good, to be able to give back to the city which had given us so much, during its hour of need.

The following week we were back training, but the city was still in pieces, and so many distractions remained. Trying to balance focus on high-performance sport and our various roles in the recovery was something we would work on all season.

It was particularly acute in the early days and weeks. We all had our own issues with housing and amenities. Training was relocated, and a number of the older guys had families who desperately needed them through that period. The administrators were scrambling to try to relocate our home games, but they were caught in the same bind the whole city was: how to honour the dead and the tragedy, while still dealing with the realities of trying to rebuild life in the city.

Right through it all there was the sense that this particular team was special. That year might have been the strongest Crusaders side I've ever been involved in. Chris Jack had returned to lock alongside Brad Thorn. Sam Whitelock was also there and making a big impression. Sonny Bill was in the side, with Robbie Fruean outside him coming on strong, and it was Israel Dagg's debut season for the Crusaders. It was just an extraordinary rugby team, right across the park. But this immense challenge wasn't easily resolved. People didn't have places to live — team members were really struggling.

It wasn't just the team. One of our board members, a good Ashburton man named Philip McDonald, died in the quake. It was that kind of event — everyone had people around them who lost their lives, and that sense of loss permeated the city and the season.

The most pressing problem was where we would play that weekend, with our home, our stadium, chained up and fenced off. There were so many decisions to make, and no time to make them.

We ended up turning out mostly in Nelson and Timaru. They

embraced us at a time when the region needed, for 80 minutes a week, something to take its mind off what had happened. This is what we became during those next few months.

The following year the new stadium at Addington was remodelled in 100 days, which was a miracle. I love playing there — and the fact that opponents hate its bare-bones set-up. But nowhere I've ever played or ever will play will equal the emotion and thrill of playing at the old Lancaster Park.

To see it still standing, looking proud but desolate, is heartbreaking. I feel such a pull towards that place and I drive past it whenever I'm nearby, drawn in by the good memories, but also a sense of loyalty. I hate seeing it the way it is now, behind chain-link fencing, with the grass grown long and wild.

It's part of the sense of loss the city feels all the time. So many of the buildings and monuments that made up the city in your mind are gone. I look around sometimes and feel sick about it: see open air where a building once stood, or the vacant lots that still litter the city centre. I understand the desire of heritage advocates to try to save as much of what remains as possible, but personally I wish we were moving faster to fill the voids. I talk to friends and they have the same sensation, and avoid the city centre on trips home. Because there's nothing you can do. Personally I'd like to see faster progress on the rebuild — I'm excited about the new Christchurch which is going to rise out of this tragedy.

I visited the stadium for the first time since the quakes in early 2015. Despite my regular drives past, I had never stopped and looked at it again until then. I hung on the fence on an overcast day and took in this place, once so magical, now locked away. I remembered playing here for the first time, in under eights, running across the width rather than the length of the field. I remember the queues outside the stadium in the lead-up to game time, the energy and anticipation. I remembered climbing the advertising hoardings and perching there for the whole game, with my legs hanging through, way above the ground in a way you'd never get away with today. Then running onto the field afterwards, hanging out for autographs in little tribes until the last player had escaped to the changing room. I was so shy that I didn't get many. I'd never ask, just hold out my pen and paper. I remembered, years later, the rough and rowdy concrete embankments where I'd go as a student. Some of the happiest memories of my life.

Then, in my playing days, the vast changing rooms, the feverish atmosphere, feeling near invincible on that ground. That Crusaders team, in any other season, would have revelled in the atmosphere at AMI Stadium. Instead, we were forced to play in unfamiliar environments, even jetting over to London for a game to help compensate for the massive loss of earnings which occurred due to our lack of a home ground with a large capacity.

In comparison to everything which the city and its people suffered, it doesn't rate at all. But every game that season felt like it was for something bigger, and we desperately wanted to demonstrate to the world that this city was battered but not beaten by these forces.

The season went pretty remarkably, in the end. We played the game at Twickenham in late March, a high-scoring win over the Sharks which got a lot of publicity for the earthquake relief efforts. But the endless travel really took it out of us. In the last few weeks we were forever on planes: Perth, Bloemfontein, Cape Town, Napier, Sydney, Timaru — with no chance to settle and few home games to recharge and surge.

We beat the Hurricanes in the last game of the regular season, the first of the longer 15-team competitions. We played and won a tough game against the Sharks in Nelson, and our reward was a return to Cape Town, where we beat the Stormers by 19 points. That set up a final with the Reds, who had played brilliantly all season. We'd only lost by a point in Brisbane a few rounds previously, and felt like we were peaking at the right time.

We came desperately close, battling through everything that had come at us, both as players and as a province. The first half was tight, as expected, but in the 34th minute I grubbered and scored to give us a 7–6 lead at the break. In the changing room we felt confident, as though momentum and a sense of history was on our side. We wanted so badly to do this for Christchurch, and had positioned ourselves perfectly. Only 40 minutes stood between us and the title.

After the break we traded points, and the game was tied at 13–13 heading into the final quarter. But all of a sudden the fatigue seemed to engulf us. The toll of all that travel — something like three seasons' worth in one — arrived at once. I remember looking around at my teammates and thinking we were in trouble — that our control of the game was waning, and their hunger rising. Sure enough, Genia broke our line and ran 30 metres to score a brilliant try with 10 minutes to play. In my heart I knew we would struggle to come back from that, and it proved the last scoring play of the game.

The Reds were deserving champions — they had been the most impressive and dynamic team of the competition all year. But after everything we had suffered through, as Crusaders and Cantabrians, it was an awful burden to bear, and there was a dark mood in the changing room. We had felt fated to win, but rugby doesn't care about fate. The season ended in agony, and a palpable sense of guilt, that we couldn't quite finish the job for our province and home-town.

FINAL YEAR DIARY: Auckland, 5 August 2015

Recorded via cellphone at the Auckland Airport Novotel, hours prior to departure for Sydney to play the Wallabies.

When the test in Samoa was first announced, I hoped I'd miss it. Not because I wasn't excited about the opportunity to create history, but because I wanted to win one last Super Rugby title as a Crusader. That didn't happen, and by the time the game came around I was way up for it. There's something special about the first test of the year, and for it to coincide with our first-ever game in the Islands meant it was doubly special.

We landed to an incredible reception: utter chaos, with thousands of people at the airport to greet us. It was easily the biggest and most boisterous crowd I've witnessed outside of New Zealand, post the World Cup win. All in another country! We boarded a bus for the 40-minute journey to our hotel, and every village we passed through was a sea of All Blacks and Samoan flags and banners. The entire nation was focused on nothing else.

The following day we boarded a windowless bus for another parade through the streets of Apia. It was pandemonium of the best kind, and led us to a ceremony welcoming us to the country, which only served to heighten the sense of occasion. We'd all dressed in lava-lavas, which was fun, though Luke Romano will likely regret not keeping his legs closed while sitting in the front row. He gave the cameras an eyeful, which circulated widely on

214

social media. The guys won't let him forget that in a hurry.

On the day of the test we were very conscious of the heat. The only time I've ever played in similar conditions would have been pre-season games in Brisbane, which are very different to a test against a Samoan team as fired up as they're ever likely to be. As we walked out the crowd were extraordinary — so passionate, which made you acutely aware of what a special and likely unique match it was.

The test itself didn't live up to the occasion. The game's proximity to the Super Rugby final — exacerbated by it being contested by two New Zealand teams — meant that there were a lot of new combinations, and some players gaining a cap who might never otherwise have been called up. But the selectors had no choice under the circumstances.

Our performance was also a function of their brilliant play. The speed of their defensive line meant I put up a few cross kicks to the opposite wing, what we call a 'kick-pass'. These were signalled for by the wingers, and one came off in pretty spectacular style for George Moala, who brilliantly regathered my kick to score on debut. But otherwise it was an error-ridden performance, though take nothing away from Samoa — they were immense.

I think I played an okay game generally, though I was pleased with my boot, but was most happy to make it through uninjured, and to have had a good run at 10 for the All Blacks. Every game in the jersey at this point feels very special.

The following morning we flew back to camp in Christchurch ahead of the opening of the Rugby Championship against Argentina. With the arrival of the

Hurricanes and Highlanders the squad swelled to 41, the biggest I've been part of, and we barely fit on the team bus. It was another goodbye in a year full of them. My last test in Christchurch, and perhaps my final ever game in the city. It was also my first All Blacks test there in some time, too, and I was happy to once again start at 10, and show some improvement. I'm not yet satisfied with my game, but just having time in the jersey and a prolonged period without injury is a great feeling after the past couple of seasons.

In the sheds after the game, Steve approached me to let me know I'd be missing the trip to South Africa. My immediate reaction was one of disappointment. Ellis Park is one of the most hostile environments in world rugby, and I relish the challenge of withstanding that onslaught. But I understood the reasoning, and felt fortunate to have had the first two starts of the season.

It also gave me some more time at home with the family. Young Fox is growing up fast. He's four months old and rewarded his tired mum by sleeping through the night for the first time on 1 August. It was nice to have a brief spell where I was something like a normal dad, and able to get some sustained time with the children.

Despite missing the test, it wasn't much of a break. Nic Gill thrashed me with my training regime, so I've been falling asleep more exhausted than ever. It feels good, though, and my body is responding well to the work.

I was as surprised as anyone when Lima Sopoaga was given the start over Beauden against the Boks. That said, he played brilliantly, and I really rate the guy, having roomed with him in Christchurch. He's level-headed and asked all the right questions. I think he'll have a terrific career and be a real asset to the All Blacks in years to come.

More than anything, I'm happy with the amount of game time I've had. Starting my third test of the year, as I will this weekend, makes me feel like the jersey, once slipping from my grasp, is mine again. In less than two months we'll be into the teeth of the World Cup. I can't wait.

13

Watching History from the Stands

One of the good things about losing a Super Rugby final is that you don't have a lot of time to dwell on it — there's always an All Blacks game the following weekend. This was truer than ever in 2011, when even the warm-up games had an edge to them, with the World Cup imminent, and everyone wanting to book their place in the squad. This was magnified by the compressed international season that year. We had one warm-up, against Fiji, then a shortened Tri-Nations, before rolling into the World Cup in September.

In the week leading into the Fiji game we came up with a leadership group of management, players and coaches to talk about how to prioritise the year's competitions. We had the World Cup, the Tri-Nations and the Bledisloe Cup. The way we saw it there was one must-win (the World Cup, obviously), one we'd like to win (the Bledisloe) and one we didn't mind too much about (the Tri-Nations). Funnily enough, that ended up being exactly what we got. Back then, had you offered it to us as a result by the season's end, we'd have been elated. But I can't imagine the current All Blacks side conceding the Tri-Nations so casually.

Our mindset has changed so much — now we want to be the most dominant team in the history of world rugby. So, if you're striving for that, you won't be satisfied unless you win everything.

The Fiji game went well. Having made the Super Rugby final, some of the other Crusaders and I skipped it, and we assembled in Wellington to open the Tri-Nations. There we punished South Africa, 40–7, setting up a good but not great Tri-Nations, one through which we really struggled to maintain concentration. The World Cup, at home, loomed so large we could never quite block it out. Particularly as it seemed likely to be the last for so many of us. A whole generation of guys were at what should have been their peak, and were thought likely to retire or head to Europe in the years to come. As it turns out, a number of them — me, Richie, Ma'a and Conrad among them — would still be there four years on. But we went in as if it were our last roll of the dice. One made all the sharper by being in front of our own fans.

Looking back, we were a different team in 2011 to the side which wears the jersey today. Still number one in the world, and coming off a great season in 2010. But not quite as ruthless as we are today. We conceded the Tri-Nations with the last game before the World Cup, courtesy of a tight 25–20 loss to Australia in Brisbane. It didn't mean a lot at the time, but we were surprised by how much was read into it by some. There was this idea circulating that it meant we were beatable, whereas others thought it was good to have a loss to sharpen your minds. To us, it just didn't mean a thing — mentally we'd already moved on.

All the conversation going in was about whether we'd be able to handle the pressure of the public. The international media went so far as to speculate whether it was even an advantage to be hosts. The theory went that because we're such a rugby-mad country, the pressure would overtake us. That seemed silly to me. We were in familiar surroundings, in front of our own crowds. Yes, there was pressure to perform, but we would have felt that anywhere. Here there was that, but also the indescribable excitement of playing the best teams in the world at our own stadiums.

Leading into the tournament we did a nationwide tour promoting the All Blacks to the nation. We went all over the country to small rural towns and centres, the kind which would never normally get to see the team. It was a fantastic way to roll into the Cup, because we got to witness a level of excitement you often miss in the big cities. They were just fanatical. We would have 300 people following us everywhere we went, every car tooting their horn, people leaning out the side, yelling and every face in town lit up. A few of us went to Te Puke and felt like visiting royalty; we toured schools and the local rugby club, and the whole town just stopped for the day.

After that it was time to head into the tournament. We reassembled, all pumped from having those experiences, and had our final week's training ahead of the tournament opener against Tonga. As usual, we stayed at the Heritage Hotel, an ornate former department store in central Auckland, a place so familiar it's like a second home. A fanzone, The Cloud, had been set up not far away on Queen's Wharf, and we could hear the opening ceremony happening there as we ate dinner. The whole central city was boiling, in a way which I've never seen in Auckland before. The following day we tried to stretch out our normal pre-match routine, as the games were starting later to fit northern hemisphere time zones.

We had a pre-match meal four hours out from kick-off. Most

of us then went back to our rooms to sleep for a half hour or so. I never have trouble sleeping, no matter what. But today was different — I was so excited, and the noise of the city meant I could never mentally escape what was coming. We assembled at the bus, and drove in along the fan trail. Normally you wouldn't see anyone until you're right at the stadium, but this was different. The whole way in was lined with people, on the street or out front of their houses. You couldn't miss what it meant to the country.

The game itself was a typical Tongan test. They came out with brutal aggression and fire, but we knew that if we could absorb that things would start breaking our way. They did, but the game never really took off. We lacked a bit of cohesion, for some reason. Whether it was nerves, or excitement, or knowledge that we were meant to put on a show for the opening game . . . who knows? Still, it was a comfortable win, 41–10, which was all we required from it. In time that Tongan team would prove themselves one of the surprises of the tournament, which casts the result in a somewhat better light.

In the days which followed we started to deal with the typical problem of World Cups — maintaining your momentum. Six weeks is such a long time to be in the midst of something as consuming as this tournament. You have to be constantly building to a peak, rather than ebbing and flowing. The end-of-year tours are four or five weeks long, and often the last two weeks you're just counting down the days, which is why you'll sometimes see us slip up in the last or second-to-last game of a tour. Guys are just spent by then. So the World Cup, at six weeks, is a real challenge mentally. That's where the depth of your squad comes in, and your creativity within the team, with elements such as the entertainment committee. That, and taking advantage of your days off. That was another plus of being in New Zealand: if you were in your home town on your day off you could see friends or family. That's what I'd do: go home to familiar surroundings, see Honor and avoid that staleness which comes with living hotel life for too long.

I sat out the Japan game in Hamilton, which was always the plan. During training that week I tweaked my back doing squat jumps, so back spasms restricted my training. Your back's a funny thing — it's really hard to know how serious an injury is. It was sore, but very manageable, and I wasn't particularly concerned. I was at a public event in Hamilton when all that changed. It went into spasm so badly I could barely move. I ended up having to take a lot of tramadol to get enough pain relief to calm it down. It remained tight, and I started to get anxious about it coming right ahead of the pool game against France. That was our one serious hit out ahead of the knockout stages, and I needed to play it. I was still taking lots of tramadol leading into the week, but thankfully it began to settle down as we approached the weekend.

I remember being so relieved. Given the history between the sides it felt so important that we execute it right. And we did, emphatically, in a 37–17 win. Izzy Dagg was unstoppable, and the whole team gelled in a way which gave us a tremendous amount of confidence. I felt my running game was as good as it had ever been, and the game was the best I'd played in three World Cups. The only black spot was Richie's foot. It would be a problem throughout the tournament, but it's a sign of his mental strength that even though he couldn't train, and could barely run, he never seemed to consider quitting the team. Like me, he'd skipped the Japan game, and it was clear that it was really bothering him. He gutsed out the game against France, but was touch-and-go for Canada.

223

Coming off the French game I felt so buoyant heading into the Canada test. It was a Sunday game, which is unusual in New Zealand. Normally the day before a game involves some promotional work, but I'd been given the Saturday morning off, so had a lie-in. We were staying at the Intercontinental, in downtown Wellington. Ma'a and I went off to his local café in Lyall Bay, trying to avoid the crowds. We were sitting having a coffee when I got a phone call from Darren Shand, our manager. He told me that Richie's foot hadn't come right and he was pulling out of the game. Shandy told me I'd be captaining the side, and I was needed back at the hotel to do media. I hung up, momentarily stunned, and told Ma'a what had happened. He drove us back into town.

I'd been vice-captain since 2009, around two and a half years by that point. But I'd never captained the All Blacks, because Richie and I had always played together through that span. The games he missed, I missed too. So Mils Muliaina got to captain the side, as did Kevvy Mealamu, in the pool match against Japan. While I never begrudged them or Richie, I was so happy to be finally getting the honour. I called Dad, who was incredibly proud, and headed off up to the press conference. There were a bunch of questions, asking how it changed things, and I gave stock answers. It truly didn't change much at all. I've learned so much from Richie over the years, principally that captaincy is driven by your actions on the field. As first-five you're already a big part of tactics and strategy anyway, so there were no nerves to speak of. I was just tremendously excited about the opportunity.

After the press conference we had lunch together in the team conference room. Richie's injury wasn't thought to be too serious, so there wasn't any major concern in the air. Management explained that I was now captaining the side, and we talked about how the captain's run would play out. We'd warm up, play a bit of touch, do the captain's run, then we're done. We didn't need a big session that deep into the tournament, when your preparation is already well advanced. The only unconventional part was that as Westpac Stadium was occupied that evening, we'd do the run at Rugby League Park, in Newtown.

The ground was stickier, which isn't ideal, and the conditions naturally somewhat different. But it didn't seem a huge deal. I felt good throughout the warm-up, then rolled my ankle a little during a game of touch rugby. We were only running at half pace, but I went to step and it rolled. So the rest of the game I hung out on the wing and tried to run it off. I could still feel it during the captain's run. It was a short and sharp pain, and refused to come right the way these kinds of minor tweaks tend to. But I didn't want to disrupt my routine, so when the run ended I thought I'd go through my normal kicking session before I saw the physios. After a captain's run I'll always do 15 or 20 goal-kicks, and a few drop-kicks. But because my back had been tight, and my ankle a little soft, I thought I'd limit it to four goal-kicks, just to make sure I had my timing down. My plan was to do two from right in front, then one each from either side, 15 metres in from touch.

The two from out front felt fine. My dodgy ankle was on my plant foot, and it wasn't 100 per cent, but I was certain it would settle down ahead of the game. As I prepared for my third kick, I put the ball down, and knelt on one knee to place the ball on the tee, before pushing up with my left foot. It's the kind of ritual that all kickers have, and this was no different to thousands I've run through before. Just as I stepped up with my left foot I felt my groin twinge a little bit. It was odd, and a little unsettling.

But bodies are always giving off phantom messages, so I didn't think too much of it. I stepped back, ran in and kicked the ball. Black dot. No problem.

One more kick, I thought, then I'll go and get that ankle seen to. I went through the same routine, and as I got up I felt my groin twinge again. Not enough to worry, just enough to be aware of it. I shrugged the sensation off, and stepped to the back of my run-up, then paced in to kick the ball. I approached and swung through my kicking arc, just the same as ever. Only this time the result was very different. At the moment of contact, when my foot struck the ball, my leg just buckled beneath me. I felt this pop from within, and collapsed to the ground, screaming in agony. The ball dribbled 10 metres in front of me, and I lay there, crumpled in a heap.

Everyone around me assumed it was a joke. It was such a routine kick, and I have a reputation as something of a practical joker, though I'd never do that in such a serious situation. I stayed down, clutching my groin, and soon people surrounded me. Deb Robinson, our doctor, asked what had happened. I was in such acute pain I could barely speak. I just stammered out that it was my groin.

After the captain's run the backs do their kicking drills and forwards do lineouts. Then the media come in. Deb realised that media would be there any minute, and wanted me off the field and in the changing room before they arrived. She asked if I could walk. I tried, but couldn't, and had to be helped off the field. When I sat down, I was in shock. It didn't seem possible that it could be happening — again. I looked down at my groin and it kept moving, grotesquely, in spasm. Deb felt around it, and I sat there mute. I was in so much pain, and the potential implications for the game and tournament were just starting to dawn.

The rest of the team slowly finished training, and began to filter into the room. I had questions running around in my head: how serious is this? Is this my World Cup over? I had no way of judging the scale of the injury — whether it was just a tear which would heal in a couple of weeks, or a complete rupture. I just didn't know.

Deb is outstanding in these kinds of stressful, emotional occasions. She has an infectious calm about her. She told me not to jump to conclusions; that something had happened, but that we should wait until we'd had scans and a firm diagnosis before we figured out what to do next. I called Honor, who was in Wellington for the game, to let her know about the injury and that I was going to get a scan. Then Deb and I headed back to the hotel to wait until an appointment could be procured. I sat, trying not to worry, until the phone rang that evening, and we headed across to Wellington Hospital, passing waves of supporters on their way to the stadium.

After the scan I sat in the waiting room while Deb and the specialist went through the results. I didn't want to be involved in the conversation; I just wanted to know if my Cup was over or not. I'm not a religious man, and never have been, but I was praying that it was just a partial tear, that I might somehow recover in time for the final. Eventually they called me through and pulled images up on the screen, and told me the news I'd been dreading: a torn adductor muscle in my groin. It was the adductor longus, a key stabilising muscle which runs from the pubic bone down to the thigh. It would have been a major injury for anyone, but it was particularly serious for kickers — our accuracy relies on the repetition of a very specific action. The longus is the source of a lot of the thigh's fine motor control. Mine was shot — the MRI showed that the muscle had torn clean off the footplate.

I asked if that was my World Cup over, already knowing the answer. They confirmed it was, that three months was the most optimistic recovery timeframe. My heart sank. I said nothing at all.

We got back in the car. Deb sat up front with the liaison officer who'd driven us there. I leaned back and welled up with tears. All my questions were whys: Why here? Why now? Most of all: Why me? This tournament had meant so much to me, and had just been wrenched away doing something so ordinary, something I'd done dozens of times a day for virtually my entire life. It was a freak injury, one which could've happened at any other time and had no impact on my World Cup. Kicking a ball, the action which has brought me so much joy and opportunity, had now snatched away a dream I'd been working towards, in one way or another, my whole career.

We arrived back at the hotel, and they snuck me in the back entrance. The media knew something was up. I was a wreck, so it was some small solace to be able to avoid the scrum. Partners aren't allowed to stay with players at the hotel, but Shandy said Honor could come in for the night. She was waiting for me, and comforted me through that long night. Over the course of the next few hours some key people came by to see me: Graham Henry, Wayne Smith, Richie, and a few of the other leaders. They made a point of keeping most of the team away, for which I was grateful at the time. Because none of us knew what to say. There was nothing that could be said. Facts are facts: I was out. I tried to make light of it, to crack little jokes, but my heart wasn't in it. I still believed in the team, thought they would win the whole thing, and I wanted them to know that. But as soon as they'd leave the room I'd crawl back into my hole, cursing my luck.

I barely slept that night. I was in a lot of pain, and on a lot of painkillers.

When I woke up the next morning my first thought was about how I'd get right, how I'd fix the injury. I wanted to be proactive, not just sitting there, broken and useless. For a week the debate went back and forth among medical personnel and specialists: should I have surgery to get my adductor muscle reattached, or should I let it heal on its own? One opinion was that letting it heal naturally might result in a loss of kicking power, and that surgery had proven successful for some AFL players, who kick far more than we do in rugby. I was scared of losing kicking power; it sounded like it could limit or end my career. So even though there were some key people opposed to the surgical option, I elected to travel to a specialist we'd been recommended in Melbourne as soon as possible, and have it reattached.

The next day I stayed anchored to my room. I watched the guys tear Canada apart. I watched numbly as Colin Slade injured *his* groin. I was stuck in my own world, angry, resentful, wishing I was there with them, captaining the side. I would stay in that black mood for days.

That only broke when Joe Locke, our media manager, approached me and asked if I'd like to do a press conference ahead of the quarter-final. My general attitude towards press conferences is to avoid them. I guess it comes back to that shyness. But I was aware there was a sentiment out there suggesting that the team couldn't win without me, which I knew to be untrue, and I liked the idea of being able to stand up and squash it in a very public forum. So I agreed to front the media.

The event ended up being pretty emotional. I had no option but to be candid about the fact my dream had been hauled out from under me. The wall I normally keep up around media came down. But, as draining as the experience was, I also found it empowering — like I had asserted control over the injury and the narrative, had stopped just being a victim of this awful event. I opened up about my feelings both personally and towards the team, and said I remained convinced they would win this tournament.

I was surprised by how good it felt, and gratified by the way it was received. Some people told me it changed the mood of the nation, and while I don't believe that, I do believe it helped the media and public move on from the injury, to refocus on the tournament, and the team. And that felt really, really good.

After the press conference I was determined to continue to do what I could to help the team. But first I had to have surgery. I flew to Melbourne later that week, and was actually under the knife during our victory over Argentina in the quarter-final. When I returned I had to stay away from camp. One of the most brutal things about World Cups is that you're only allowed so many players in your squad. When you're invalided out, you lose your accreditation, which makes it really difficult to even be around the team. So I couldn't attend training, or spend time with the guys. (At least not officially. Some friendly security guards would let me in.) But being kept apart from the team was very challenging mentally. I moved from feeling like a senior member of this very unified group to almost cast aside, however unintentionally.

With my injury, Aaron Cruden was called into the team. I was able to have some input with him and the other 9s and 10s, trying to mentor them a little on the occasions I could get around the squad. That felt good. I tried to focus on presenting a very positive face around the team, and in public. Over the years I've grown pretty good at putting on the mask of a happy-go-lucky guy, having a few go-to lines in response to questions. It's easier than being honest. I didn't want anyone to see me moping around, feeling sorry for myself.

When the semi and final came around, I watched from the stands with very mixed emotions. I love my team and my teammates, but I wanted so badly to be there with them, sharing the good and the bad — the nerves, the excitement and particularly the sense of satisfaction after the adrenalin of the week is resolved in a game. They were out there, doing exactly what I'd always dreamed of and worked towards. I tried not to dwell on why it happened to me, and not someone else, but it was hard not to.

The semi-final against Australia was something else. Everything clicked, and there was no doubting the result from the first whistle. I was so impressed at the way the guys handled themselves. The final was obviously incredibly tense, but we pulled it off. With the final whistle, a lot of my bitterness melted away. I was just so happy for my teammates, for the coaches, for the whole country. I got swept up in that. I was allowed on to the field, and able to finally soak in that feeling. It didn't turn out the way I'd planned, and I'd still today give anything for it to have played out differently. But in front of a packed home crowd, we'd won the World Cup. At last.

14

Marriage, a Peak and a Body Breaking Down

The final had finished just 24 hours before, a huge tournament involving hundreds of players and many millions of dollars, chasing this one object: the Webb Ellis Cup. And somehow I'd ended up alone with it, in the back of a cab, on the way to a team function in the Viaduct. I cradled it, soaking in the satisfaction of having wrestled this thing back into our possession after so many years of trying.

As we approached downtown I realised we would drive right past a bar where a number of my best friends had gathered, out celebrating the win along with most of the rest of the country. It seemed like too good an opportunity to pass up. I asked the driver to pull over and wait, then snuck into the bar, with the trophy under my jacket, and found my friends. The awe on their faces when they saw me with the trophy was outstanding. I waited long enough for us to fill it up and have a quick drink from it, before I headed along to the team event, acting like nothing had happened. The guys in that bar went home with a pretty good story to tell.

The next few days were some of the happiest I've ever spent

as an All Black. We went around the main centres, showing off the Cup and experiencing an incredible level of adulation and support. It became a blur of different parades, each one with its own distinctive character. The most important and emotional by far was in Christchurch. We'd been deprived of the opportunity to play in the heart of New Zealand rugby by seismic events beyond anyone's control. It felt so cruel, yet all the anguish of the quakes seemed to disappear, if only for a day, when we took the Cup into the city. No one there will ever forget those scenes, and the whole team, particularly the Crusaders guys, was deeply moved by the moment, and its symbolism.

After a triumph like that it's sometimes hard coming down. Luckily I had something pretty big on the horizon demanding my focus: our wedding, which was less than two months away. Some 180 guests were flying in to Blenheim, and it was a huge event to organise. Somehow we'd managed to keep it under wraps from the media, which was something of a shock, given the scale of the thing. They knew we were engaged, but had no idea where or when we'd be getting married. Unfortunately I blew it by having a stag do. Ahead of it Honor had said, 'Have fun, do whatever you like — just make sure it doesn't end up in the papers.' So that was the briefing I gave my groomsmen. How hard could that be?

We decided on a bus trip, starting at my place in Christchurch, ending in Queenstown. The bus picked us up at 10.30 on a Friday morning. We must have looked a picture — wearing Morphsuits. I've always liked dressing up, and this had the added advantage of letting us play up in public without any of our identities being revealed. We got into Queenstown 10 hours later, having stopped at various bars and completed a few activities on the way down.

We'd hired a house for the weekend, and just stayed in and had a few beers that night. So far, no media reports — we were in the clear. The following morning we were scheduled to play golf, but the hangovers were a bit heavy, so we cancelled that and headed into town for some lunch. Later that afternoon we holed up at a bar in the city which we'd hired for the night. There were a dozen or so of us, and we partied pretty hard. The Morphsuits were long gone, when at midnight it opened to the public. By then we weren't thinking too hard about who might be watching, and chased the night to a few bars afterwards, finishing up at around dawn. That afternoon we all flew home, hung over but happy, and I poured myself into bed in Auckland, thinking all had gone smoothly, that we'd gotten away with it.

The following morning I woke up to Honor, extremely unimpressed, holding the *Herald*. Obviously someone in Queenstown had spilled, and there it was, splashed across the front page: 'Dan's Stag Do'. Her one request. It didn't seem too much to ask. But I'd blown it, and now the media knew the wedding was just around the corner — oops.

We were a few weeks away from the wedding at that stage, and knowing that the wedding was out there in the public made us reassess our ideas about magazine deals. We've never done them before or since, but at that point we made the decision to go ahead, due to the security it provided. When you make a deal, obviously it's in the magazine's best interest to have it exclusively, so they really ramp it up.

It seemed like the right decision at the time. We didn't want to be getting married and to be constantly looking over our shoulders to see if there were photographers around. Even though the location of the wedding — Timara Lodge, a beautiful lakefront property near Blenheim — was private and secluded, we still wanted the extra support of ensuring that it stayed between us and our guests. We went to great lengths on that front. Invitees weren't told where it was — just that a bus would take them to the location. Catering and infrastructure was all ordered under a different name. We thought we'd done a pretty good job — but obviously it wasn't good enough, as there were paparazzi waiting at the airport when the guests flew in. You don't often see that in Blenheim, so we knew the game was up.

Despite the scrutiny, we had the most amazing time. We'd booked four bedrooms at the lodge so our parents could stay along with us. The night before we had a cocktail event for our families, the bridesmaids and groomsmen, put on by my brother-in-law Jonty Edgar. It was his present to us, and an opportunity for the two families to meet. Afterwards I left Honor for the night and went to a hotel with my groomsmen. They'd flown in from Europe and Melbourne. It was great to spend time with them before the chaos of the wedding began.

The wedding didn't start until 4 pm, so to fill the day we went to my other brother-in-law Pete Wells' house to shoot clay birds. He's got a full circuit set up, and I've shot before — but I was hopeless on that morning. I was literally shaking with nerves, knowing what was to come. We went to Herzog Estate winery for lunch, just the groomsmen. A glass of rosé helped take the edge off my jitters, and it turned into a beautiful day. From there we returned to the hotel. Crane Brothers had kitted us all out in traditional morning suits, and had flown down Carl, one of their people, to ensure we were all properly presented. It was a very traditional wedding, in many respects, and I enjoyed the process of dressing for such a serious occasion.

We drove towards the venue, and pulled over a kilometre out from the perimeter to chat with security. They said that things had gotten pretty feverish overnight. They'd found a number of photographers who'd snuck in and hidden in the gardens in the middle of the night. We knew then that the venue had been rumbled. On we drove to the gate, and it was a circus — photographers and cameras everywhere. It was annoying, having to deal with that kind of thing on your wedding day, but I had confidence in the security team that they had it under control.

Once we got in the venue a lot of the tension dissipated. You could tell it was clean, that no one had made it inside who wasn't meant to be there. I relaxed a little, but Ben Jones, my best man, was really starting to feel it. You could see him sweating his speech, writing it down on cue cards, just not at all comfortable. He hates public speaking, and the idea of talking to a crowd of 180 people clearly had him shaken. I was more worried about the weather. We'd had to make a call whether to erect a marquee 24 hours out, and had decided to trust our instincts and the forecast. The day had been overcast with rain threatening throughout. Then, an hour out from the ceremony, it cleared. We were set.

The ceremony seemed to come around quickly after that. Family and friends poured in, and soon we were being ushered to our places. That was when my nerves returned with a vengeance. I stood on the lakeside, waiting for my bride to arrive. Hayley Westenra was singing for us, and as soon as I heard her voice I knew Honor couldn't be far away. The bridesmaids appeared, and then my beautiful bride. I was determined to keep from tearing up, but couldn't help it in the end. It was a very special feeling, surrounded by our loved ones, watching her walk down the aisle.

After our vows and the ceremony had finished came an event

which was something of a masterstroke. My late father-in-law Jimma was a pilot, and he'd spoken with friends at the local aero club to arrange an old Nanchang plane to put on a show for the guests. It was a spectacular scene in itself, but the real genius of it was that it meant that the airspace was closed off for the duration of the wedding. This meant any rogue helicopter toting paparazzi was out of luck, and couldn't get clearance to come near the venue. We heard later that three choppers had been booked for the day, but Jimma's plan thwarted them all. I'm so grateful, because to have helicopters buzzing low overhead, drowning us out as we tried to exchange vows, would have ruined everything.

An hour later they had to reopen the airspace, at which point a couple of helicopters came in — but by then the big events of the day were over. We just put up umbrellas to shield ourselves. It was a bit frustrating, but outweighed by the satisfaction of knowing we'd outwitted them.

We had the reception in a marquee on tennis courts. Everyone spoke brilliantly, particularly Jimma and Jonty. I was next to last, and started pretty poorly. I just couldn't get the words out. Then I abandoned my cue cards and spoke from the heart, at which point it picked up. Next it was Ben's turn. Everyone knew he was incredibly nervous, and I think we were expecting something a bit shambolic. But he was brilliant, truly exceptional.

Later we took the guests down to the lake while the tables were cleared, before the last seriously nerve-wracking event of the night — the first dance. We chose 'Let Your Love Flow', a '70s pop-country single by the Bellamy Brothers that we both loved. We'd practised for a couple of weeks, and had a glass of champagne for Dutch courage — but were still pretty hopeless, and encouraging our friends on to the floor in no time. But it was a perfect day and night, the stuff of dreams.

The following day we returned to the venue to hit golf balls into the lake, take kayaks out and had DJs — good friends Clarke Gayford and Devin Abrams — playing throughout. In some ways I enjoyed it more, because there was no pressure, and the whole atmosphere was that much more relaxed. It was the culmination of a crazy few months for both of us, with the World Cup and injury for me, and the huge amount of planning the wedding required for Honor. Afterwards we both badly needed a break, and flew to Fiji for a week to honeymoon. It's a place we've spent a lot of time in over the years, and we love the people, the culture and climate. There was never anywhere else we'd have gone.

We returned home for Christmas and New Year, but only briefly, as we had plans to travel some more. I'd been given the first three games of Super Rugby off to allow my groin to heal, so we planned a huge trip overseas. Both of us had travelled quite extensively through Europe and Asia, but had barely spent any time in the Americas. The next two months would remedy that.

We started in LA, then travelled to Big Sur, the Napa Valley, Yosemite, San Francisco, before heading south for a couple of nights in Las Vegas. From there we flew to New York for a week, before travelling on to Buenos Aires. We had an incredible few days on the Galapagos Islands, then went to Machu Picchu, though we took the train rather than walking the trail, I'm ashamed to say. Finally, we took a cruise from Buenos Aires around to Rio in time for Carnival, which was absolutely mad, and incredible fun.

While I was in Brazil, I happened to catch a game of Super Rugby on satellite TV. I realised I'd be playing in just three weeks, and found myself wincing at the prospect. While my groin was feeling better, I had only been training at hotel gyms, and hadn't kicked a rugby ball since the injury all those months ago. I knew it was time to head home, get my head out of the clouds and return to rugby.

No sooner had we landed in Auckland than I was on a plane to Christchurch, ready to rejoin the Crusaders. After going through my medicals and working with the physio team, the day came when it was time to kick a rugby ball. I still clearly recall the first time I stood at the back of my run-up, staring at the ball and feeling utterly tormented. The memory of what had happened at the World Cup had mentally scarred me, to the point where I'd have done anything to avoid taking the kick. I had no clue whether my groin would hold up through the kicking motion, and was in no hurry to find out.

Eventually I could wait no longer. I ran in, and completed a truly awful kick. My groin *was* still a bit sensitive. But I'd done no damage, and was back on the road to playing. I was helped by having Tom Taylor in the side. He handled the kicking while I rounded back into form. It ended up taking six months before I truly regained my kicking confidence, and throughout that period I was often in knots about the process. Kicking had always been something I'd loved, and had come easily. Now every time I stood looking at a ball on a tee, I had to fight to get away from the memory of that afternoon in Wellington, and it was a long time before I could finally rely on my groin, and stop worrying that I would break down with every place-kick.

Away from the field, the big change was a new All Blacks coach. My first contact with him came with the leadership group meetings, during the Super Rugby season. Steve Hansen was now in charge. He'd been on the coaching staff since 2004, and

I knew him well. But I hadn't really been coached by him a lot, because the majority of that time he looked after the forwards, the breakdown and areas we're less involved in as backs. When he was appointed I wasn't sure how he was going to go. We had just won the World Cup, had been through a period of incredible success. To be perfectly honest, I had my doubts.

But as soon as we had those first leadership group meetings and I saw the vision that he had for the team, I knew he was going to do something special with this team. When we first heard him articulate his plan, it was somewhat daunting. He wanted us to try to attempt challenges which had never been achieved before. Your first instinct is to doubt and deny. But there was also the competitive part of you which wanted to embrace the challenge. It was ample motivation for me and the rest of the leadership group as we worked through the Super Rugby campaign.

The Crusaders' season went well enough. I was extremely focused on my rugby, as I am every year following a serious injury. It seems to instil in me a desire to reaffirm to myself and the world my quality as a player. We had a strong Crusaders team, but ran into a Chiefs side which was on another level that year. Nothing was keeping them from the title.

I had expected it, in a way. When I heard Wayne Smith was leaving the All Blacks set-up to go and assist at the Chiefs, I was gutted. I knew that he was going to have a huge effect on that team. I could immediately see that influence, the detail with which they approached games and the hunger that they had, especially on defence. It was obvious they were a new side, and a force to be reckoned with. They had an outstanding year and were deserved winners.

I knew, too, they weren't going to be a one-year wonder. It

was clear they were building something solid and lasting. It is instructive when outsiders know that you've got a really good set-up and culture by the way you are playing. Sometimes that's how you're best judged — by people who aren't involved in the environment. You could just sense their passion and how much each game meant to them in the way that they were playing for one another. You need that if you are going to win titles, and it was no surprise to anyone in New Zealand rugby when that started to happen for them.

Our All Blacks season started with a trio of tests against Ireland. I felt great about my form through the series. It was comfortable, apart from the second game, in Christchurch, which was so brutally cold that we never seemed to get into our game. I ended up having to kick a dropped goal at the end to sneak a win. It wobbled over unconvincingly, but was enough to take the game. Then the boys ran rampant in Hamilton, which felt like a reaction to how ordinary we'd been the week before. I missed the game after straining my calf muscle during the week. I played the opening two matches of the Rugby Championship, but injuries kept me out of the next two.

It was the first year of the Rugby Championship, the competition which replaced the Tri-Nations. It came along at the right time — I was so over the Tri-Nations by that point. You'd just finish playing against South Africa and Australia at Super Rugby level, then have to turn around and do it all over again. The same players, in the same stadiums. Different jerseys, sure, but it was hard to stay motivated when you've been doing it for so long. Argentina provided that in spades. Particularly playing over in Buenos Aires — it refreshed the whole calendar.

We went through the Rugby Championship undefeated, thanks largely to Steve providing a framework to focus us for the year. The first thing that he had pointed out in those early leadership group meetings was that every single team that has won a World Cup had been awful the following year. So that became our goal — a World Cup-winning team trying to better itself. We didn't want to have a World Cup hangover, so our main focus in 2012 was to avoid conforming to the historical trend. That was a real driving force for us, and in striving to achieve that we had an almost perfect year.

When we approached the end-of-year tour, I started to become aware that I was approaching a personal milestone. I was in the 90s for All Blacks games played, and in my head I had worked out that my hundredth could well be at home in Hamilton — where my test career had begun. I thought that was pretty cool, enjoying the symmetry of it, and the idea of it happening in New Zealand. I played the first game in Europe, against Scotland, which kept me on schedule. The next game was against Italy. I was named on the bench, and thought I'd get 10 minutes or so at the end of the game to keep myself on track for Hamilton.

Towards the end we were beating them comfortably. Steve had really wanted to give Aaron Cruden a go in that test, to get his confidence up, and to his credit he'd had a great game. But we were up over 30-odd points, and I selfishly thought I might get on for a few minutes and get an extra cap. I knew I shouldn't be thinking that way, but couldn't help myself.

As the minutes ticked down, I started realising that I might not get on at all. For some reason it really made me angry, and for the last part of the game I waited on the side of the pitch, ready to get on. There was a bike there, so I warmed up, without being instructed, and I kept looking up at the coaches. 'Put me on,' I thought. 'We're killing them out here.' They didn't put me in, and I ended the game seriously, irrationally angry.

We did a fitness session afterwards, and played a bunch of anaerobic games — touch and other sprint-focused sports. I was still steamed from the game, and so thrashed myself throughout. I probably pushed myself too hard, and my right Achilles — not the left one I'd done in France — started getting a bit tight.

Normally I'd ease back in a situation like that, but I was so angry I thought I'd run through the aggression. I've never been very good at telling the coaches what I'm thinking, and that inability to articulate my anger just made me push even harder.

The next day I was talking to Steve Hansen and I asked him why he didn't put me in the game. He explained his thoughts around giving Crudes some extra game time. I told him that I had been keen to get on in that game, so that my hundredth test would be at home. He'd had no idea — and why would he? It just made it clear to me that I needed to be more open with my thoughts to coaches.

I moved on and we went to Wales for the next game. The training field was awful — worse than a club field. It had been raining for days, and was just so heavy. As I warmed up my Achilles got more and more sore. I pulled out of training, then we didn't train again until Thursday.

By Thursday it had failed to improve. I was limping around and had to pull out of the weekend's game. So here I was having missed Italy, and now the following week's test because I'd tweaked my Achilles running around like a fool. The final game of the tour was against England and I couldn't train all week because of my Achilles, but I really wanted to play.

I was hobbling still, but the whole team was in trouble come Tuesday, when nearly everyone in the camp came down with a vicious virus. No one could get away from the bathroom, which tore apart our schedule for the week.

Even at the Thursday training there were a few guys who couldn't train — they simply couldn't get out of bed. I was one of the handful of players who didn't get hit. The energy of the team was really sapped, which would have been hard at any time, but was particularly difficult at the end of a gruelling season. We didn't want to let that be an excuse, and still prepared as well as we could have.

I had extra motivation to play, as it turned out. Before the game, I had heard that I was narrowly ahead of Richie for IRB Player of the Year going into the last game of the year. We're both pretty competitive people, and I wanted to keep him out. The top three players from each game are awarded points, so any result was possible. As it turned out, my Achilles gave way early in the game. I was out. Luckily for me, Richie had a very rare off game, so the results stayed unchanged. We lost the game, 38–21, and with it our shot at an unbeaten season. But while I was gutted to lose the game, I was proud of our bounce-back year after the World Cup, and couldn't help but feel elated at winning the IRB award for a second time. Particularly after the disappointment of the previous year, it felt like a kind of vindication.

The only disappointing part was that when I won, nothing was announced. I think my manager told me on the Sunday afterwards. There was a low-key IRB dinner on a Sunday night — one which I didn't really know anything about. I think Steve Hansen and Richie went along, and Steve accepted my award on my behalf. I was away in Germany doing promotional work.

It was just all a real anticlimax, particularly for something that should be such a big occasion.

Worse was to come at the Steinlager Awards. After winning the IRB award, and playing the way I had throughout the year, I felt I had a reasonable shot at doing well there. But I wasn't even nominated for player of the year. It left a sour taste in my mouth. I don't play for the awards, but if I was good enough to win the IRB award, it felt like I should at least be nominated in my own country.

So despite being more than satisfied with my work for the year on the whole, I ended up in a somewhat negative frame of mind. The awards were one thing, but the Achilles injury began to really play on my mind, and started a spiral of negative thinking towards rugby which would peak with a long, low period the likes of which I'd never before experienced in the game.

FINAL YEAR DIARY: Wellington, 30 August 2015

Recorded via telephone in Wellington at the Intercontinental Hotel ahead of the naming of the squad for the World Cup.

I remember being really tired in Sydney. We'd been getting so much content, so many new moves. At the same time we were learning new combinations and assimilating a very different team to the one which had played the earlier tests. So while we were very up for the game, with hindsight I wasn't surprised when we lost.

I don't blame the unfamiliarity between players or with the game plan, though. Sometimes you just don't front up as a team, and that was what happened in Sydney. We had a strong side, probably the best of the year to date. We walked in confidently and we got smoked.

Ahead of the test the new strategies seemed to make sense. We had quite an open game plan, involving moving the ball wide to get it to the edges. We thought Australia might be more vulnerable there — and we were wrong.

That flowed into the big change from the first Bledisloe Cup match into the second. We stripped all that noise out, and played a game which was really simple and direct. We felt like we had to go through them first, and *then* get the ball into the space.

That was something the leadership group really drove. This team functions so much better when the leaders and the players are driving the game plan and the messages. It was only a couple of little changes, really, but it just made such a big difference to the result and the mindset of the players.

During the week leading up to the Eden Park game I spent a lot of time with Ian Foster. He really drove into me: 'This is your team, I need you to drive the team, I want you to direct the guys around the field. You've got this game plan, but if you want to change something — it's your team — you just go out there and own it.'

The conversations gave me a real sense of responsibility — and I loved it. It might seem strange, given the length of my career, but because I've been in and out of the team for so long lately, I haven't been able to own the team in the same way I once did.

Fozzie pushed me on that, and I felt like I responded well. One example which stood out was our lineout calls. We had a sequence which should have dictated our plan for the lineouts in a particular order. But during the game, I began changing the sequence to reflect what I was sensing, and calling what I felt appropriate at the time. It worked really well. Coming away from the game, it's elements like that which give me more satisfaction than anything else.

The week was special for a number of reasons: our last home game of the year, the last of our careers for a number of us, and a record-breaker for Richie. But the most memorable moment came in the build-up. Our defence this year is named Wiremu, after Willy Apiata, New Zealand's only living Victoria Cross winner. Wayne Smith, our defensive coach, has done a few presentations about him and relates our defence to Willy.

On the Thursday before the game, Willy was there in the room. He wasn't planning to speak, but at the end of the meeting he decided to say a few words. It was incredible —

he's probably one of the best and most motivating speakers I've ever witnessed.

Everyone walked out of that meeting room so fired up and pumped. I believe it was a big part of why we stepped up and performed the way we did at Eden Park.

I had felt a bit of pressure going in. A part of me wanted to play well for selfish reasons, after copping some criticism following the previous tests. But mostly I just wanted to retain that Bledisloe Cup. I can't emphasise enough how much I love the Bledisloe. I've never lost it, and desperately wanted to keep that record intact. It was also a rare playoff-style game. You don't get a lot of those do-or-die scenarios in New Zealand rugby. The game had that intensity, and it was an immense relief that my final game in New Zealand was a win, and a pretty emphatic one.

The week after was fairly quiet. The group which weren't returning to the ITM Cup assembled in Tauranga for camp. We mainly focused on conditioning, so Pete Gallagher and Nic Gill thrashed us pretty hard. Afterwards I flew back to Auckland for a night at Vector Arena. Richie and I hosted an event for our charity iSport, formerly known as For Everyone. I think we got close to $200,000 out of the night, which is just incredible. Ali flew in and made a very funny speech, Richie spoke brilliantly on leadership and John Campbell was the MC. There was just a great feeling in the room.

We had some time off after that, ahead of the team being named. I, predictably, filled mine with commitments to some of my individual sponsors. They turned out to be some of the most fun of my career. MasterCard was running a 'surprise' campaign. They organised for me to turn up to an under-8s rugby training in tackle pads and helmet. The kids thought I was their coach and went hard at me. The look on their faces when I took off my helmet afterwards was . . . you know the drill.

Even better was an event in Christchurch. We were shooting some video, for another campaign — or so I thought. I spent the morning doing voice-over interviews about my formative years in rugby — about Southbridge.

We moved to the Canterbury training ground to shoot video in the afternoon. I went through a particular motion a half dozen times. The next take I walked around the corner to a rugby team charging at me. I had no idea what was going on, and thought I was about to get smashed. I barely had time to register that they were wearing Southbridge club jerseys. They pulled up just before tackling me, and I finally got a decent look at them.

It was three teammates from my very first midgets rugby team — none of whom I'd seen in 15 or 20 years. It was such a deep, lasting shock, and such a sweet surprise. It ended up being a very special day, reconnecting with those guys.

My phone call came this morning. I was chilling with Fox and Marco in the playroom when Darren Shand rang. It never gets old that phone call. Even now I'm still buzzing.

That was this morning, about 9 am. By 10 am I got the flight information and the plan for the next couple of weeks. By 2 pm I was on a plane to Wellington. As soon as we landed we had a meeting about the announcement. Steve talked about the Rugby World Cup, congratulated us and spoke of the expectations. It filled us with adrenalin, and we walked out ready to play. And in less than a month, we will be.

15

I Wish I Could Retire

The thought crept up on me slowly, but once it took hold, it refused to let go. It would sneak into my mind during training, when I was pushing weights. Or in the dead of night, when I couldn't sleep. Most often, it made itself at home during rehab. Endless, thankless rehab, trying to heal a broken body. The thought was: Why am I doing this? Why don't I just retire?

Players retire every year, but when it's your peers it starts to wear on you. I was hit the hardest by the loss of Jimmy Cowan and Ali Williams. They were two of my closest friends in the team — we became a tight-knit trio off the field. I'd known Jimmy since our age-grade teams, and he's got the biggest heart. Status means nothing to him — he's just so grounded, so real. Ali was a different kind of friendship. That nickname 'comical Ali' is bang on. As an All Black it's very easy to lose yourself in the pressures and expectations, particularly for someone as prone to introspection as me. Ali would never let me get too far down that road — his pranks and jokes meant what we were aiming for stayed in perspective.

When they left Super Rugby to head north I felt lonely, like I had lost some of the sense of fun I had around the game. Particularly within the All Blacks.

There was a young group coming up that were great mates, incredibly tight on and off the field. They liked the same music, ate together, hung out together, played video games and cards together. Just as Ali, Richie and the rest of us used to do when we came into the squad over a short time span, at first overawed, then increasingly feeling like the team was ours.

These young guys were all of a similar age and generation. I watched Aaron Cruden come up, saw what he could do, felt both admiration and slightly threatened. But while I respected his game immensely, I still felt I had something to offer the team. I wanted there to be good, friendly competition for positions, and have never minded when new players came along with big raps on them. That competitive side of me relishes the challenge.

At least, I always had to that point. Now my body was shot. I was stuck in what felt like an endless cycle: play a few games, get a new injury, then give in to weeks of rehab again. I had no confidence in my body. Every time I stepped onto the field I would wonder which part would give way next. My mind was full of what-ifs and fears I couldn't speak aloud. That's not how your mind is working when you're on top of your game, and I never got close to finding a rhythm as a result. It was the winter of 2013, and rugby — for so long a joy — had become a prison.

Injuries really start to weigh on you as you get older. They feel like a betrayal, like your body letting you down. There was nothing catastrophic, but it felt like every time I'd work through one issue, another limb would give out. It got to the point where whenever there was any odd ache or strange feeling in my body, I'd start to assume the worst. I'd think it was a sign of something major looming, another session with sports physician Tony Page and muscle therapist George Duncan, assessing the physical damage, and Gilbert Enoka, assessing the mental.

Then it would be back to the stands on game day. All that time on the sideline I'd stare out at the team, the joy they felt, the explosive athleticism they displayed, and a loneliness would set in. Watching the young guys I felt a real sense of loss. I'd been that way once, through the 2000s. It felt like the whole team was a big gang of friends. You'd train hard, play hard and then socialise together afterwards. We felt indestructible. It was a fantastic lifestyle.

Now I was down the back of the bus, and was lucky if there were half a dozen guys I was truly tight with scattered around those seats. Coming and going, as they dealt with their own injuries. And every so often disappearing forever, when they headed north to chase the twilight of their professional vitality. Every time that happened, I'd feel a new loss, as that sense of connection with the core of the team began to slip away.

Having a wife and young family meant I didn't enjoy being away from home the same way, and sponsorship commitments meant that, even on tour, almost all of my free time was spoken for — there were emails to answer, events to attend, promotions to shoot, hands to shake. The game which I had always loved had become a ferocious beast, one which drained me of energy without restoring it the way it once had. Every week I would be haunted by this thought which refused to leave me alone: I wish I could retire.

Often the following day, I'd wake up and something would remind me of how much I loved the game: a pain-free training session, a conversation, occasionally even a game. Then a few days later I'd be back in the hole, wishing I could give it up. My mind would drift back to 2011, when I signed my four-year contract.

I knew in my heart that if it had been a two-year deal I'd have been gone. It was exhausting. It's hard enough playing the game, going through rehab and the grind of professional sport, without having to battle these demons telling you to quit.

The one thing which kept me sane through this period was my sabbatical. It was booked for the end of 2013, and became a beacon to me. If it hadn't been there, I'd probably have just walked away from it all. But I knew every day was bringing me closer to that break. I thought if I could just drag myself through this season, it was there waiting for me. A chance to get away from the game for six months, get my body right, get my mind right. Then maybe things would freshen up, and I'd regain my love for the game.

The worst part was that I didn't feel I could talk to anyone about these thoughts, couldn't breathe life into them by saying them aloud. It's not how rugby players are supposed to feel. We're marketed as if we're made of granite. That image helps pull in spectators and sponsors, but it can also mean you feel like you have to live up to a particular kind of rugged image, regardless of how you're feeling inside. It's a brutal sport, and exacts a heavy toll. I'd speak to Honor about it endlessly. She really coaxed me through those months, with empathy drawn from her own experiences as an athlete.

Along with the sabbatical, one number dragged me forward. I'd never cared about them before. I'm the highest points scorer for Super Rugby. The highest points scorer for international rugby. I barely noticed when I ticked past them. They weren't why I was playing the game. But when I started to limp from injury to injury, I became obsessed with one exclusive club.

One hundred tests. Richie got there first. Then Mils Muliaina,

Keven Mealamu and Tony Woodcock. I'd been cruising there for a while, playing 35 tests between 2006 and 2008 alone. But as these injuries kept creeping in I stayed longer and longer in the nervous 90s. I'd play a test or two, then be out for a month. At times I felt like fate had decided I wouldn't get there — the same way it had struck me down during the most routine of kicks at the 2011 World Cup. That fed into the fear about my body. I'd be running along in training, get the tiniest twinge and think: 'Is that my calf? I've done my calf!' Then a couple of minutes later I'd realise it was nothing.

All these people were appearing out of the woodwork, saying they could fix me. Being such a public figure, every doctor or chiropractor or neurologist in the country had a theory about why I was breaking down. They'd call Mum and Dad saying they knew what the problem was, that they could cure me. I never took them up on their offers. Mostly because I thought it was terminal. My Achilles tendon was still tender from the previous year. That seemed to flow up into my calves, then my hamstrings. My whole body — that mass of interconnected bone and tissue — was a mess of different weaknesses and flaws, each revealing themselves one by one. Some well-known, others lying in wait.

Never getting a consistent run of games meant my performance when I *could* make the field was suffering. I have incredibly high expectations of myself — I want to be the best player in the world. But through 2013 I wasn't even close to the best player on the field. And all the time my friends, the players I came up with, were dropping away. It felt like every week another would sign a contract in Japan, or France, or Ireland. Between that and the injuries the question was unavoidable and recurring: Why are you still here?

The sabbatical represented time away to rebuild my body and rediscover my love for a game which had dominated my life since I could walk. I come from a line of rugby men, and from the moment I first picked up a ball there had never been anything I'd rather have been doing. For over 20 years my body was rock solid, my love of the game unquenchable. Until now, when almost anything else seemed more appealing. The sabbatical was one thing, but it was still months away. While it was good to have Honor to confide in, her advice was more along the lines of 'brush it off, you'll feel better tomorrow', which was mostly true. But what about the following day, when often as not I'd be back in the black?

I decided to treat my mental issues the way I would my physical — to go and get help from professionals. Fortunately the All Blacks have, in Gilbert Enoka, one of the best mental skills coaches in sport. I started spending more and more time with him and Ceri Evans, another top mental skills guy I'd dealt with through the All Blacks. I put a real focus on remembering that I didn't have long left in what is one of the best jobs in the world. That I was incredibly fortunate to be there. To most people, it looked like I was paid very good money to do gym work, throw a ball around, have banter and coffee with teammates and friends. All while most people were stuck in an office. The other side is the constant demands of sponsors and media, which means a day without some form of commitment is almost non-existent, and many last from before dawn until well after dark.

The only issue was that as much as I wanted to be open and honest with Gilbert and Ceri, I always held back a little because I knew that they were part of the coaching infrastructure of the team. I knew I could trust them, but at the same time the idea of

Steve Hansen or the other guys knowing I was feeling this way filled me with dread. So instead I concentrated on processes to shorten my thinking, structures which could get me through those dark patches.

The whole time I was terrified of Steve finding out I had these feelings. Our relationship had deteriorated badly in 2013, to the point where I wouldn't talk to him about anything — I'd just bottle it all up. I would look at him and think about how busy he was, how many people he had to juggle, and think: 'I don't want to bother him.' He's not a naturally open guy either, so we each ended up making a lot of assumptions about what we were thinking or feeling.

In my mind, I started to doubt his faith in me. I thought, 'Steve Hansen doesn't want me in this team any more. And why would he? I'm injured all the time, he can't rely on me.' Those doubts wouldn't leave me alone.

Injuries bedevilled my season. I missed the opening two games of a three-test home series against France with a broken bone in my hand. Then, in the middle of the Rugby Championship, I got smoked at Eden Park by Springboks hooker Bismarck du Plessis. We were going backwards, and I received the ball from Aaron Smith. They were right up on us in defence. He timed his hit perfectly and just demolished me. It was a completely fair hit, but I was cut in half, and popped the AC joint in my shoulder. That put me out for six weeks, and meant my Rugby Championship was over.

The following morning I started to think about when I was going to play my hundredth game. I was stranded on 97, and it started to eat away at me anew: What if it never happens? It got to the point where I was having major doubts that I'd even be selected for the end-of-year tour. I'd been a huge part of the team for a decade by then, but in my mind it was history and not form or ability that was keeping me there.

During that particular rehab, things got really low. To compensate for my inability to lift, I started to run a lot, one thing you can still do with a shoulder injury. One session I was trying to pound out the frustration, and went too far, causing my Achilles to flare up again. That pushed me out of the frame for the last Bledisloe of the year, for which I'd had an outside chance of returning. It was my fifth injury of the year, and I started to spiral down.

Gilbert picked up on it, with his usual intuitive power. He finally teased out of me some of my doubts regarding my future, Steve, and my place in the team. To his credit, Gilbert realised that there was a huge gap between my assumptions about Steve's thinking, and what Steve's impressions and intentions were. Gilbert suggested Steve and I start meeting for coffee once a week, to talk about rugby and our plans and so on.

We had the first session in September, and it was revelatory. When I opened up to him about my thoughts he was shocked. He couldn't believe what I'd been thinking. That was a huge relief, and started me thinking more positively about this end-of-year tour, viewing it less as make-or-break for my career and more as an opportunity to get some game time, without worrying too much about its quality.

I met with Tony Page, who'd taken over from Deb Robinson as All Blacks doctor earlier in the year. Everyone knew how much I was fixating on 100. I even had a special commemorative pair of adidas boots they'd helped me design. They were gold and red, in an edition of 100, and I couldn't wait to wear them. But the longer time dragged on, the more I wondered if I'd ever put them on. Eventually we settled on a cortisone shot, into the sheath around the Achilles tendon — not the tendon itself — which would help dull the discomfort enough for me to play. I was told it would last around three or four weeks, and should allow me to run, which it did, but little else.

We played Japan first, on the way out to Europe. That was my ninety-eighth game — the first of the three I needed to get to 100, and get that monkey off my back. I played around 50 minutes, but they were deeply ordinary — some of the most compromised of my career. My Achilles was so tight I could hardly run or train. In any other circumstance I'd have shut it down, but at that time I had a real desperation about getting to my hundredth. I truly had no idea whether I would get another shot. The coaches knew it, and so did the medical personnel. I had no idea what the sabbatical would do to me, whether I'd even want to play again after experiencing life without rugby. I wanted to go in with that milestone ticked off, otherwise it would have haunted me throughout my time away.

The next game was against France. I started, and played 50-odd minutes, running far more freely than I had against Japan. Once I warmed up I couldn't feel the tendon, which was a huge relief. That set me up for my hundredth game, against England at Twickenham. There are no bigger stages in world rugby, so in some ways it was a perfect way to ring it up.

It was an amazing test lead-up. Dad came over to spend the week with me, which was beautiful, as he's always been my biggest supporter and mentor in rugby. I conducted a press conference which felt very special — because of the focus on looking back across my career, I was able to get a sense of the totality of its scope for perhaps the first time. The English press can be hellish, but they know how to contextualise such an event, so it was good to be in London for the occasion. The England team acknowledged it too, presenting me with a signed jersey after the game.

Despite the elation, I was a long way from fully fit. I could run, but not freely. It was week three after the cortisone shot, so I knew it would soon be wearing off. In my mind, though, I was so determined to get on the field that I almost didn't care what happened beyond then. Running out onto Twickenham, in my golden boots, was an extraordinary feeling. The crowd was so generous, and gave me a huge ovation. I had goose bumps, and do even now thinking back to it.

Then we did a haka, which featured Liam Messam, who was leading it that day, pulling me up by the jersey. It was completely unplanned, and unexpected. I almost didn't know what to do, and was nearly overcome by the moment — it's a mark of respect which is very rare, and has only happened to players very occasionally during my career.

The game started brilliantly. I was loving the occasion, playing better than I had in months. All the agonising doubt was being washed away with every step, pass and punt. Then, 20 minutes in, I received the ball, stepped, and took it into the tackle. As I went down, I felt my Achilles. It wasn't just tight — it was a sharp pain. I got up, and hobbled through the next five minutes. But I knew it was over. I realised that I wasn't helping my team, hanging around on one leg, and very reluctantly went off. It was a horrible way to end the game, especially after the energy of the week. Worse still, a year earlier I'd left the field for the same reason. Only this time I knew the injury was more serious.

As I limped from the field my thoughts moved inexorably

to my sabbatical. It was meant to be a time to rest, recuperate, retune my body and rediscover my love of the game by testing life without it. Now it would be dominated by another rehab. At that moment I believed there was a very good chance I'd played my last game of rugby.

16

Patriot Games

It was a typical winter's day in Boston. Crisp, clear, freezing cold. It was the start of my second sabbatical in late 2013, and I was determined to get a long way from rugby, to try to rekindle my love for the game. I was with a friend, Luke Lloyd Davies. He's a sports agent and knew I was a fan of the NFL, so he had arranged for the pair of us to head up to tour the New England Patriots' facilities following a round of promotional work for AIG in New York.

We pulled up to the stadium on a Monday, and walked into reception. It was the day after a home game, and the building was open, but mostly empty. At the desk they welcomed us by name, as if we were arriving for an appointment. That was my first inkling that something was up. The next thing I knew, a couple of scouts came out, and asked, 'Where are your boots?'

They thought I was there to try out for the team! I was floored, and a little wistful. Part of me would have liked nothing more than to give it a shot, just to see what it was like. But I'd just torn my Achilles tendon, and was months away from being able to kick again.

They looked downcast, as if they'd been misinformed about the purpose of the meeting. It was all so surreal — I'd been under the impression we were going to wander through the facilities like tourists; the team clearly had a very different idea about our purpose. I still don't know where that came from. We chatted with the scouts a little more, then they said: 'Mr Kraft wants to meet with you.'

Mr Kraft was Robert Kraft, the team's legendary owner. He'd made his money in paper, before making a series of smart real estate moves around the Patriots' stadium, which culminated in his purchasing the NFL team for $172 million in 1994 — at the time the highest price ever paid for a sports franchise. I couldn't believe that this guy wanted to meet me.

We were taken through a series of open-plan offices on the way to his area, deep in the belly of the stadium, then sat waiting with his secretary for a few minutes. Eventually she went into his room, and emerged to say, 'Mr Kraft is ready to meet with you now.' It was all incredibly formal.

We walked into a room which reeked of success. It was all wood trim, framed memorabilia and trophies. Very old-school. You could see how he'd become so successful, because he cut straight to the point with a series of very direct questions.

'Do you want to play football?'

'What are you going to bring to this team?'

'Do you think you can make the transition to the NFL?'

There was nothing resembling small talk with him. I mumbled my way through some answers, looking across to Luke, who seemed equally lost. He'd thought the visit was a relaxed walk-through, too. We spent 10 or 15 minutes talking through the realities of the sport, and whether it was plausible for me to transition to football.

If I'm honest, my interest *was* piqued a little. I don't think any competitive athlete could walk into an environment like that, be received in that way, and not feel a desire to rise to the challenge. Who knows what I might have done had I not sustained that injury at Twickenham? But the injury made the conversation somewhat immaterial, and Luke steered it towards an only slightly more relatable topic: the Elton John concert at Madison Square Garden on Wednesday. That was, in a funny way, the reason we were there.

Luke worked for Rocket, the entertainment and sports management arm of Sir Elton's empire. They manage everyone from artists such as Ed Sheeran to athletes such as Tour de France cyclist Geraint Thomas. I had met Luke a few years earlier, and we'd become friends. Elton — Luke's boss — was close friends with Mr Kraft (no one called him Robert), hence our being granted the audience. After we finished up, we were sent downstairs to meet with the head of the team's scouting programme, and had another very serious conversation about my playing.

He talked me through their processes, from recruitment, to testing, to training. He spoke of how they would adapt them to deal with a player from outside coming into their system. That was the point when I realised just how difficult it would be for me, competing with the wave upon wave of young athletic talent thrown up by the college system. But, as the scout explained, Mr Kraft loves doing things out of the ordinary, recognising the power of a story like mine with the media and fans. So as much as it felt like a strange fantasy to me, everyone at the organisation was treating me as a serious prospect, albeit an unconventional one. I ended up sitting with the head of special teams, who works with kickers and other specialists, and watching tape of elite place-kickers for a couple of hours, while he talked me through their technique.

I've worked with some incredible kicking coaches over the years, in Daryl Halligan and Mick Byrne, ex league and AFL players respectively. Mick, in particular, has played a big role in my success. But we'd never gone into anything like this level of precision. The scout and I talked about the placement of the plant foot, the angle at which we position ourselves to the ball to open up the sweet spot, and the various parts of the ball. We went through film of six different NFL kickers in minute detail.

I'd walked in thinking you just put a helmet on and kicked the ball, but the conversation made me realise the extent to which your success as a place-kicker is dependent upon your teammates positioning the ball during your run-up. It also made me imagine how different it would be running in aiming for clear air, just trusting that a ball would appear, perfectly placed and angled away from you, versus our traditional kicking tee. At the end of the session, he handed me a beautiful NFL game ball and told me that he wanted to see tape from me in six months. Even though I was contracted through the end of 2015, they seemed willing to wait. He gave me a timeline for receiving tape, trying out, and team selection.

I walked away with my head spinning. That morning I'd thought we were just going for a wander through another big stadium. By lunchtime all I could think about were the possibilities the visit had opened up. It gave me new impetus to rehab the Achilles injury, to see whether this was real, or just a sabbatical day dream.

After we finished up, Mr Kraft offered to lend us his driver, and fly us back to New York in his private plane. We declined, as we had an appointment that evening, but it was a little window into the money and the professionalism at which the NFL operates, and it was hard not to be swept up in it all.

The rest of the week was similarly surreal. I went to an Elton John concert with Jack Tame, the TV One reporter who's a friend of mine, and watched Elton at Madison Square Garden. It was one of the best concerts I've ever seen — despite his age, Elton still has an incredible presence and charisma. I realised how many of his songs I knew, and how much I loved them. Towards the end of the show, Luke found the two of us and asked, 'Do you want to meet him?'

We trooped backstage, and spent 15 minutes with a living legend. I was dumbstruck — what do you say to a guy like that? But Elton made it easy. He's a serious sports nut, and congratulated me on the All Blacks' just-completed perfect season. It was Jack, Luke, Elton and his then-boyfriend, now-husband David. We chatted about sports for a while, then Elton leaned in and asked, 'What are you doing next year, around March?'

I told him about the sabbatical, my six months off. He said, 'You're going to have to come to my Oscars party then.' I told him that sounded good to me. And it did — an invite to one of the flashest parties in the world for Honor and me. I still shake my head at it. After the show it was time to head home. I flew back to New Zealand and returned to my regular life, spending time with family and relaxing.

The relaxing never really stopped. That summer was the laziest, most indulgent and enjoyable I'd had since leaving school. It was just such a good time, and exactly what I needed. For all of December and January I forgot about rugby, about the All Blacks and about Super Rugby. Most of all, about training. For a guy who loves to train, and had been either running, lifting or rehabbing for 25-odd years, this was a major change. My body needed it. As a professional athlete, you get used to playing with, through and around injuries. That word 'niggles' gets used a lot, and it's both useless in its lack of specificity and entirely apt in describing the gathering of various issues into a small but palpable physical problem.

By the time I hit my thirties, my body sometimes felt like it was entirely composed of niggles. One perched upon the next, linking my bones and muscles into a web of old injuries, full of the kind of workarounds your body makes when one part of it isn't functioning as it should.

Most of my current problems seemed to radiate up from my ankle. Following the tour I had it cleaned out, the surgeon delicately plucking out bits of bone fragment and other debris floating loose around the joint. It wasn't bad enough to stop me playing — thanks to the occasional cortisone shot — but did mean I couldn't put my knee over my toe. That in turn affected my calves and hamstrings, the injury echoing up my legs.

At the same time they did an MRI of my Achilles, finding a tear from that England game. The best way to heal a tear is to let it rest, rather than have surgery. That's just one small window into the way injuries travel in a chain, the result of dozens, if not hundreds, of small knocks and strains which, due to the demands of games and schedules, are never allowed to fully heal. The sabbatical was a chance to recover my love of rugby mentally, but also get my body working closer to the way nature intended.

After two months I was healing — still in pain, but also desperate to start conditioning. I'd dropped eight kilos — I lose weight, rather than gaining it, when I stop working — and was the thinnest I'd been since 2001. I was now ready to rebuild my body.

On 1 February 2014 that process began in earnest. I scheduled a meeting with All Blacks physio Pete Gallagher and strength and conditioning coach Nic Gill. To start that process we convened at the Les Mills gym on Victoria Street, Auckland to test where my baseline fitness sat. Then we headed up the road for coffee at Best Ugly, and put together a four-month plan to make a new Dan Carter, and try to iron out some of the worst of the kinks which existed in my battered old bones.

I had lost a lot of muscle, but they weren't too bothered by that. I'd become too big — up to 98 kg at my peak, which is four or five kilos north of a good playing weight for me. Carrying too much muscle was putting a strain on my joints, which would feed into injuries and create extra wear and tear.

What they found was predictable — the problem area was my core, which has always been really weak. Most specifically my hips. We decided to meet once a month, assess my progress and put together a new plan. The first, for February, was very basic — body weight movements, body weight squats — just realigning and rebuilding my body. I could do that stuff anywhere there was some open space, or a neighbourhood gym. The process would necessarily be relatively slow, both because we were unwinding years of issues and because my priority remained getting a break from rugby, travelling and spending time with my family.

We put in place rules to avoid stressing or reinjuring myself. Chief amongst them was that I wasn't to train the day after travelling. That was a little problematic, as I had a few amazing trips planned over the next couple of months, mostly to sporting events I was keen to check out. There was also Elton's Oscars party invitation still there, hanging in the distance, equally attracting and repelling us.

Honor and I are both small-town people, and big swanky parties aren't really our scene to begin with — let alone the most glamorous event in the world. We thought we'd be so out of place, and for a while convinced ourselves that we shouldn't go.

Eventually we came to our senses, and realised that this was an opportunity most people would crawl over broken glass for. No matter how uncomfortable we might be, we wouldn't want to look back on this in our old age and wish we'd done it. So I called Luke, and he said he'd sort everything — all we needed to do was book our flights.

As soon as they were booked, a fresh worry descended: What are we going to wear? Particularly for Honor. We ended up going back to the people who'd served us well through our wedding. Honor had an Anna Schimmel dress made, while Crane Brothers again came through with a black tie number for me. That issue being resolved, we jetted into LA, and spent a few days exploring the city. I don't love LA at the best of times — the Hollywood fakery gets a bit much. That was particularly acute during Oscars season. But we saw friends and enjoyed a wee break from being parents — we'd left Marco behind with Honor's mum and a nanny for a few days.

Soon it was time for the party. We got dressed up, took a deep breath and headed to the event. It's a screening party and auction, hosted by Elton, to raise money for the Elton John AIDS Foundation. We went along to the event with Luke, who cajoled us into walking the red carpet. We stood watching the scene for a minute or two, dreading having to walk down it. Just ahead of us was Sheryl Crow. The crowd and paparazzi went crazy for her, flashes going off over and over. Then we headed down. The announcer called out our names: 'Dan and Honor Carter!' Tumbleweeds. A couple of photographers yelled to us, but more out of pity, I felt. It was pretty embarrassing, but also hilarious.

Once inside we were full-time celebrity spotting. The first one we came upon was Ed Sheeran, who happened to be standing alongside us. He's a lovely guy, with an affinity for New Zealand, and later dueted with Elton on 'Candle in the Wind'. Soon we were seated, and the enormity of this event really washed over us. We looked around and saw Lady Gaga at one table, the Kardashians at the next, Britney Spears one over. The stars were everywhere you looked. Directly across from us on our table was Tim 'The Tool Man' Allen!

Honor and I started talking to the woman next to me. She was a real character, and we were having fun chatting. When she left for a moment the man next to her said, 'Do you know who you're talking to?' 'Sorry, I don't,' I replied, adding by way of explanation or apology, 'I'm from New Zealand.'

'It's Tatum O'Neal!' he said, in a way that implied I was well out of line for not recognising her. 'That's awesome,' I said, still not really knowing who she was. 'She's the youngest ever Oscar winner!' he hissed. I knew that wasn't true. 'Nah, it's Anna Paquin,' I said confidently. 'She's just over there.'

'She's the second-youngest,' he snapped. I thought I'd better get on Google and see what was up with this woman, and why her mate was so fired up. I slipped my phone out and discovered that O'Neal had won an Oscar at 10 and had a crazy life — married to John McEnroe, drug problems, the works. She was an incredibly famous person, and I'd just been chatting away, completely unaware. That set the scene for the night.

At one point I bumped into Robert Kraft, who surprised me by not only remembering who I was, but asking whether I'd made that tape for his scouts. I laughed it off, but I was flattered that he was still interested. The idea was still floating in my mind a little.

Soon Steven Tyler took the stage to commence the auction, which showed you the unbelievable wealth which was in the room. Elton's signed piano went for $500,000 to start us off. I kept my hands firmly underneath the table. Afterwards we saw Tyler in the crowd, and Honor asked if she could have a photo with him. He was very enthusiastic about it, though much less so when I asked.

The whole night was filled with moments like that. We got as much as we could from it, then left them to it. The next day we flew home, back to Marco, friends, family and normality.

This whole time I had been waiting for the love for rugby to return. I expected to get that familiar pull as the season came into view, of wishing I was out there playing. But it wasn't happening. I was barely paying attention to rugby. I'd watch the Crusaders sometimes, if it was on, but mostly I just left it alone. It bothered me. I started to wonder if it would ever come back. That I'd get to the end of the six months and still have no desire to return to the game. I was enjoying the fitness and training work I was doing. But if you'd told me I had to play that Saturday — I couldn't think of anything worse.

Luckily, there were other events to distract me. Honor and I flew up to the Laureus World Sports Awards, which were in Kuala Lumpur, Malaysia, towards the end of March. The All Blacks had been nominated for Team of the Year, but because the guys were playing and coaches working, no one could make it. So I was asked if I could go along and represent the team. We had been looking at flying Malaysian Airlines. Then MH370 disappeared. We were spooked, and went with another carrier.

The event was conducted in the shadow of the missing plane. Being in the city then was a very sobering experience. You were acutely aware of the grief and mystery engulfing the families of those whose loved ones were on that plane. The event itself was toned down as a result — no one felt like it was appropriate to be celebrating in that climate.

That said, on the night it was hard not to get swept up by the stars in attendance. It was like a sports world version of the Oscars. There were Formula One drivers such as Lewis Hamilton and Sebastian Vettel, ex-athletes such as Carl Lewis and Sebastian Coe — everywhere you looked there were famous, award-winning sportspeople. So even though the All Blacks lost out — Bayern Munich took the team award — it was still a spectacular time.

Afterwards we flew to Hong Kong to spend time with Honor's sister and brother-in-law, and attended the Sevens. It was my first time at the event, one I enjoyed doubly due to it being a rugby tournament upon which nothing was riding for me. There was no training, no playing, no media or commercial work. I was just another spectator. The demands of our seasons mean that while we play in the great stadiums of the world, we don't often get to attend big sporting fixtures and just watch. It was great attending huge international sporting events just as fans, and we'd set up a couple of them in a row.

Honor then flew back, leaving me to continue on. The next stop was Augusta, for the Masters. I met up with Chris Liddell, a good friend of mine, and his business partner, Craig Heatley. Heatley is a legend of New Zealand business, having founded Sky and worked across Brierley Investments and Woolworths in the '80s. He's also a very strong golfer, with wins in a couple of big pro-am tournaments in the States. That might be why he's one of the select few with membership of Augusta National — and the only New Zealander.

Whatever my experiences over the years, nothing prepared me for Augusta. The history, the tradition and the etiquette — all things which are lost at a lot of modern sporting events. You aren't even allowed to take your phone in, as they don't allow cameras. You sensed how prestigious the event was, and how fortunate you were to attend.

Craig is head of the media committee for the tournament, which meant he was able to give us unbelievable access. I sat in on Adam Scott's press conference, and met him afterwards, and I got to walk the course, which was an extraordinary experience.

The whole time, though, I was still having to keep up my training regime. I was onto my third monthly programme, and starting to feel pretty good about what I was accomplishing — though I still had no desire to test my fitness on a playing field. While at Augusta I found a gym at a complex near the course, and had noticed a few golfers coming and going. I know what it's like to be a professional athlete and be recognised and approached when you're trying to get through your work, so I kept my head down and left them to it. One day I was in the middle of a session, going pretty hard, when I saw Rory McIlroy out of the corner of my eye. I left him to it, but caught him glancing my way a couple of times. I didn't think much of it, and didn't want to trouble him while he was out there trying to win the biggest golf tournament in the world.

All of a sudden this thick Irish accent booms across the room: 'Dan Carter! What the hell are you doing here?' It turns out he's a huge rugby fan, and we ended up having a chat about rugby, golf and life. It was another cool, strange moment among many in that period.

At some point, though, it all had to come to an end. After capping the trip with a few amazing days at the music festival Coachella, I flew home, and started to really ramp up my training. As the end of my sabbatical came into view, and I started doing more rugby-specific work, I finally started to feel that hunger come back. I became more engaged with the Super Rugby season, and aware of the looming international calendar. But the curve seemed too steep, to go from flying around the world, training on my own, straight into top-flight rugby.

I decided to ease back into it. Rather than starting at the top of the rugby tree, I wanted to play a few club games first. Because of the timing, I was playing club rugby while the Crusaders were training and All Blacks were playing. So I had the singular experience of training with the Crusaders, while playing for Southbridge on the weekend, then watching the All Blacks play on the big screen at the clubrooms after the game. Watching the team play without me, at such a remove, really helped light a fire in me to push on with the rehab and return to the team.

First though, I had to make it through the final stages of the Super Rugby season. We'd done the typical Crusaders thing, starting relatively slowly before gathering momentum at the right time. Colin Slade had started to play really well, and we were looking at a playoff berth should we maintain our trajectory when I returned to the side. I was asked if I would play second-five, so as to not upset the rhythm the team had established, which I was more than happy to do. And it seemed to click. Perhaps because I wasn't playing first-five, and over-thinking things through all the tactical elements, the game seemed really clear to me. I was playing good, attacking rugby, with a confidence I hadn't felt in two years.

We were seeded second going into the playoffs, and played the Sharks at home in the semi, a game we won very comfortably. After losing to the Chiefs twice over the previous couple of seasons it felt good to make a final again, though we had huge amounts of respect for the Waratahs, who had been outstanding all season. We flew to Sydney confident in the way we'd been playing, and well prepared for what was coming.

Or so we thought. They came out of the gates with monumental energy, and within 15 minutes were leading 14–0. Matt Todd struck back, and it felt like the momentum had shifted. We believed we'd absorbed what they had and were ready to hit back. Andy Ellis ran a bit, before he passed to me at 12 to take the ball into contact. I was collected by Hooper, their captain, and their hooker, Polota-Nau. Immediately I felt my leg go completely dead. I thought it was just a good deep bruise, so I got up and tried to run it off. It was my plant foot, so Sladey took the kick. Then he called me over to kick from a breakdown, giving me no choice but to test the leg. I gritted my teeth, swung through, and collapsed with the pain.

I knew something was wrong, but it was a final, so I kept trying to run it off. It soon became clear it wasn't going away, and I reluctantly limped off. I watched us lose by a single point — another gut-wrenching finals defeat for this era of the Crusaders.

Afterwards I decided to just retain my focus on returning to the All Blacks. So when everyone else had a beer to toast the end of the season, I just went to my room and iced my leg. I'd decided when I returned to playing to give up drinking for a spell so as to maximise my chances for the year. The following day we flew back to Christchurch, and I was named in the All Blacks that morning. That gave me further motivation, so I passed up the team function to continue icing my leg, which was refusing to come right.

I saw Dr Deb the following morning, and told her that the leg was still troubling me, so she booked me in for a scan. When I emerged I could see the damage to the muscle, the kind you always get with a haematoma. But they found something else, too. A small crack in my fibular. And just like that, I was out again. Six weeks. After all that I'd been through to rebuild my body, I was back here again — just me, an injury and my black thoughts.

When it came out in the media, the story on me quickly became 'injury-prone Dan', which frustrated me no end. It was a freak contact event which could just as easily have happened to a 20 year old. That only increased my despondence. We had another team function that night, and I decided I'd have a drink — why was I bothering abstaining, if this was where it got me? I ended up enjoying my time with the team, even though I felt slightly distant from them, due to only having played the last five games.

The next morning I flew up to Auckland to try and get back to my disciplines. The only solace I took was knowing that my body was fundamentally in good condition, and that it was just a piece of bad luck in a contact sport. That helped a little, but I was still pretty down as I watched the All Blacks from my sofa. Beauden Barrett started to get some game time. He was coming on strong for the Hurricanes. Sladey had been playing well for the Crusaders in the 10. So all of a sudden it's not just Crudes

— it's Beaudy, Crudes and Sladey, all lining up for the 10 jersey. I watched glumly, thinking I was giving them way too many chances with my injuries. That was the first time in a decade that I truly felt I didn't deserve to be the number-one 10 for the All Blacks.

Even in 2013, when I was at my lowest, I'd always felt that if I were fully fit I was the first choice. Now it was a lottery — whoever is playing best deserves the jersey. That felt like a permanent change; whoever dominated Super Rugby in 2015 should earn the jersey. Whereas in the past I felt I had a claim to it, and could play my way into form without worrying about anyone getting ahead of me. The fact was that I simply hadn't had form for the All Blacks since 2012, and just when I start to round into form again I'd broken my leg.

After a week or so of wallowing, I dragged myself up and returned to Ceri and Bert. Together we worked on narrowing my focus, rather than spending too much time gazing off into an uncertain future. That helped. I went back to Canterbury, with whom I hadn't played in years, and started training with them. I was scheduled to play 40 minutes against Southland, but after 20 took a whack on my leg. I refused to come off, even though I was limited in the aftermath, and gutsed my way through to halftime.

That started a deeply frustrating cycle of recovery and setback. I would lock up to the point where I could barely walk, then it would disappear and I'd be fine. The next couple of days I'd train well, and start thinking I was ready to play. Then boom — a hit and my ankle would be completely immobile. Sometimes it would last a day or two, sometimes a few hours. It would rear up at odd times, like driving or lifting Marco. It was at that point the medical staff realised it was more complex than they'd originally thought, and a six-week injury turned into 12. I was back to the lows of the previous year, only worse, because this time no one seemed to really know exactly what was wrong.

All the while the heat around the World Cup was building. I was sitting in interviews, asked about the following year, and forcing myself to talk about how much it meant to me. I found myself wishing I'd retired a couple of years earlier, at the sabbatical. I found it as challenging a period as I'd had as a professional.

I was talking with Steve Hansen regularly by then, at Gilbert's suggestion, and told him how much I wanted to play. But the ITM Cup was nearing an end, and I still couldn't make it on to the field. I was targeting the last round of the regular season, just to try and sneak into the squad for the tour. Canterbury were keen to have me too, as they'd lost Sladey to the All Blacks, and would regularly call trying to get me into the team. I would have given anything to play, but the leg just wasn't quite there.

My body never did come right in time to play, and as the announcement for the end-of-year squad loomed, I started mentally preparing for the call. The one telling me I'd missed the team. It never came, but on the morning it was announced I was incredibly nervous, sure I'd missed the opportunity to prove my fitness. I listened to the radio, waiting and hoping. Sure enough, there I was, in between Sam Cane and Dane Coles. The relief was immense, and after a couple of very difficult years, I felt like I deserved this break, and the chance to build a case for making one last World Cup.

FINAL YEAR DIARY: Swansea, 12 October 2015

Recorded via WhatsApp call at The Marriott Swansea, Wales, ahead of the quarter-finals.

There have just been so many hotels, it feels like we're forever moving. Just another hotel to sleep at; another little town to train in for another week.

The travel is wearying, but everything else has been incredible. I'm so conscious that these are my last days as an All Black, and the team has done a great job of making us aware of that. We each got presented with an All Blacks book. We've had them before — there's a little about the All Blacks jersey, the history of being an All Black, the haka, the All Blacks cap and ties, the trophies we play for. I wrote a section in it about the series against the Lions in 2005 and what that meant to me and the team. It helps you realise, again, why you're here, what you're playing for.

To help continue that feeling I've been making notes in the back of my book. I thought I'd write down how I feel before each match. I wrote just before the Argentina game:

— I'm so pumped right now.

— Just make sure I do the little things well.

— I need to talk all day.

— Enjoy.

I remember being so excited for the game. We hadn't played for over a month and I was so pumped up to be playing in front of some 80,000 people. The Argentinians took it to us and it was actually a really tough one. I was reasonably happy with the way I played. We didn't gel greatly as a team, but I felt like I was doing the basics well and controlling the game. I walked off the pitch reasonably satisfied, which is a good way to start the tournament.

With the game against Georgia, I was seriously pumped up, and I thought I was going to do really well. I wanted to have a huge game. For some reason I didn't write in the book before that game; it just slipped my mind. The match didn't start well. I missed a couple of kicks early on and they put us under so much pressure. The game wasn't going the way we expected it to, and although we found our feet and scored some good tries late in the game, I walked off that pitch gutted with the way I played — as were most of the guys in the team about their performances.

I sat down and reviewed the game with Fozzie [Ian Foster]. He brought up some good points, and suggested that I see Gilbert Enoka to really nail what the bigger problem was. It had nothing to do with my preparation and my skills; it was something more on the mental side. After seeing Gilbert, it was just so obvious that I was too focused on outcome and results. I went into the game wanting to be the man of the match, I wanted to kick all my goals, I wanted to be setting up tries. Then, suddenly, I make a mistake or miss a kick and I can't reach the result. That's why I got into this 'red head' state, playing with frustration — because I could no longer reach those goals. It was a huge lesson for me.

The following week they gave me another crack, against Tonga, and for me the whole week was all about the process — forget about the outcome. I was a lot more at ease, more controlled and relaxed out on the field, and I had a much better game — back up to the standard I wanted.

When the game had finished, I walked around the field with Ma'a, who was celebrating his 100th test match. He's such a team man, and I've been there since day one with him. I could just see how special that week was for him and was so proud of my mate achieving what he has. He's been through some ups and downs, been in and out of the All Blacks, and missed the 2007 World Cup. To deal with that adversity and come back and be such a world-class player and such a valuable member of this team — I was really proud of my brother.

Now we're starting the real World Cup, the knockout phase. We know the French are our opponents. Effectively this could be my last game in an All Blacks jersey. I just found out today that I'm starting, so I'm pretty excited about that. I've got one more definite game as an All Black and I don't want it to be my last. I have to make sure I do everything I possibly can this week to help the team fight to live another day.

There are no guarantees. England are already gone. I've sat and watched a lot of the other teams play. There have been some huge games: Australia versus England, Australia versus Wales. You can just see the intensity and the physicality in those games. It's a huge step up.

It feels like it's our turn to have one of those games.

Final Year Diary

Surrey, 26 October 2015
*Recorded via WhatsApp call at The Oatlands Park Hotel,
a day after the All Blacks' 20–18 semi-final victory over the
Springboks at Twickenham.*

Leading up to the last round of pool play we repeated the
line over and over: that it didn't really matter whether we
played France or Ireland. We probably meant it at the time,
but as soon as we found out we were playing France, my
immediate thought was of 2007, and losing the quarter-final
to them 20–18.

I didn't talk about it in the media — I didn't want to fuel
the fire. But at the same time it was hard *not* to think about it.
There was a big part of me that wanted to right the wrongs
of 2007, and felt this was a perfect opportunity. The way I
saw it, there were two ways we could go about it: either
let it daunt you and worry that it might happen again; or
walk towards it, embrace it, view it as the opportunity I've
wanted ever since that day in 2007 — playing the same
team, in the same stadium . . . but this time succeeding.

It wasn't just the opposition sharpening our minds. There
was some genuine fear early in that week, because we
hadn't been performing throughout the Rugby World Cup.
In patches we had played okay, but never across a full 80
minutes. Between that and the parallels with 2007, there
was a real edge to training.

To help our head game we met with Ceri Evans, the
psychologist. He showed us a clip of a cliff diver aiming
for a little hole in a rock. We talk about do or die, but it's
very literal for those extreme sportsmen: if they get it wrong,

they're dead! They have to be so focused on the moment. The talk made us recalibrate and really focus, again, on the process, rather than the outcome.

You don't know exactly what drives a performance. But for whatever reason — the opponent, the venue, Ceri's talk, or genuine fear about the way we'd been playing — everything just flowed. We played brilliantly. We learnt from 2007 and 2003, when we had looked too far ahead, that nothing was guaranteed after that quarter-final. So, we saw this as our final. That's all we had guaranteed in this tournament. Afterwards we were just so happy to give ourselves another week.

For 24 hours after beating the French we let the performance wash over us, allowed ourselves to reflect on one of the best games we've had as a group. But come Monday, after the review, we put a full stop on the quarter-final, and started looking forward to South Africa. It was actually really hard, because as the week went on we were still hearing about it: from fans; from friends; from the media. It was challenging at times to forget about it and concentrate on the Springboks.

I had bigger issues than concentration to worry about, though. Just before halftime in the French game, I developed a sore right knee — affecting my plant foot. I told the training staff at halftime, but never considered coming off. All the same, it was uncomfortable, and compared to the first half I was pretty quiet. I thought it was just a bruise, even after I started cramping up in that calf towards the end. After the game I iced it and took it easy, thinking it would be right in the morning.

The next day, though, I could barely walk. Monday was as bad, if not worse. By Tuesday I thought I wasn't going to play the semi. I caught up with the team's medical staff, and they realised I'd tweaked my MCL [medial collateral ligament]. I was given a cortisone injection, and didn't train at all on Monday or Tuesday. Wednesday was our day off, so I focused on getting right for Thursday, and figured I'd know then what my chances of running out that weekend were.

Throughout that time I was fighting to avoid thinking the worst — that all my training and rehab was for nothing, that I'd miss out on the big games *again*. I spent time with Gilbert, which helped. He broke my day into two-hour blocks: the first would be gym and recovery; the next spent doing media — it gave me control and something on which to focus.

Thursday came, and with it two training sessions. The morning was really light. I had a wee run around, and it felt a lot more stable. But I still wasn't confident on it — between the pain and the messages it sent to my brain I couldn't play with the necessary freedom. After my morning run I decided to get a local anaesthetic in my knee, just to take the pain away. That allowed me to — finally — get in a good, hard training session, which was a huge confidence booster.

With my leg better — or at least much improved — it was time to focus properly on our opponents. There is just something about the Springboks. They're such tough adversaries, very similar to us, and they play with so much heart and spirit.

The game was incredibly tight, but I never felt worried.

It's easier to play than to watch those games. I remember having to watch the last World Cup and, honestly, it sucks. You just can't enjoy it when it's so close and so tense. But when you're actually out there playing, you have control: the outcome is in your hands. Even when it was close, even when we were down, I was confident we'd find a way to win. It's something this team has done time and again these past four years, so despite the pressure of the semi-final, I knew we'd figure it out. And we did.

I don't like to show a lot of emotion, but after the last whistle I couldn't help it. I was just so pumped to reach the final. One step closer to a dream of mine coming true. It meant we had the opportunity to do something no other team has done before. Something we've talked about for four years: repeating as champions. It has always been in the distance, but to finally be one game away was such an immense relief.

Last year was such a challenging one for me. Lingering injuries and elusive form combined to make me doubt my ability to ever reach this point. There were so many times when I wondered if I'd made a mistake by re-signing, that my body wouldn't allow me to fulfil this dream, one I've nurtured for a dozen years now.

But to be in this situation, my body feeling great, playing good rugby — I'm just so grateful. All the pieces of the puzzle have fallen into place. Now I just really want to finish the job — not only for myself and what I've been through, but for this team and what we've created and achieved over the last four years.

It will be defined in just one game.

Acknowledgements

I'd like to thank Dean, Simon and Lou for their guidance over the years. It has been invaluable. Mum and Sarah, for always being there for me. Dad for constant encouragement and unquestioning belief in me and my game from the day I was born. Ben Hurst for being a great mate, and casting his eye across my book. To all my coaches past and present, for everything they've done for me as a player. I'd also like to thank Richie, Aaron, Deb and the Essentially guys for giving up their time to contribute to the book. Finally to Honor, Marco and Fox for putting up with a dad even more absent than usual over the last year. That'll change in France.

Dan Carter, September 2015

***

Thanks to Warren and Kevin at Upstart Press for their faith in me, support through this project and calm when months and months would pass without new chapters. Dean, Lou, Simon and all at Essentially for their help and willingness to discuss areas such as contracts and sponsorships which instincts suggested might be better kept private. All my editors, particularly those who've published my sportswriting: Simon Wilson, Scotty Stevenson and Eric Young. Alex Casey for running 'The Spinoff' while I was away or distracted. Honor for letting me take so much of

Dan's time while she was pregnant, then raising a newborn *and* a toddler. And Dan, for committing so thoroughly to this project, and for trusting me with such a personal story.

And my family. My mother for raising me to love books, and my father to love rugby. My wife Niki and my perfect kids Jett, Robyn and Vivienne, for dealing with a harried and often absent father and husband through this period. I truly couldn't have done it without you.

Duncan Greive, September 2015